CUBBINGTON

CUBBINGTON

Reflections on Village Life

Domesday to 1970

Millennium Edition

G. F. PEPPITT, A.C.P.

THE PLEASAUNCE PRESS
A.D. 2000

First published MCMLXXI
by The Pleasaunce Press

Second, Millennium edition published MM
by The Pleasaunce Press
at 60, Clinton Lane,
KENILWORTH,
Warwickshire,
CV8 1AT

ISBN 0 902372 10 6 Paperback
0 902372 11 4 Boards

British Library Cataloguing in Publication Data
A catalogue record for this book is available from the British Library

Printed and bound in Great Britain at the University of Warwick.

CONTENTS

PREFACE to the First Edition

Three miles from one of the recognised spots marking the centre of England — seven miles from Coventry, twelve from Rugby, fifteen from Stratford-on-Avon — lies the ancient village of Cubbington, abutting Leamington Spa and housing about four and a half thousand people.

The village had developed slowly through the ages until the public sewerage system was introduced in 1953. In 1086 there were 88 inhabitants, in 1665 257, in 1821 614, and in 1931 1,264. Thus in 110 years between 1821 and 1931 the population had increased by only 650. Between 1951 and 1967, a period of 16 years, the population had increased by 2,857. The village in the 1800's consisted of terraced cottages, some of them back-to-back so that there was only one outside door to each house, with a small garden in front and a larger area of garden some distance away where the toilets were situated. Most of the cottages were built on the edge of the pavement without any front gardens but with a considerable piece of garden to each at the back. You might have called it a 'Compact Village'. Many of these properties were not owned by a Lord of the Manor of Cubbington but by the tradespeople of the village, the tailor, the baker, the retired farmer, the saw-mill owner and the blacksmith. For a number of years the Lord of the Manor had not lived in the parish and this created amongst the inhabitants a healthy spirit of independence. This is illustrated in many ways in the following pages. An opportunity was given to the ordinary villagers to fill posts of responsibility in the administrative offices. The tailor, baker, farmer and tin-smith were very successful in the respective offices they filled as Overseers, Churchwardens, Surveyors, and Chairmen of the Parish Council.

Also, there arose a wholesome enthusiasm for non-conformity but not in the narrow religious sense, and this was vigorously shown by the Wesleyans — now known as Methodists — in building three successive places of worship and also running a day school; but the two denominations of Church & Methodism lived harmoniously together. By the creation of a healthy non-conformity the actions of the community were not controlled by the whims of a Lord of the Manor, nor by the mass hysteria generated by a few, as at the present time.

What of the newcomers during the last few years? Several large estates have accommodated them. They have been welcomed by the members of the prevailing churches and other organisations and all would seem to have benefited. New organisations have been formed by them. The Community spirit is maintained.

I hope what is written in the following pages will create a greater interest in the village. I started this work about 40 years ago by making a pictorial list of interesting features and records. I was spurred on to do this by being shocked one day to find that demolition men had taken the Dovecote down without any previous warning being given. As a result of this I took photographs and collected records so that now I have about one hundred lantern-slides illustrating interesting features which have since disappeared. A few years ago I realised that a more permanent record must be made than the scattered notes I owned. The following pages, then, are the result, arranged to guide the reader from Domesday to the present time.

I have derived great interest and pleasure in compiling them and I hope the readers will enjoy the same experience.

PREFACE to the Millennium Edition

It gave great pleasure and satisfaction to 'Gus' (Gustavus Frederick) Peppitt to see his book in print at the very end of his life. (He died on the 6th of January, 1976, at the age of 85.) He had worked long and hard at it, as he had worked long and hard for the well-being of his beloved Cubbington. But not only did *he* derive pleasure from the book: so did the many who read it. Even after nearly thirty years, the bulk of his work is still fascinating, relevant and, often, droll. The Publisher has not seen fit to make any changes from the first edition except where misprints had slipped through or illustrations have had to move from their original positions, perforce — some of the originals of pictures that appeared are now no longer available, and copies of them are too poor to be reproduced again. As a result, a few of the pictures have changed (hopefully for the better), but the Publisher nonetheless apologises to anyone whose favourite view or group is no longer to be found! Appropriate substitutes have been provided wherever possible.

On the other hand, there is now a supplementary section at the end of the book designed to bring its coverage up to the end of the second Millennium. It has been kept separate from the contents of the original book in order to preserve the latter's integrity as an historical record in its own right.

In this new section are to be found short accounts of what the various village societies and industries have achieved in this time, what changes have taken place in local government affecting Cubbington, and what alterations have taken place to the landscape. These changes are accompanied by photographs kindly lent by many interested people, some of whom are resident and some distant but nonetheless closely and fondly attached to the village.

Since every effort has been made to seek permission of copyright-holders to reproduce illustrations, the publisher can only apologise if any have slipped through, and asks the holder for his or her kind indulgence on this rare occasion.

From the response to requests for material for the new chapter, and from the enthusiasm for a new edition of this book, it is quite clear that the vibrant Spirit of Cubbington is as strong as ever. May it continue in the Third Millennium!

Note: Inflation has affected Britain greatly since 1971. In order to understand some of the figures quoted in the material of the first edition, the reader should know that one pound sterling (£1) in 1914 could buy a basketful of goods that, in 1997, cost £56.25; £1 in 1938, at the outbreak of war, bought £35.80's worth of goods in 1997; and £1 in 1970, £8.51's worth in 1997.

The average weekly household income from salaries and wages in 1996/7 — the latest figures available — was £256.28; overall weekly income from all sources was £396.86. This amounted to an annual income of £20,637. This can be contrasted with the £3 *a year* earned by a labourer at the time of the Dissolution of the Monasteries (1536-40), the £7 a year pension of the canons of Kenilworth and the £100 pension of the Abbot when they lost their Abbey to Henry VIII.

An index and list of illustrations have been added for the reader's convenience.

ACKNOWLEDGEMENTS: First Edition

I am most grateful to the following for their assistance in providing material for the book.

The Ministry of Agriculture, Fisheries and Food for permission to use extracts from their Crown Copyright booklet 'At the Farmer's Service';

The Coventry Evening Telegraph for the article on 'The Old Manor';

The Cubbington Freeholders for permission to quote from the Minutes of their meetings;

Warwickshire County Records Office for the use of records, and the kindly help of the Staff;

The Heart of England Newspaper Company Limited for photographs and news items from the Leamington Courier; and the report from the Warwick Advertiser of 1832;

Mr. Victor Bonham-Carter for permission to quote from his book 'The English Village';

The WCC Planning Department for the plan and notes on the Conservation Area;

The Reverend Glyn Lewis, Vicar of Cubbington, for permission to use Church documents in the care of the Diocesan Records Office;

The Librarian and Staff of the Leamington Spa Reference Library, for their courtesy and help on many occasions;

The Librarian and Staff of the Warwickshire Headquarters Library;

The Clerk and Staff of Warwick Rural District Council for willing answers to requests;

The County Education Office and the School Managers;

The late Mrs Mary Bastock for programmes and letters willingly supplied;

Mr. A. Hedderwick for his tremendous help with photographs;

Herbert Associates Ltd for their photograph of the Bechler AS 10 Automatic Lathe;

and the many villagers who have lent photographs over the years.

ACKNOWLEDGEMENTS: Millennium Edition

The Publisher sees a new edition 'Cubbington' as a fitting memorial to dear old Gus Peppitt, and hopes that perhaps, thirty or fifty years later when he himself is just a memory, someone else will produce yet a third edition to keep Gus' memorial thoroughly alive.

However, the 'Millennium' edition would never have come into existence if it had not been for the determination of Margaret Walters, known to many Cubbingtonians as Margaret Rose. She ran the Publisher to earth in his home not long after he had returned to live in Kenilworth, having moved house no less than seven times in the intervening years. This was no mean feat. Persuading him to take the risk of a second edition of a book peculiar to a village of only four thousand people, a book which would have to cost ten times as much as the original, was an even greater feat! Everybody reading this page has only her to thank. And, of course, the Publisher has also to thank her, because without all the effort she has put in to finding lost photographs, into proving that people would buy the book if it were published, into persuading people to both support and provide a very parochial advertising campaign, he most certainly could never have succeeded in bringing it to the light of day. In the end, he came to share in her enthusiasm and enjoy all the work involved, and he wishes to express here his heartfelt gratitude.

The Publisher would like also to thank those many people who have made their invaluable contribution of material, advice and time for this new edition. It is difficult to see how the project would ever have been completed without so much willing co-operation.

A special note of thanks is due to the following:

Marion Avern
Brian Bass
John Cain
Karen Chambers
Joan Clark of the Mothers' Union
Councillor Clifford Cleaver
Nigel & Jane Coad of the Manor House
The staff at Warwickshire County Records Office
The Coventry Evening Telegraph
Gill Dillow
Ray Elliott
Sally Ellis of Cubbington Village Stores
Christine Fairbrother
Freda Goddard
Elaine Golder
Colin Hughes
Robert Inman — Clerk to the Parish Council
John Judd
Sue Kendall of the Silver Band
The Manager & Staff at Kenilworth Connection
Ron Key of The Freeholders
Connie Lambert
John Lambert
The Leamington Spa Courier
The Reverend Kenneth Lindop
Frances Merriman
David Morris of the Albion Football Club
Maureen Pedley
John Randerson for detailed information about the Methodist Church
Gill Sawyer
Michael Serhyniuk of the Old Age Pensioners Association
M.B. (Betty) Taylor
Warwickshire County Council & Warwick District Council staff for help with statistics
Peter Webb, Red Cross Branch Director

All those who provided photographs, acknowledged with the captions wherever possible

ON THE MAP

WHAT'S IN A NAME?

One explanation of the name is that it comes from the 'town of the descendants of Coba', and an ancient spelling — Cobynton — seems to give some support to this theory.

Dugdale, the great Warwickshire historian, tells us that the place is written in Domesday Book (1086) once Cubitone, twice Cobintone, afterwards Cumbynton, which shows that it had its name originally from its situation in a low or deep hollow, 'for the word Cumbe doth signifie as much'. (Examples — Ilfracombe, Combe Martin, etc.)

Looking at the village, nestling in a valley and picturesquely surrounded by elevated ground, there can be little doubt that the name Cubbington is derived from the situation and signifies 'the town in the hollow'.

We have abundant proof that there was a village here in Saxon times. The Parish was owned in the time of Edward the Confessor by

1. The Church of Coventry.
2. Lewin and Chetelbern.
3. Tabern.

What we should today call the rateable value is stated to have been then £5 per annum. (The rateable value on the 1st April, 1970 was £155,039).

Soon after William the Norman had succeeded in planting himself in this country of his conquest, there appeared the famous Domesday Book of 1086, a minute record and exhaustive survey of all the land in the realm. The reason assigned for this survey was that everyone should be satisfied with his own right and not usurp with impunity what belonged to another. A further reason and, I suspect, more true, was that those who possessed landed estates now became vassals to the King, and paid him so much money by way of fee or homage in proportion to the lands they held, and William wanted to know exactly how much!

The population of Cubbington consisted of seven villeins, six bordars and five bondmen — eighteen families with an estimated population of eighty-eight. The present population — June 1971 — is estimated at 4,400.

The following entries respecting Cubbington appear in Domesday Book of 1086, but an explanation of some of the words used in these extracts may now be necessary.

'Hide' or 'Ploughland' was the amount of land annually ploughable by one team of oxen. Its extent varied from 100 acres to 220 acres, according to the stiffness of the soil. In this district it appeared to be about 120 acres. 'Plough' refers to a plough and team of oxen. 'Demesne' was the home farm of the Lord of the Manor.

LAND OF THE CHURCH OF COVENTRY IN STONELEI HUNDRED

The Church holds in Cobintone 2 hides. The arable employs four ploughs. Half a plough is in the demesne and 2 bondmen. There are 5 villeins and 1 bordar, with 1 plough. There are 8 acres of meadow. It was worth 20s., now 30s.

LAND OF THE EARL OF MELLENT

The Earl himself holds in Cubitone 3 hides and Boscher of him. The arable employs 3 ploughs. One is in the demesne with 3 bordars. There are 8 acres of meadow. It was worth 40s., now 30s. Lewin and Chetelbern held it freely in Edward's time.

LAND OF ROGER de IVERI

Roger de Iveri holds of the King as it is said 5 hides in Cubintone. The arable employs 4 ploughs: 2 are in the demesne and 3 bondmen. There are 2 villeins and 2 bordars, with 1 plough. There are 15 acres of meadow. It was and is worth 40s. Tubern held it freely in King Edward's time. This is a fee of the Bishop of Baiena.

In 1236, during the reign of Henry III, the part belonging to the Prior of Coventry was held from that Monastery by Simon de Cubinton, and 16 years later by Henry de Cubinton. The part owned by the Earl of Mellent and which Boscher held of him, came to the monks of Stoneleigh.

Of the part owned by Roger de Iveri, Dugdale says 'Hastings of Allesley became anciently enfeoffed, by one of which line it was given to Semely (Lord of Radford Semely) and to St. Maure'. He cannot trace succession of Semely's part, but it was undoubtedly the same land which in the reign of Edward IV (1473) was given by John Hugford and Thomas Waldeyve to the monks of Stoneleigh. It consisted of 5 messuages, eighty acres of land, three acres of meadow and four acres of pasture.

St. Maure's portion does not seem to have remained very long in that family, for Henry de St. Maure, having committed a murder during the reign of King Edward I, fled, whereupon his Manor, which then yielded twenty-five shillings, was seized by the King and given to the Knights Templars who, in 1278, are recorded to have held here 'three yerd land in Demesne and a certain grove enclosed like a Park'. Soon afterwards it was transmitted to the Knights Hospitalers, and continued with them until the general Dissolution of the Monasteries, as did that also which the monks of Coventry and Stoneleigh held.

Finally, the Manor passed through the Fawkoners, Sadlers, Fishers, Watsons, Hickmans, Shuckburghs, Greswoldes and Wises to the Knightleys of Offchurch.

In 1767, Manorial rights in Cubbington were disputed between a Mr. Blissett and a Mr. Wise, and 'settled' in favour of Mr. Blissett by the tossing of a halfpenny.

His widow Susannah and son Charles were in possession in 1780 and 1782 respectively. His son Charles sold the estates for £3,800 to Dr. Crines of Kenilworth (whose son-in-law John Stanton sold them in 1820 to the Earl of Aylesford for £14,000), and the royalty of the Manor, without any land, for £300 to John Whitwick Knightley of Offchurch, whose grand-daughter held it in 1834. She married the Earl of Aylesford and died in 1911.

THE VILLAGE IN NORMAN TIMES

It is impossible to imagine the conditions of life in the village in Anglo-Saxon days. There would be about 20 families in the parish. The land was divided into three portions. There was the village itself in which the people lived in rough houses built of wood or rough stone work. Around the village were a few small enclosures called crofts for rearing calves and other animals; this was the common farmstead. Around this was the arable land where the villagers grew their corn, oats, wheat, rye, beans and barley and around this the common meadows, or pasture land, held by the whole community. Each family could turn its cattle into the common land, subject to the regulations of an officer elected by the people, whose duty it was to see that no one trespassed on the rights of his neighbours, or turned too many cattle into the pasture.

Around the whole colony lay the woods and uncultivated land which was left in its natural state, where the people cut their timber and fuel, and pastured their pigs.

The cultivated land was divided into three large fields, each field being ploughed into strips about a furlong in length and two or three poles wide, each strip being about half an acre. These were separated by unploughed belts of grassland, usually called baulks. The groups of strips were called furlongs.

The Norman Conquest made little difference to the work of the tenants and labourers in the fields.

At the head of the rural society were the freemen — they paid a fixed sum as rent for their land, either in money, in goods or in labour. They were not bound to the land like the villeins, and could leave their homes when they pleased.

Villeins held about 30 acres each in scattered strips in the three-field system. These lots were scattered in various parts of the fields, so that the good land might not all be assigned to a few privileged mortals and the bad land left to the unfortunate. A rotation of crops was rigidly enforced, and every man was obliged to sow the same crop as his neighbour. Another rule was that each field should be fallow once in three years.

When the corn was reaped and the harvest gathered in, the arable fields were all thrown open for grazing. The same plan was adopted with the meadowland after the hay had been gathered in.

Each villein supported his wife and family from the 30 acres he held, and in return he had to render certain services to his lord, to work on the home farm and provide two or more oxen for the manorial plough team. His work was of two kinds — week work and boon work. The former consisted of two or three days a week, while the latter was performed at harvest time, and the like.

Other members of society were known as bordars. They held 5 acres of scattered strips. They supplemented their income by doing piece-work or day-work for others.

The third group of members of the community were bondmen, annexed to the person of the Lord and transferred at his pleasure.

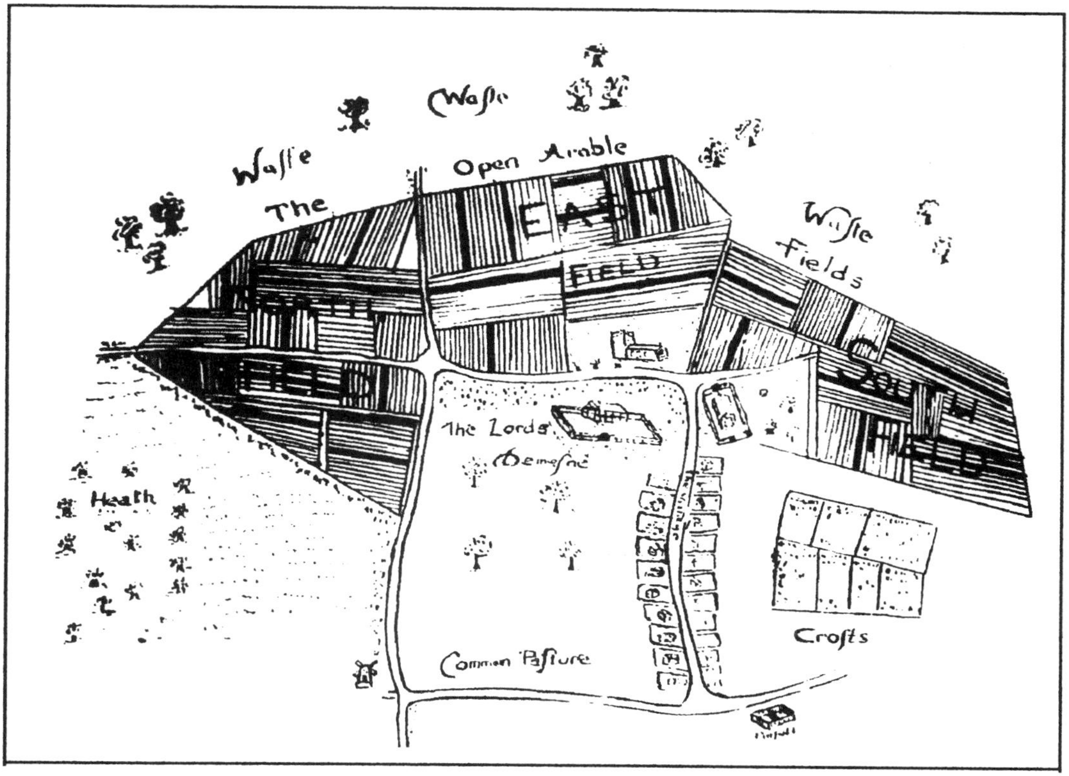

The sketch shows an imaginative plan of the village in those days. The street going through the village is now known as High Street and Queen Street. Many of the half-timbered houses along these streets have since disappeared but there are still traces of them. The Pinfold is at the bottom right-hand corner and the Windmill on the left-hand corner at the top of Windmill Hill.

It also shows the Three-field system of farming which worked well for about two hundred and fifty years. The Church, the Old Manor, the Manor House and the Heath (the area now approximately covered by Heath Farm) are all shown.

The Church before restoration in 1885

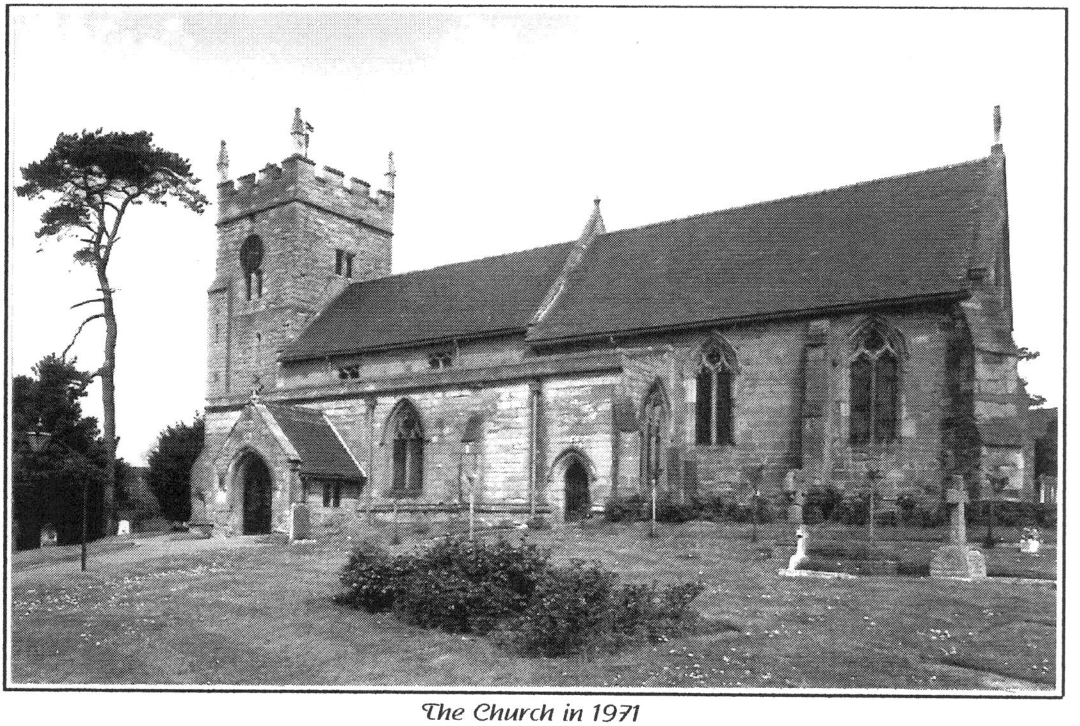

The Church in 1971

THE CHURCH

As the Church of Coventry was an owner in Saxon days, we may reasonably assume that even at that early date there would be a Church at Cubbington, and provision made for the spiritual needs of the place. No trace, however, remains today of the building in which our Saxon forefathers worshipped.

Undoubtedly, however, by far the most ancient object in the Parish — the work of men's hands, but built to the glory of God — is our fine old Parish Church, dedicated to 'The Nativity of Our Lady', a rather unusual dedication. The first record of the observance of the day is in 687 when Pope Sergius I placed the Nativity among the Festivals kept in memory of the Blessed Virgin. In the Eastern Church the day is kept with great solemnity. The Patronal Festival of Cubbington Church is the nearest Sunday to September 19th.

Situated as it is on a gradual ascent from the village street, our admiration is at once claimed for the site chosen for the House of God as picturesque and commanding.

A considerable part of the Church, as we know it today in its rugged grandeur, dates back to the Norman period. The Church in Norman days consisted of Tower, Nave, South Aisle and a small chancel, and must so have remained for 250 years. The Tower (with the exception of the uppermost portion, added about 1857), the Nave and the South Aisle have stood very much as we now see them for over 800 years: In the great Abbey of Westminster are pillars, AD.1066, surmounted with capitals and arches, of which these in the South Arcade are an almost exact reproduction.

In 1346, the Papal throne was filled by Clement VI, a Frenchman by birth, formerly Cardinal of St. Nereus and St. Achilles. This Pope ordained Cubbington a Vicarage, with Vicarage House, Mortuaries, Altarage and small tithes.

Previous to this date the services probably had been conducted from Coventry, then from Wootton, of which Cubbington is said to have been a Chapelry, and finally by the Canons of Kenilworth, the patronage of this living having been vested in the Prior and Convent of Kenilworth from 1309 until the Dissolution of the Monasteries in the reign of King Henry VIII. Dugdale gives the names of three of the Clergy who ministered here prior to Cubbington becoming a Vicarage: Thomas de Harewell (presbyter) 1309; John de Shotteswell (acolyte) 1313; Robert de Fitzwith (presbyter) 1342. An acolyte is the fourth Minister of the Altar.

The first Vicar was Adam de Thorpe Mandeville — his name pointing to the place of his birth, Thorpe Mandeville near Banbury.

To this period when Cubbington became a vicarage we are greatly indebted for the improvement of the Church. The Porch, the doorway on the South side, the Chancel and the North Aisle were added at this period. The South wall of the Nave was raised so as to admit the insertion of the Clerestory windows. Thus, by about 1350, the Church may have presented a similar appearance to what it does today. The organ chamber was added during the Vicariate of the Rev. B. M. Bean, 1885. The vestry was also added during his Vicariate, 1896. In 1885 the Church was restored at a cost of £1,000.

1. The West Gallery and high backed pews, erected in 1829, were demolished.
2. The Belfry was thrown open once more to the rest of the Church.
3. The plaster was removed from the walls.
4. A modern slate roof which blocked the Clerestory windows on the south side was removed.

In 1897 the Chancel was re-roofed at the expense of William Henry, Lord Leigh (Lay Impropriator).

In 1898 the Nave was re-roofed.

On entering the Church, we are at once struck by the curious appearance of the walls, which give the impression of having departed from the perpendicular. This design is often found in ancient churches. The word 'nave' is from the Latin 'navis' meaning a ship, and in constructing the walls in a ship-like form, the old builders evidently wished to symbolise the Church as the Ship of Salvation.

THE CHANCEL

Within the Sacrarium, on the North Wall, there is an Easter Sepulchre where the Host was placed on Good Friday after the Ceremony of the Adoration. The veiled crucifix had been uncovered gradually, with the words 'Behold the wood of the Cross, on which hung the salvation of the world'. It was kissed by the Clergy and the congregation, all kneeling, and then also laid in the Sepulchre until Easter Day, thus commemorating and symbolising the descent of the Lord's body into the grave.

Chancel & Sanctuary

Easter Sepulchre

In the South wall of the Sacrarium are a Credence (kre-dens), a small table on which the bread and wine are placed before being put on the altar ready for consecration; a Piscina — a niche with a small basin and water drain, into which the priest empties any water used; and the Sedilia or seats for the Clergy.

Although the number of these seats varies in different churches it is usual, as here, to find three, one for the Celebrant — the priest officiating at the Eucharist — one each for the Deacon and Sub-Deacon who assist him. Also in the Sacrarium is the Memorial Chair to the Rev. B. M. Bean:

TO THE GLORY OF GOD

In loving memory of the
Rev. B. M. Bean
Vicar of this Parish for 37 years.
This chair is the gift of Parishioners and friends.

The chair, with the exception of the upholstery and brass plate, was made in the Village. The three figures of the bottom rail of the back represent Faith, Hope and Charity.

A brass plate fixed to the North wall of the Chancel reads:

IN LOVING MEMORY

The Reverend B. M. Bean
Vicar of this Parish from 1880 - 1917
By his efforts the Church was restored,
A vestry and organ added and
during his Vicariate the schools were
enlarged and improved.
This tablet is placed here by his
Widow and Sons.

COMMUNION RAILS

In heavy brass work, these are the work of the famous Skidmore of Coventry, and the gift of Rev. George Leigh Cooke, Vicar, 1820 - 1853.

THE ORGAN

was placed in the Church in the year 1896 and was built by Sweetland of Bath.

On the brass plate are the following words:

SACRED TO THE MEMORY OF THE
REV. P. T. BROADWAY LTh
VICAR OF THIS PARISH
1918 - 1951

During his Vicariate
the Tower was Restored and the
Churchyard enlarged

This Tablet and the Litany Desk
were placed in this Church by his
Parishioners and some Local Government
Associates.

THE CARPET IN THE CHURCH WAS GIVEN
by the Mother' Union in memory of
Mrs. Eva Gordon
their Enrolling Member who died
29th August 1954.

There is also a Memorial Tablet Sacred to the Memory of

RUBY BROADWAY
wife of REV. P. T. BROADWAY
an Enrolling member of the Mother's Union.
This tablet is placed in this Church by
members and friends of the Mothers' Union.

Aumbry, Piscina and Sedilia

Nave, looking east

Font

Abraham Murcott's Memorial

He was appointed High Constable of the Knightlow Hundred in 1664 and was generally active in Local Government about this time particularly as inspector of repaired bridges. In 1668, John Murcott was appointed treasurer of the County stock. A member of the Murcott family was among the principal landowners in 1768.

THE NAVE

and South Aisle, 800 years ago, must have looked very similar to what they do today. In the South Aisle is a Credence and Piscina. At this spot stood an altar.

The North Aisle was added about 1346 - 1350. In the North wall is an Aumbry or locker, an oblong opening in which the sacred vessels of the Altar were kept. Here, in olden days, stood an altar, possibly a Chantry, where masses would be sung for the repose of the dead. Also in the North wall is the Devil's Door, and tells of the provision made for the exit of the evil one after being exorcized by the administration of Holy Baptism.

The Devil's Door

ESCUTCHEON TO ABRAHAM MURCOTT

This hangs on the North side of the Chancel. It shows the captain standing on one side of the Shields of Arms, with his feet in a small boat with seaweed around it. On the other side is a figure representing Neptune, with the lower part of his body ending in a mermaid's tail. Upon the shield is painted 'Abra. Murcott Marriner 1702'. At the top of the escutcheon is a small figure holding a telescope. Below this are the Royal arms.

This Murcott is reported to have been lost on the Scilly rocks. The following family tradition is taken from 'Unknown Warwickshire' by Miss Dormer Harris.

This brave mariner's ship (unnamed) was filled with gold-dust, and having brought their precious burden so near land and safety, he and his men were tempted to refill their glasses with overmuch freedom, so that they were caught unprepared by the storm with tragic result.

On Friday and Saturday the 26th and 27th November, 1702 the most terrible and dreadful storms visited the country, hence Queen Anne's Declaration of a Fast.

COMMUNION SERVICE

This is singularly handsome, of silver gilt of the Queen Anne period, given to the Church by the Honourable Mary Leigh, sister of the last Baron Leigh of the old creation. This lady, who is said to have been of very benevolent disposition, made handsome gifts and presents to churches and parishes. The service consists of a very noble flagon, two massive chalices, a paten and spoon, all, as was characteristic of the period, almost devoid of engraved ornamentation.

Additions were made to the Communion Service in 1962 by Mrs Mooney and her brothers in memory of their mother and father. The gifts consisted of a Ciborium, a wafer box, and a pair of silver cruets. These were presented to the Church 'To the Glory of God and in loving memory of Charles and Ellen Stone. Ellen Stone 1878 - 1957. Charles Stone 1877 - 1961

THE WINDOWS

Storied windows richly dight
casting a dim religious light.

Dugdale mentions stained glass windows presumably as existing in his day, which have since been taken out.

It appears that in the East Window of the chancel were the Arms of Albany, Earl of Arundel, and other arms apparently unknown.

In a north window of the chancel were the Arms of Benedictus Shuckburgh (1594), son of Thomas Shuckburgh, of Shuckburgh Superior.

In a south window of the chancel are the Arms of Edmund Johnson, and underneath the following quaint words:

Who lies here dost thou wonder
Loe - my name is written under
What I was wouldst thou know,
Flesh is frayle and I was soe
Who Almighty is yet may
Convey to Heaven this lump of clay.
Edmund Johnson. Ob. Feb. 3rd, 1635.

In the east window of the north aisle were the Arms of (1) Beauchamp, (2) Henry, Earl of Lincoln, (3) England, (4) Clare, Earl of Gloucester.

It does not necessarily follow that all whose arms appeared in the Church were owners in the parish. Often the arms of the same family are to be found in a large number of churches. Nor was this merely for the purpose of self-aggrandisement. The explanation is that the ancient dead desired thus to keep their memories in evidence to command the attention, and still more, the prayers of the faithful of future generations, for the well-being of their souls.

EAST WINDOW

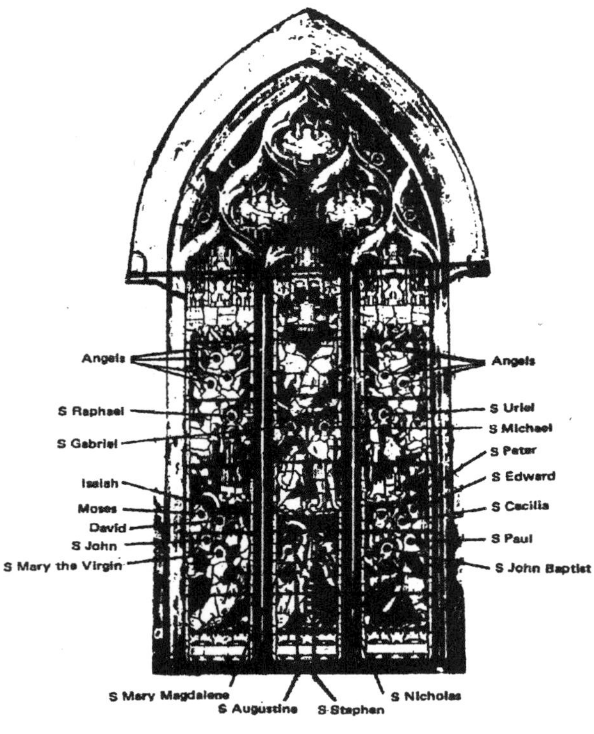

To the Glory of God
this tablet and East Window has
been placed by his surviving
children in memory of
Edward Lamb Parsons
born Aug. 10th 1805, died Jan. 8th 1832
of a family connected with this
Parish for many generations.
John E. Parsons of New York and
Lennox in the State of Massachusetts;
William H. Parsons and Mary Parsons
of Rye in the State of New York.

The window was dedicated June 22nd, 1902, and replaced a memorial window, also of stained glass, which was taken out and stored at the Vicarage.
It is a gift from the Parsons family who now live in the USA. Their forefathers were farmers who lived at Furzen Hill Farm. A family grave is at the East end of the Church. In fact, some of the relatives who were buried in the Manchester area were re-interred at Cubbington about this time.
It is known as the Te Deum window. In the lower part the Church Militant is depicted, with the Church Triumphant above.

The East Window

West End, Tower & Ringing area

In the south aisle are three windows:-

(1) In memory of William Ledbrook and Elizabeth his wife. (2) In memory of William and Ann Murcott. (3) In memory of George Bostock and Mary his wife.

In 1909, a member of the Parsons family filled windows in the north and south walls of the chancel, the subjects being Aaron and Saint Peter in the north, and Saint Ambrose and The Blessed Virgin in the south.

Also in the chancel on the north wall are two old stained glass windows, one showing Jonah being thrown out of a boat with a whale waiting to receive him, and the other the body of Christ being attended to, having been taken from the Cross.

In the south wall of the chancel are three stained glass windows. One shows Judas at the Last Supper, another depicts almsgiving and the third is a Magnificat window.

In the west wall of the north aisle is an epiphany window in memory of Lt. Col. Samuel Walker and Arabella, his wife.

In the north wall is a window in memory of Edward J. Walker and E. M. Kenny. Also in the north wall is a window in memory of Arthur William Ledbrook. All the windows in the chancel and nave are stained glass, the only windows not stained are the one in the belfry and the clerestory windows in the nave.

SEATING

In the early days, seats were not provided as worshippers either stood or knelt at services. Stone seats were placed against the walls for the old and infirm; hence the saying 'The weakest go to the wall'. Stalls or seats were provided in the chancel for those who ministered or sang.

About the end of the 14th century, fixed seats were introduced. Later, when long sermons formed part of the service, more comfort was needed and box pews were introduced. Seats were arranged on all four sides of these and entrance was by a door. In fact, these pews were like boxes without lids. Cubbington once had high-backed pews, entered by a door, but these were removed in the 1885 restoration and the present seats substituted.

At one time in the church's history, members of the congregation could pay a pew rent for the particular seat of their choice. The dividing line in our church between these seats and the free seats was the aisle leading from the front door to the north wall. The seats on the belfry side of this aisle were free seats: on the opposite side were the rented pews. The centre portion of the latter were the pews rented by the occupants of the large houses of the parish: the Manor House, The Old Manor, The Grange, Stonehouse, West Hill and the farm houses.

On the north side of this area were seats allotted to the servants of the above households and on the south side seats were rented by the tradespeople — blacksmith, baker, grocer and so on. The remainder of the seating was called free and was for the use of the general public.

Long after pew rents were abolished and all the seats had been declared free, tradition had built up the custom and as late as the early 1900's the seats were occupied by the respective households as before.

About this time it was usual at the Evening Service to see a goodly number of young men occupying seats in the north aisle. Most of them would be wearing sprays of flowers in their buttonholes, this being the fashion at the time. A gardener in the village made these up for sale.

An employer expected his servants to attend church and the story is told that a farmer missed seeing one of his labourers at a particular church service. On questioning the labourer about his absence, the farmer was told, 'I'm not going to serve God on the Sabbath and the devil the rest of the week.' I am sorry that the story ended without telling us what further action the farmer took over this incident.

BELLS

The use of bells is so ancient that it is impossible to say by whom they were first manufactured.

Bronze bells were found in the excavations carried out at Nineveh. They are found among the ancient Jews, Greeks and Romans, but it seems that none appears on any of the Egyptian monuments. In the Mosaic Church we read in the Book of Exodus, chapter 28, verse 33, a description of the robe of the Ephod of the High Priest.

'And beneath it (the Ephod) upon the hem of it thou shalt make pomegranates of blue, and of purple, and of scarlet, round about the hem thereof; and bells of gold between them round about: a golden bell and a pomegranate, a golden bell and a pomegranate, upon the hem of the robe round about. And it shall be upon Aaron to minister: and his sound shall be heard when he goeth in unto the holy place before the Lord, and when he cometh out, that he die not.

The bells being removed in November, 1960, preparatory to restoration

In the early days of the Christian Church, when persecution made it necessary for the services to be held secretly, there would of course, be no bells used. Their use, therefore, probably began when the conversion of the Emperor Constantine the Great (312) gave liberty to Christians to worship openly. As early as the fifth century a bell is recorded to have rung in France to call the monks to service. From early days bells have been used to denote the hours of devotion and to summon the people to church. In connection with the tolling of bells for deaths and burials, the Venerable Bede speaks of the passing bell being heard at a great distance when St. Hilda, the Abbess of Whitby, died in AD. 680.

An order of Bishop Grandison of Exeter in the early part of the fourteenth century is interesting and quaint. The order says that great people are to be rung for with big bells and many bells, and little people with small bells and few bells; the bells are not to be rung too long, nor early in the morning, as is the custom at Exeter, because 'sounding brass or tinkling cymbal profits not the departed souls and much harms ears, building and bells.'

Cubbington has a peal of four bells, all dating to the stormy times of King Charles I, two being erected when that most lamentable of all conflicts, Civil War, had begun. When the tramp of soldiers was heard on these roads, and some had, doubtless, gone forth from this village to share in the deadly conflict, some people turned their thoughts to more peaceful subjects.

The dates on the bells are as follows: One, 1626; one, the tenor, 1640; the treble and the remaining bell 1646. On three of the bells is inscribed

I.H.S. NAZARENUS, — REX IVDEORVM
FILI DEI — MISERERE MEI

which means, 'Jesus of Nazareth, King of the Jews, Son of God, have mercy on me' The other bell bears the inscription in English, 'God save the King'. The date on this bell is 1646, which is significant, as the Battle of Naseby in 1645 completed the King's overthrow. Charles surrendered to the Scottish army, who handed him over to Parliament.

Did the church authority in this village in consequence of the event, being fearful of what might happen to the King and also to show their loyalty to his cause, decide to inscribe the 1646 bell with the words 'God save the King' — in all sincerity, a prayer. Charles was nonetheless beheaded in 1649.

The passing bell was tolled at 8am. after a death in the parish: for the death of a man three strokes, for a woman two strokes, and for a child one stroke. A common variant was three times three for a man, three times two for a woman, and it was not uncommon to conclude by tolling the age of the deceased person, one stroke for each year. This custom was followed at Whitnash Church. It has been suggested that the old saying 'nine tailors make a man' is a corruption of 'nine tellers make a man' since the tolls on the bell are often called tellers or tailers. When the time of 'gleaning' arrived a bell was tolled at 8am.

A Sanctus bell in earlier days was tolled at the singing of the Sanctus — Holy, Holy, Holy — and at the moment of the Consecration in the Communion Service, in order that the sick, and others unable to be present, might join in the worship of the congregation. All who heard the bell were bidden, if possible, to fall on their knees in prayer.

At a later period a bell was rung after the morning service; an old verger told me it was called the 'pudding bell', and was sounded to inform the servants in the large houses that the service was over, and they could expect their masters and mistresses to return shortly.

Happily, some provision has been made for the supply of bell ropes for all time. A lover of bells, possibly a bell ringer, left a small field of about one and a half acres, known as 'Bell-rope Close'. This was sold in 1859, with the consent of the Charity Commissioners, and the money invested in consuls.

1969 saw the commencement of the £14,000 Restoration of the Church project. The bells were removed so that the tower could be restored. This also provided an opportunity for the bells to receive the attention they needed and to add two more, thus making a peal of six.

THE CLOCK

The following is taken from the Rev. B. M. Bean's book: 'Cubbington Ye Ancient Dates'.

Here my master bids me stand
And mark the time with faithful hand.
What is His will is my delight
To tell the hours by day, by night.
Master be wise and learn of me,
To serve thy God as I serve thee.

It would be ungracious not to add a word on our clock, to whose face we have long turned as to the face of an old friend, always receiving encouragement or well-merited reproof. This friend has always struck me as being singularly honest and truthful: yet local tradition says it was stolen from a neighbouring parish. My curiosity has often been aroused by the desire to know who were the thieves. Could the Vicar and his churchwardens possibly have instigated the theft? Was it committed by day or by night? Peaceably or by violence! Where was the constable of the despoiled parish?

These disquieting questions, have, however, ceased to trouble me. 'Truth is great and will prevail' — so, at the sacrifice of tradition, I must tell where it was bought and how paid for!

A Memorandum in the Register dated 1741 says,

Whereas ye Church Clock was become very old, and ye materials thereof so much decayed that it could not be duly kept in repair it was agreed by ye Minister and Churchwardens to have a new one put up who accordingly agreed with Thomas Paris of Warwick for a new clock (exclusive of a dial plate) to be set up by him for twelve pounds, besides allowing him ye old clock.

But for the case of ye Tenants, who had been at great expense in other accounts, it being further agreed to raise only 5£ part of ye said 12 by levy and the rest by Subscription, it was thought requisite to set down ye names of ye several proprietors of Lands & Tenements in ye Parish of Cubbington, and likewise of such of ye Inhabitants as were pleased to contribute to so useful a work.

The names and sums by each contributor viz:

	£.	s.	d.
The Right Honble Dowager Lady Leigh	1.	1.	0.
The Right Hon. Lord Leigh	2.	2.	0.
James Wright Esqre Patron	1.	1.	0.
Joseph Greswolde	1.	1.	0.
Edward Horne Vicar		10.	6.
Mrs. Dorothy Russell		8.	6.
William Parsons		10.	6.
Mrs. Tarver			
Mrs. Wigg			

THE VILLAGE ORCHESTRA

Two of the instruments used in the Church Orchestra

This story does not concern Cubbington but it shows the versatility of village orchestras.

I am sure our own village orchestra could play Christmas Carols in the Vicarage and Manor House with the decorum necessary for the occasion, while the next night they could be blazing away in the village pub clubroom to a hearty party of dancers.

In the story that follows concerning a village that shall be nameless, these musicians at the various Christmas festivities had been in great demand. Continuous late nights for over a week found them exhausted through lack of sleep. The Sunday afternoon after Christmas found them in their usual places in the gallery of the church ready to supply the music. The strain of the previous week and the length of the sermon had a marked effect, for they all fell asleep.

'Twas a very dark afternoon and at the end of the sermon all you could see of the inside of the church was the light of the candle by the pulpit.

The sermon ended at last, the Vicar announced the evening hymn, but sad to relate there was no response from the orchestra. For a moment, which seemed endless, there was complete silence. The people began to turn their heads to learn the reason why.

A small boy who sat near the gallery, nudged one of the musicians and said in a hoarse whisper, 'Begin, begin'.

'Hey, what?' asked the nudged one. His head was so muddled and the church so dark, that he thought he was at the "Fiddlers' Arms" where they had been playing so vigorously the night before and immediately struck up one of the most popular dance tunes.

The small boy bolted down the gallery and out of the church homeward like lightning.

The Vicar's hair fairly stood on end; he held up his hand and said, 'Stop! stop!' but he was not heard owing to the noise of the playing, and the more he called the louder they played.

Then the Squire came out of his pew which was lined with green baize – where the visitors to the Hall were worshipping – and stood in front of the gallery, shaking his fist at the musicians shouting, 'What! In this holy place? Never shall one of you villainous players sound a note in this church again'.

Then the unfortunate church band came to their senses and realised where they were. 'Twas a sight to see them creep down the gallery stairs, with their fiddles and clarinets, all looking like naughty schoolboys.

The Vicar would have forgiven them when he learned the truth, but the Squire would not. That very week he sent for a barrel organ that would play two-and-twenty psalm tunes, so exact and particular that it was impossible to play anything else. He had a really respectable man to turn the handle and the players played no more. The members of our church orchestra had a more dignified exit; they gave way for a harmonium and in 1896 this was supplanted by the present organ.

WEDDINGS AND FUNERALS

A tremendous amount of sympathy prevailed in the village. There was feeling for the joyous events as well as the sad, and as the village was small, the date of a wedding of a villager would be known well beforehand. The invited friends of the bride and bridegroom went into Church, but curiosity was shown by a goodly number of ladies at the church gate, watching the bride enter the church. Comments about the dresses of the bride and bridesmaids, chiefly flattering, were heard.

Sympathy was shown at funerals. During severe illnesses, practical help was forthcoming very readily from neighbours. Offers of help to sit up during the night to care for the sick, to look after the children, or to help in other ways, were freely given. Delicacies suitable for a sick person's diet would be taken to the house. Beef tea and egg custards were often carried from our house to the invalids, while my mother frequently took turns in sitting up at night with sick friends. This practical help from all was done voluntarily.

The signal that a death had occurred was given by the tolling of the church bell on the morning after the death. As has already been related, the particular way the bell was tolled denoted whether it was a male or female who had died. It was also the custom to invite friends of the deceased to view the corpse.

At the time of the funeral, the blinds of every house on the route of the funeral procession were drawn. The people were too poor to afford hearses and funeral coaches, so the coffin was carried by the bearers, and the mourners walked. A bier (a vehicle made specially to carry coffins) was available. This had to be pushed. It had iron tyres and as the roads were not tarmacadamed at this time, the bier made a rattling noise. On this account, very little use was made of it, even when rubber tyres were substituted for the iron. Consequently, the coffin was carried by four or six men.

The method of carrying was webbing passed under the coffin and through the handles. The bearers slipped their hands through the webbing. This meant a heavy strain on the hands and necessitated a change of hands if the journey was long. So that this could be done with dignity, villagers along the route, perhaps at one or two positions, placed two kitchen chairs on the pavement, and if the undertaker thought it advisable, he quietly fetched them, the coffin was placed on them and the bearers changed sides. The chairs were returned and the procession would proceed. Wreaths were carried by the mourners.

The funeral over, the procession returned to the house and a meal would have been provided for the bearers, generally cold ham and ale, while the relatives took tea in another room.

THE CHURCHYARD

A Saxon phrase describes it as 'God's Acre'. Now it is often called a 'Garden of Rest'. The Churchyard has been enlarged at least three times. In the 14th century the whole of the south side of the Churchyard formed the vicarage grounds. The vicarage was situated slightly towards the west corner. In 1855 the old Churchyard was enlarged by enclosing a timber yard and surrounding ground, given for the purpose by the Wise family.

There are many ancient memorials, but owing to the soft character of the stone employed, in the majority of cases the inscriptions are no longer legible.

At the south-east corner of the chancel is a very characteristic and decidedly ancient tomb. The walls are of massive stonework rising to about twenty inches above the surrounding ground and covered by a heavy slab. The position chosen for the tomb undoubtedly points to its having contained the body of a dignitary of the church, possibly the remains of one of the priors of Kenilworth.

At the east end of the chancel is an area enclosed by kerbing. Here are the remains of the Parsons family, a branch of which lived at Furzen Hill. On one of the stones are engraved the names of members of the family who have been buried there since 1602.

We do not know how our Churchyard looked then, but we do know that the herbage was grazed by sheep, and the hinges of the gates which protected the porch from intrusion can be seen at the present time. In some Churchyards crops were grown. The story is told of a Rector (not a Cubbington incumbent) who had sown his Churchyard with turnips, to the annoyance of the Archdeacon. That dignitary is said to have reprovingly told the Rector that he hoped he would not find turnips there next year. 'Certainly not', was the reply, 'Next year it will be barley'.

It was the custom then and for many years afterwards to leave mounds to indicate where the graves were situated. When the use of sheep was discontinued what a lot of work was needed to keep the Churchyard tidy! Men were employed to mow with scythe and sickle.

A transformation has taken place since then. It is now a real Garden of Rest. Scores of rose trees are in bloom, and the closely mown turf is neatly edged. Our Garden of Rest is one of the best in the County.

The following record of results in competitions deserves the warmest praise from parishioners as a whole. All this has been done by a small band of voluntary workers. Many hours of devoted effort goes into that accomplishment. The result is not unrecognised.

In the competition for the Best Kept Churchyard in the Warwickshire Rural District Council, Cubbington won in 1961, 1962, 1963, 1964, and 1965.

Cubbington was also the winner in 1964 of the Trophy awarded for the Best Kept Churchyard in the Diocese of Coventry and received Certificates of Merit in this Competition in 1962, 1963, 1964, 1965.

As I am writing this on a July evening, the following quotation comes to mind:

With the kiss of the sun for pardon,
And the song of the birds for mirth,
One is nearer God's heart in a garden
Than anywhere else on earth.

How aptly this applies to Cubbington Churchyard, our 'Garden of Rest' — a beautiful garden.

THE REGISTERS

The Burial registers date from 1559 but they are wanting 1642-1719; the Marriage registers from 1590 but wanting 1643-1719, and the Baptismal registers from 1606 but wanting 1643-1707, — irregular and scanty to 1730.

QUAINT EXTRACTS

1636 *Paied unto Thomas Buxton for lodgeing of William Grundie on our ladie daie:* 2s. 6d.

1640 *Payd for a warrant for Anne Lapworth, who would not abide at her service.*

1645 *Sept. 18th.*
To the Constable of Cubbington.
I pray certifie your neighbours that I intend (God willing) to keep Thursday the 25th of this instant September, a day for hiring of servants at Bubonhall. *To. Deane.*

1658 *Item given to goody Allibone for tending Anne Allin when she lay sicke.* 4s. 0d.
Item, given to William Hands for going with the Constable to Warwick for two warrants for William Garlicks daughters. 0s. 6d.

1661 *Item payd Joane Greene her quartridge.* 2s. 6d.

1668 *Payd for a warrand for such as would not pay the levy.*

1671 *Payd misstress Grisold for rente for the house that ye Widow Harte liveth in and Sara Twitty.*

1679 *Elizabeth Lapworth was buryed in Wollen according to ye Late Act of Parliament and John Jepson buryed in Wollen which are all ye burials that have been in our Parish since ye act.*

John Price, Vicar.

In 1678 an Act of Parliament required that all persons buried should be wrapped in woollen shrouds with a view to encouraging the wool trade, and an affidavit that this had been done had to be brought within eight days of the burial.

1682 *Given to Martin Gardiner having been under ye Sargen's hand, powder and shot.* 1s. 4d.

1689 *Sept. 19th funerall charges for Sutton* 5s. 0d.

Memo. his apparell sold for 2s. 6d.

1693 *for a warand for seasing ye woming at Will Rees.* 1s. 0d.

1694 *paid to Mr. Price* (Vicar) *for money he payd To John Reynolds for twice going to Coventry & for Post letters and for his own journey to Coventry & expence & letters* 2s. 6d.

1698 *Payd for old Martin Garnor his duty to the King for his buriall*

1708 *pd Abram Morrol for a load of wood yt Joseph Wright had when he was sicke*

1725 *Feb. 15th. pead too William Waranam for Crokepin* (probably crow-keeping?)

1768 *Dec. 2nd. Paid for two foxes* 2s. 0d.
Dec. 10th. Paid for Edge hog 4d.

1769 *May 13th. Paid for Sacrament Wine* 4s. 0d.
14th. For a Church Broom 1s. 0d.
16th. For a Edge Hog. 4d.

1769 *June 1st. Sparrows* 2d.
2nd Ditto 2d.
Church Prayer Book 18s. 0d.
3rd Paid for Four Foxes 2s. 0d.

1770 *Ap. 26. For writing the accounts* 2s. 6d.

1779 *paid William Draper for wringing* (sic) *the bells* 14 shilling

Interior of temporary Roman Catholic Church (c. 1948)

HIRINGS

September 18th, 1645. To the Constable of Cubbington. I pray certifie your neighbours that I intend (God willing) to keep Thursday the 25th, of this instant September, a day for hiring of servants at Bubonhall. To Deane.

These hiring sessions were held once or twice yearly at Michaelmas and Whitsun and were attended by farmers and farm servants. The farm servants indicated the particular work they sought by wearing an emblem in the lapel of their coat, or some other sign: the waggoner, a piece of whipcord; the cowman, a wisp of straw; the shepherd carried a crook. These sessions were called by various names: the Hiring, Mop or Statute Fair, so called after the Statutes of Labourers passed in 1349. Sometimes a Runaway Mop was held a week or two later, for the benefit of those who had made a bad bargain.

The Warwick and Stratford-upon-Avon Mops are relics of these Statute Fairs.

The ravages of The Black Death of 1348 had some alarming results. The death of about half of the population through the plague made agricultural and other labour almost impossible to obtain. Wages rose; prices of food rose also. Labourers wandered away from their villages to seek higher wages elsewhere.

There were many landless men wandering about who could have found work if they had wished, but preferred the wild, free life of the woods, and became bandits and beggars. This state of the country caused the Government to pass an Act in 1349 known as the Statute of Labourers. It ran as follows —

Every man or woman of whatsoever condition, free or bond, able in body and within the age of threescore years, and not having of his own whereof he may live, nor land of his own, about the tillage of which he may occupy himself and not serving any other, shall be bound to serve the employer who shall require him to do so, and shall take only the wages which were accustomed to be taken in the neighbourhood where he is bound to serve.

If a man refused to obey the laws he was sent to prison.

LIST OF VICARS

A. de Thorpe Mandeville	1346
H. Aleyn	1348
T. Silverstre	1349
W. Haywell	1349
J. Blackfordsby	1401
T. Halford	1402
T. Hulle	1410
J. Marshall	1421
W. Lydom	1422
R. Wylkins	1425
J. Hall	1427
W. Loweles	1428
R. Wells	1437
S. Percivall	1439
J. Gubbys	1441
J. Huggeford	1444
R. More	1450
W. Sheydun	1454
R, Marten	1457
R. Alryche	1511
W. Wylliamson	1533
J. Steoynson (dec'd)	1548
J. Olde	1548
W. Ludmans	1554
T. Gardiner	1557
J. Lounde	1561
W. Catherall	1564
R. Barker	1569
G. Barley	1572
R. Marrell	1581
J. Harper	1626
J. Price	1672
G. Greenway	1699
R. Blore	1719
G. Huddesford	1731
E. Horne	1732
T. Welsh	1763
J. Dodson	1764
C. Dodson (dec'd)	1792
J. Austen	1792
G. L.Cooke	1820
M. Anstis	1854
T. Edge	1865
B. M. Bean	1880
P. T. Broadway	1918
M. Gordon	1952
E. Smith	1957
D. Glyn-Lewis	1968

INCUMBENTS OF NOTE

J Olde Presented to this living by King Edward VI — 'the true Patron hereof'. This was, no doubt, brought about by the confiscation of the possessions and rights of the Canons of Kenilworth by the Crown when the Monasteries were dissolved by Henry VIII. Mr. Olde is said to have entertained one or more of the Great Reformers at Cubbington.

Richard Blore 'Rector of Corley and Vicar of Cubbington, buried in the Church of Cubbington, near the Reading Pue. March 23rd, 1729'

G. Huddesford Vacated living on being elected President of Trinity College, Oxford.

C Dodson Tablet in Church — 'in him the Parishioners lost a faithful and good Minister, the poor a true friend, and the world an honest man.'

James Austen The brother of Jane Austen, the famous novelist.

George Leigh Cooke At one time Tutor at Corpus Christi College, Oxford, he also occupied the Chair of Sedleian Professor of Natural Philosophy at Oxford. Amongst eminent men who had the benefit of Mr. Cooke's instruction may be mentioned the famous Dr. Arnold of Rugby, the Rev. John Keble and Sir John Coleridge.

— † —

A Sermon preached at Cubbington Church, September 24th, 1865, by the Rev. M. Anstis, MA., Vicar, Late Fellow of Exeter College Oxford.

The author of this Sermon, having been requested by his friends to print it in justification of the step he is about to take, viz. the resignation of the living of Cubbington, feels that, by complying with their request, he may prevent much misrepresentation of both his motives and his words.

SERMON

The 1st Epistle to the Thessalonians,
Chapter 5, verses 12-13:

And we beseech you, brethren, to know them which labour among you, and are over you in the Lord, and admonish you; And to esteem them very highly in love for their work's sake.

By the good providence of our God, we are brought round once more, to that Sunday which is known to most of you as the 'Wake' Sunday, and although the name stamps the day and the week with a character anything but religious, yet I think we should remember, on each returning 'Wake', that this was the season at which our Church was first consecrated to the service and worship of Almighty God, this, the first Lord's Day on which the blessed sounds of prayers and praises were heard within these hallowed walls.

From the services, however, of our Sanctuary, our thoughts are naturally led on, to the Ministers who perform them and the people who join in them. Saint Paul, in the text, tells us the relationship that should exist between these two classes. He tells all Christian men how they should regard those who are set over them as their spiritual guides and teachers — they are 'to esteem them very highly in love for their work's sake'. In another place, the apostle writes, 'Obey them that have the rule over you, and submit yourselves, for they watch for your souls, as they must give account'. Also, he enjoins Timothy, 'Let the elders that rule well, be counted worthy of double honour, especially they who labour in the word and doctrine.'

Now, I think we cannot dwell on such passages as these, without seeing at once, how they are totally disregarded amongst ourselves. In this respect, the Parish of Cubbington presents a strange anomaly, such as cannot be accounted for on any Christian principles.

The chief rate-payers of the place profess themselves to be Churchmen, some of them are pretty constant attenders at Church, and occasionally partake of the Blessed Sacrament at my hands, and yet, instead of esteeming the Minister of Christ, set over them for this work or his office's sake, instead of paying him any respect, they are never so well pleased as when they can be vilifying and insulting and lowering him in the estimation of their dependants and poorer neighbours.

Insult offered to me personally, that is, in my character of a neighbour, I am not going to notice. It is beneath me. Supposing it to proceed from ignorance, I shall treat it with contempt, and pity those who offer it. But insult to my sacred office and the work I have been appointed to do in this Parish as the Minister of Christ, I am bound to rebuke if I am to be loyal to my Heavenly Master, and honestly teach you your duties to God and man.

Now, the office of teaching and admonishing in a Christian Minister is most properly exercised in these three places — the Church — the Schools — and the sick chamber. My time as Vicar of this Parish has been spent chiefly in ministering to my people, old and young. But what is my reward for attempting to perform these duties to the best of my ability?

I have no means of learning the feelings of the parishioners at a Parish Meeting, in a body, on such a subject, except I would ask them first, what is my reward for giving to my people in this Church, as reverential and as ably a performed service as is to be found at any Parish Church in the County, and giving it quite as much at my own expense, as at that of the Parish — for my offerings towards the due performance of Divine Service in this Church have equalled, during my incumbency, all that has been given by the Parish, whether voluntarily or by the Church rate.

What is my reward for this? At a Vestry meeting, the moment Church matters are referred to, the whole assemblage is in an uproar. A volley of abuse has been fired at the Vicar, such as he would not have to encounter at a low public house, because on one occasion, finding people standing in the aisle of his Church, he shewed them into seats, that would certainly not be occupied by their supposed owners.

What every right-minded man would have called a kind and Christian act, draws from Cubbington Vestry, nothing but abuse and insult. One farmer gives him the lie to his face, in a threatening attitude, as if about to strike, declaring that he would rather believe a former drunken Sexton, than the Vicar.

Another accuses him of misapplying (I almost said 'robbing', for the words would bear that meaning) the Sacrament money, he having the strictest account of every farthing he has ever received and spent, since he first became Vicar.

Another, with an awful lie on his lips, tries to get up a scene in the House of God, by claiming a pew, to which he has no more right than has a man living in London.

Another, since the meeting, swears several oaths at the Vicar in the public streets, and another tells him in earnest (the man meant what he said) that it was all one to him, whether Cubbington people went to hell or to heaven.

Be it remarked, all these men profess to be Church people, who go to no other place of worship but the Church, and men who have their children taught, as is right, their duty to God and their neighbour, that duty which tells each to submit himself to all his governors, teachers, spiritual pastors and masters.

Whence, then, proceeds this grievous inconsistency? If these men differed from me in their religious opinions, one might have accounted for the insults, by ascribing them to an ignorance of the Christian duty of toleration. If they had been men of a very low grade of society, one would have said that they did not know any better, that they did not know how to behave in the presence of a gentleman. But they have no such excuse, for most of these men aspire to a higher place in society than that, to which by their occupation, they are entitled.

However, let them not think that they can treat a Minister of Christ thus, and escape the judgement of God even in this world. The master who, by his life, teaches his servants to despise the spiritual pastors, will one day find those servants rise up against himself. The parent who, by his example, teaches his children to neglect the duty of public worship will live to hear those children cursing him in his old age. Nor let anyone think that the conduct of which I complain, is the conduct of a few. If few are the chief speakers or actors at these meetings, there are many to encourage them, laughing aloud at these insults offered to their Vicar, as if at a good joke.

I never had a word of sympathy, nor did I hear a cry of 'Shame!' when the most dire insults were being offered to me in the presence of the largest rate-payers in the Parish, except from my present, respected, Churchwarden.

The same account that I give of my ministrations at the Church, I can relate of those at the schools and the sick bed. At the Easter meeting of last year, it was asserted by someone, without any foundation, that our schools were declining in numbers and efficiency, and immediately there was a look of satisfaction, if not a laugh, on every face at the table.

This year, when some Parish money was to be distributed and the Treasurer was at a loss to know how to spend it, money to which the schools had the strongest possible claim, every farmer in the Parish who had a vote voted against giving to them, and applied the money to a purpose for which it had never been spent before. No vote could be more unjust, but it satisfied the farmers (as I heard it expressed) if it spited the Vicar.

I need not add, now, how many leading farmers of the Parish are continually swearing at the schools and the teachers.

Some years ago, I seldom passed a week without hearing such oaths. Nor need I dwell on the baseness of one who could abuse the present teaching in the new Government School although he owned that he had never entered them in his life. Suffice to say, that the knowledge of Holy Scripture and the Religious Instruction of the young in these schools has since that meeting, been declared by the Government Inspector, to be of a higher order than any he has found in a village school in the County — and the persecution does not end here, it follows me to the sick chamber and the death bed. Not many months ago when attending daily on a poor sick man, reading, praying with him, and instructing him in the way of salvation, I tried to procure for him, when said to be dying, the same advantages that I should probably have, if I were dying or sick, namely the advantage of second doctor, or further advice, as men call it. I had good reasons for what I did, and in nothing did I transgress my path of duty, for an old book, entitled 'The Parish Priest's Guide to the Sick Chamber' says, "When thou enterest the sick room, be earnest in prayer, rebuke with gentleness, comfort with all kindness, see that the sick man's wants are supplied and proper medicines obtained for the relief of his suffering". I remembered them in my office of Parish Priest.

What was my reward for the alms and advice I gave and for the interest I had taken in the poor man's case? I received a letter, strangely enough, from the medical man whom I had recommended, taking me to task, if not threatening me with law proceedings, as if I had libelled him. This letter was written by the Doctor, but was traceable to a farm house in the Parish. I could not visit a sick and dying man in peace!

Now, how, under such circumstances, and among such people, is a Christian minister to perform his duties? For I might add to these remarks, that the moment these men have insulted me, they will act themselves and try to make their neighbours believe that they are the injured persons and I am in the wrong. Thus, the farmer who, at the last Vestry meeting spoke of my misapplying the Sacrament money, though formerly a constant attendant at Church in the afternoon on Sundays, has never come since because I was able to answer the charge. But, some men will say, some of the many strangers now present will ask, 'Is there not some cause for all this opposition? Have you not provoked the enmity of your people by some rudeness or some unseemly behaviour?' In answer to such a question, I declare before God, in this Holy Temple, that I cannot call to mind a single occasion during the eleven years of my ministry in this place, in which I have said a rude or unkind or unchristian word to anyone. I can thank God that I am the injured man, not the injurer. I have not come into collision with a single man in the Parish on any subject of business, save a former tenant of Glebe Farm, with whom I never had an unpleasant word, till he, for whose convenience I had spent a large sum of money, to whom, as his landlord, I had never refused a favour until he insulted me — this man told me, in my own house, without any provocation on my part, that he purposely did not stop, but rather encouraged the sin of adultery under the roof of my own cottage * because he knew that by so doing, he would annoy me. These were his very words. I gave him every opportunity of retracting such words — but as he refused to do so and persisted in his iniquitous work, I turned him out of the farm — the Lord judge between him and me.

That same wicked, lying farmer, aided by a neighbouring one, as I am informed, is striving to empty Cubbington Church at this very moment, by helping to put falsehoods into the Leamington newspaper, against me and those belonging to me. Again I say, the Lord judge between him and me.

For myself, I can affirm that amidst manifold infirmities and all these undeserved annoyances, I have endeavoured to be kind and courteous to all men, to relieve distress wherever I have met with it — to instruct, and often clothe also, the children of the poor, to help the village labourer in sickness — to comfort him in death and cheer him when a mourner. How, by such acts, I have given offence I cannot imagine.

I have not been a busy-body in other men's matters, I have confined myself to a Christian Minister's work at the Church, the Schools and the sick chamber. I have been ready to show kindness to my slanderers and many of them have received favours at my hands. I challenge enquiry. I defy contradiction. Where then, is the esteem due to the Minister of Christ in this Parish?

** (this most probably refers to the cottage belonging to Glebe Farm)*

The Revd P T Broadway

Those who dissent from me on religious opinions are courteous and respectful to myself and my office, and I think, will say of me, that I try to live in all neighbourly kindness with them. Those who profess to have me as their spiritual guide, treat me in the manner I have described.

I am tempted, at times, to ask, 'Am I living among heathen men, or Christians?'

Most people, I think, would say, among the former, especially when they know that a leading farmer of this parish sent his child up to Cubbington Church to be buried without a mourner or a single attendant, so that I found it difficult to perform the Burial Service, and drove off to Warwick market as soon as the bell had tolled to its memory. Could a heathen have shown less parental affection? I can hardly believe that this was done to insult my Office, but the whole village told me that it was.

On the mention of these sad truths, and I might have added many more, you will not be surprised to hear that, after due consideration, I have determined no longer to minister in the Parish of Cubbington. I have spoken to the Bishop on the subject and within a month from this time, I hope to resign the Vicarage. I have not come to this determination without much pain, for the middle class in the Village and those who teach in my schools, with my dependants and servants, I greatly respect, but I throw aside all worldly considerations, change of residence, great personal inconvenience and heavy loss.

If my presence in Cubbington helps to foster that fearful profaneness of which I complain, it is not good for me to stay any longer, so I will obey that command of my Master, 'When they persecute you in one city, flee ye to another', nothing doubting, but that His loving kindness and mercy will follow me all the days of my life. If only by His grace, I plead the truth in sincerity and labour to win souls to Him, with greater earnestness than I have ever yet shown. No weapon inflicts so deep a wound on the soul as the cutting slander, and from such a wound I have suffered much, but I shall pray for grace to forget and forgive it all yet I bear no ill will to my persecutors.

On the contrary, I shall pray for them, that they may soon be brought to a better mind, and give to my successor in the Vicarage, that respect and esteem which they have withheld from me, and I shall pray for myself that this trial, bitter as it has been to bear, may at last, through the mercy of Christ Jesus, be found to have helped forward my own soul's salvation.

And now, unto God the Father, etc.

REV. P. T. BROADWAY

Mr. Broadway became Vicar in February, 1918, after serving several years as Assistant Curate at Christ Church, Coventry.

He took a great interest in the Church choir and during the whole of his time here was an active member (he had a wonderful baritone voice) and for many years undertook the training of the choir, which, as well as the Festival anthems, also rendered 'The Crucifixion', 'The Messiah' and 'The Story of Calvary', among others.

Accompanied by his wife, who was his helpmate in every aspect of his work, he ran the Sunday School and each Sunday found them in charge of their classes. His work for the scholars did not end with the close of the Sabbath Day, for he was to be found on two weekday evenings during the greater part of the year at rehearsals for concerts, by which the Sunday School earned the funds to provide the extras such as prizes which were won by attendance.

For Sunday School outings, Barmouth, Colwyn Bay, Weston-super-Mare, Bournemouth, Southsea, Portsmouth, Eastbourne, Ryde and Skegness, amongst other places, were visited, some more than once. These activities entailed tremendous effort and organisation by the Vicar and the Sunday School secretary.

The Mothers' Union was first formed during his Vicariate. Meetings were held weekly. They were very popular, with Mrs. Broadway as leader, assisted by her husband — whose hearty singing leading the mothers was quite a feature and is still remembered.

A Men's Service was held on the third Sunday in the month and a Women's Bible Class every Sunday afternoon from 3 o'clock to 4 o'clock These Sunday afternoon services were preceded by the Vicar and his wife having taken Sunday School in the morning and afternoon, and the

Vicar taking Holy Communion and Morning and Evening Services.

The cost of the fares for the summer treats, for Christmas parties and the prizes was met by funds raised by Sunday School teachers' concerts and so on.

The Sunday School Anniversary day was a great excitement for the whole school.

This day was looked upon as Children's Day. The infants sat in the front pews of the nave and the rest occupied the chancel for the morning service. In the afternoon the children took bunches of flowers which were afterwards taken to the sick and aged of the Parish.

During the evening previous to this service, a procession took place through the main streets of the village, headed by the village brass band. Hymns were sung at various points and then the procession returned to Church.

On Easter Sunday, at the afternoon service, the children brought eggs which were taken to various hospitals. As many as 900 have been collected.

During his Vicariate, the Church Tower was restored and the organ cleaned and renovated. Ledbrook Hall was acquired, cleaned, repaired and decorated through his initiative — when he came to Cubbington it had been empty. It was dirty and derelict but after he and his band of helpers had finished it was suitable to be used as a Church Hall, the home of all the activities of the Church, and for meetings, parties and the Boys' Club, which met there for a number of years.

At the beginning of the Second World War, Ledbrook Hall became the headquarters of the Home Guard. The Vicar became head of the village wardens, and his study at the vicarage was used as the headquarters, men sleeping there when on night duty.

At the invitation of the Vicar and his wife, a Tennis Club was formed of church workers. The court was the vicarage lawn. Mrs. Broadway kindly allowed the use of the kitchen in which to prepare picnic teas, thus adding still further to the enjoyment.

He was a member of the Parish Council, of Warwick Rural District Council and for a time was its Chairman.

In all his parochial work, he was ably assisted by his wife. A great career of service was ended by his sudden death in October, 1951.

The road, Broadway, is named after him.

The Vicarage

VICARAGE HOUSES

Apparently there have been three Vicarages at Cubbington, the plans of which, fortunately, have been preserved.

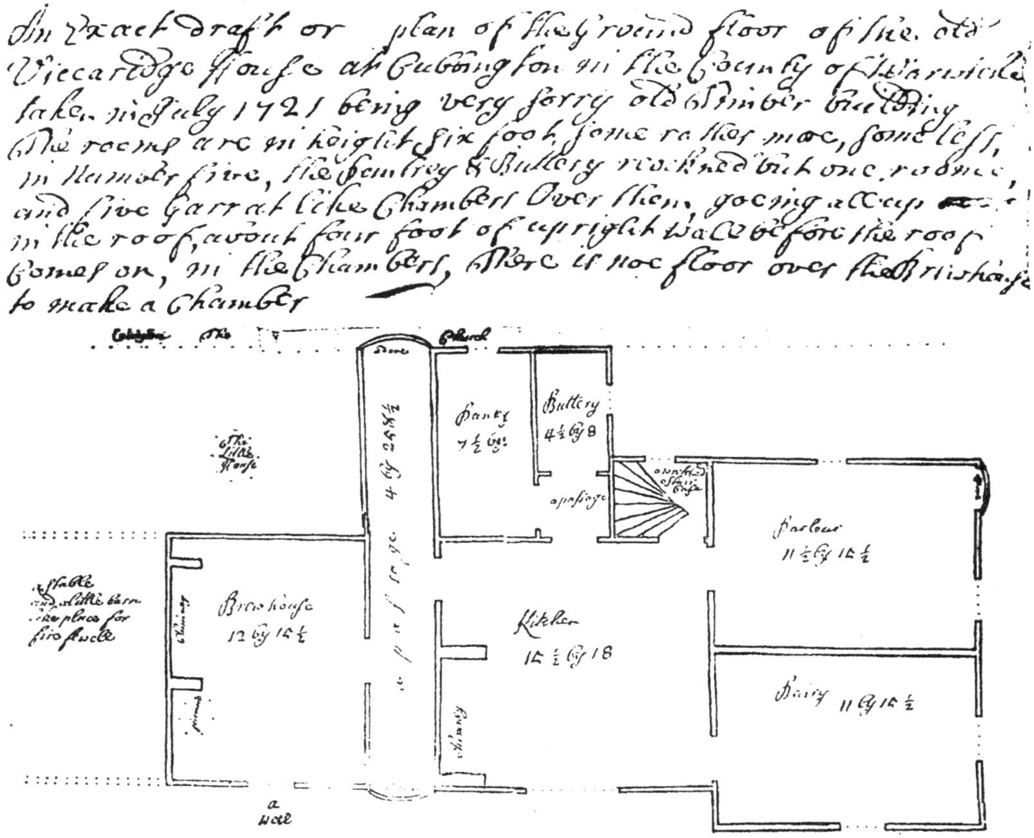
An exact draft or plan of the ground floor of the old
Vicaridge House at Cubbington in the County of Warwick
taken in July 1721 being very sorry old timber building
The rooms are in height six foot, some rather more, some less,
in number five, the pantrey & Buttery reckoned but one roome,
and five Garret like Chambers over them, goeing alleys
in the roof, about four foot of upright wall before the roof
comes on, in the Chambers, there is noe floor over the Brewhouse
to make a Chamber

The first, a 14th century house the plan of which appears above, had a long life. At this time the whole of the south side of our churchyard formed the vicarage grounds, the house being situated slightly towards the west corner. The description reads:

'An exact draft or plan of the ground floor of the old Vicarage House at Cubbington in the County of Warwick in July 1721 being very sorry old timber building. The rooms are in height six foot, some rather more, some less, in number five, the pantry and buttery reckoned but one room, and five garret-like chambers over them, goeing alleys in the roof about four foot of upright wall, before the roof comes on, in the chamber. There is no floor over the brewhouse to make a chamber.'

The new Vicarage was built in 1726 on the same site or close to it. Its plan is shown on the next page.

A memorandum in the Register says, 'This Vicarage House finished May 1726 as was ye Lord Leigh's at Stoneleigh Abbey'. The plan:

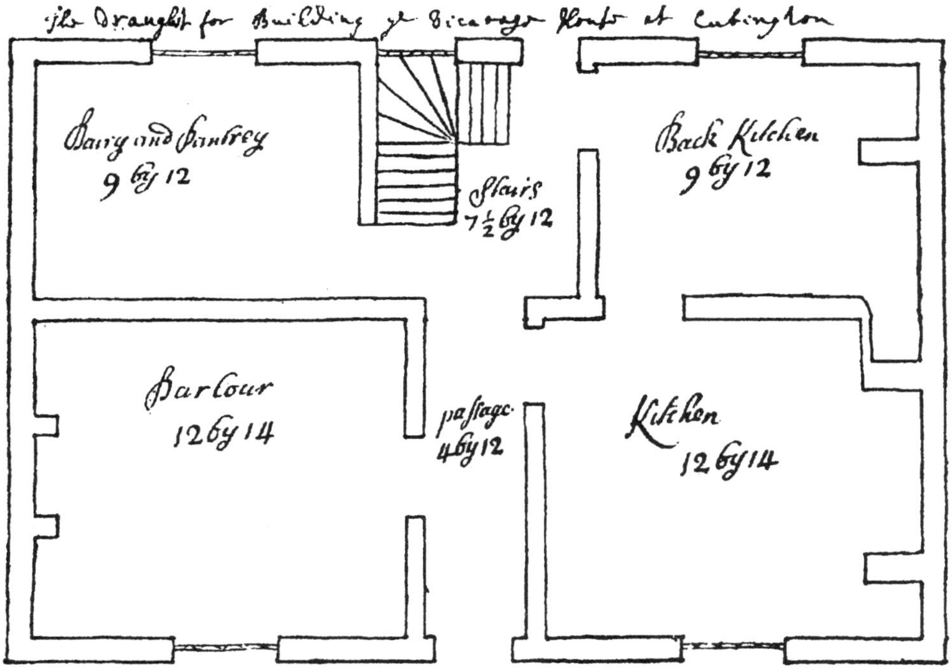

The present Vicarage was built in 1821, at a cost of £1,200 and enlarged at a later date.

LAND BELONGING TO THE VICARAGE OF CUBBINGTON IN THE COUNTY OF WARWICK

A house and two gardens near the Church in the village. The Hill Farm * is one hundred acres of Arable and Pasture. Twenty-one Acres in Coventry field and 21 Acres of land situate at Higham in Leicestershire. Purchased by the Governors of Queen Anne's Bounty.

As witness our hands this 17th November, 1801.
Thomas Warde. Curate of Cubbington.
James Smith. Church Warden.

** Hill Farm is now known as Glebe Farm.*

TITHES

As a reward for his services, a parish priest was accorded a number of privileges. He could refuse any of the civil or manorial offices, all military duty, membership of a jury, and, up to the sixteenth century, he was exempt from civil jurisdiction.

His house, and the lands that he cultivated, were free of rents in terms of money, produce or service, other than the exercise of his calling. Gradually his standing improved but, while continuing for centuries to farm his own glebe, he was not financially independent, and increasingly relied upon the community for support in the form of tithes.

Now this was originally a voluntary offering, consisting of one-tenth of the annual yield of stock and crops, or the products of personal industry, and had been devised either for the relief of the poor or to the general expenses of the Church. From about the tenth century onwards, it became a compulsory tax and was levied for the particular benefit of the priest.

Stoneleigh Abbey

Hill Farm House

Half-timbered barn on Offchurch Road

Tithes were either 'great tithes' calculated on corn, hay and wool, or 'small tithes' on everything else.

In early days, when land was granted or willed to cathedral chapters, monasteries or other ecclesiastical bodies, it was the custom for the latter to appropriate the great or rectorial tithes, and leave the small to the priest or vicar (deputy) who was appointed to the living.

At the Dissolution (1538) most monastic possessions including advowsons and rectorial rights passed into the hands of laymen.

When agriculture was carried on in the open fields and commons system, tithe collection in kind was feasible. The produce was stored in the tithe barn — often a place of architectural note.

At the beginning of the nineteenth century, the demand for the general commutation of the tithe had become insistent. The clergy opposed this because the commutation value was estimated as likely to be less than the value in kind, and so attempts to alter the custom were temporarily frustrated.

Even so, in many cases of enclosure, it was possible to extinguish tithe by allotting land in lieu to the tithe holder as it was in the Cubbington Enclosure Award 1768. This stated that the said Edward Lord Leigh was allocated three allotments of land, totalling 195 acres 2 roods 21 perches in lieu of impropriate tithes.

Earlier in the Award it declared that the Right Honourable Edward Lord Leigh was owner of the Rectory Impropriate of the Parish of Cubbington aforesaid and also Patron of the Advowson of the Vicarage there.

A Lay Rector is a layman receiving the rectorial tithes or in whom the rectory is vested.

Impropriate means to place tithes or ecclesiastical property in lay hands.

It appears that the Churchwardens were responsible for the fabric of the church, except the chancel, which was the responsibility of the rector or lay rector. The lay rector was responsible for the repair of the north, east and south walls of the chancel, and the roof. The Church Council is now responsible for the nave, which is considered to include the chancel arch.

THE TERRIER OF THE VICARAGE OF CUBBINGTON IN THE COUNTY OF WARWICK FOR THE YEAR 1809.

In the Parish of Cubbinton one hundred and twenty one Acres and Vicarage House and Garden.

Lands purchased by Queen Anne's Bounty at Higham on the Hill in the County of Leicestershire Eighteen Acres, 3 Roods and thirty one Perches as witness my hand

Sept.4th. 1809.

Thomas Warde — Curate of Cubbington.
Church Wardens — Thomas Smith
J. Murcott.

There is no Stipend or Tithe whatsoever Paid to the incumbent of the vicarage of Cubbington nor no other income than what arises from the Lands before mentioned.
Thomas Warde. — Curate of Cubbington.

A TERRIER OF THE VICARAGE OF CUBBINGTON FOR THE YEAR 1828

A new Vicarage House of one storey built by the present incumbent consisting on ground floor of two large sitting rooms, one small do., two kitchens with nine sleeping rooms in the upper storey.

Courtyard adjoining house enclosed round with two stables, coach house and other offices.

The Homestead comprising two grass fields of about four acres, one small kitchen garden adjoining Churchyard where old Vicarage House stood, also the Churchyard.

In Coventry field commencing from Rugby Turnpike Road and running north three contiguous closes containing about seventeen acres.

An Allotment of land called The Hill Farm, lying in south south east of Parish beginning from Offchurch Road, divided into several closes containing one hundred acres, having also on it a large new Barn, Cow Pens and cottage built by the present incumbent also an old Barn altered into a stable.

Lands purchased by the Governor of Queen Anne's Bounty at Higham on the Hill in the County of Leicester containing twenty one acres.

George Leigh Cooke, — Vicar of Cubbington.
Thomas Smith — Churchwardens of
George Hinde — Cubbington.

Aug. 6th 1828.

CHURCH RESTORATION ACCOUNT

In sending this Balance Sheet to the Subscribers to the Restoration Fund, I would venture to express the opinion that the work has been well done, and would take the opportunity of offering my grateful thanks to both Parishioners and Non-Parishioners for their kind and generous help.

Cubbington Vicarage.
October 1885. B. M. Bean.

CHURCH RESTORATION ACCOUNT

RECEIVED	£	s.	d.
Subscriptions	838	1	0
Offertories	21	0	7
Interest (Greenway & Co.)	5	15	7
Collected in Box	0	15	9½
	865	12	11½

SPECIAL GIFTS

Oak Reredos	The Misses Ledbrook
Brass Altar Desk	Mrs. Bean
Brass Altar Vases and Service Book	Col. Walker
Brass Pulpit Desk	Mrs. Fielding Harding
Book Markers	Miss Walker
Kneeling Cushion for Altar Rails	Miss Ledbrook
Chancel Stools	Miss E. Ledbrook

PAID	£	s.	d.
Mr. G. Smith	836	4	0
Mr. Ingleby	9	0	0
For Faculty	7	16	6
Mr. E. Duggins	6	13	8
Jones and Willis		6	9
Brown and Son		8	5
Carriage of Goods		10	8
Printing		15	0
Small Expenses	1	10	6
Mr. J. Bastock	1	11	6
	864	17	0
Balance in Treasurer's Hands		15	11½
	865	12	11½

CHURCH RESTORATION FUND

LIST OF SUBSCRIBERS

	£	s.	d.
Miss Bodington (for re-seating)	200	0	0
J. Y. Robins, Esq. J.P.	100	0	0
Mrs. Woodhead	100	0	0
Rev. B.M. Bean	50	0	0
W. Ledbrook, Esq.	50	0	0
The Lord Leigh	21	0	0
The Lord Bishop of Worcester	20	0	0
J. H. Bodington, Esq.	20	0	0
Mrs. John Ledbrook	20	0	0
W R. Mann, Esq.	20	0	0
Lieut. Col. Walker	20	0	0
J. Kidd, Esq.	10	10	0
Mrs. Barton	10	0	0
A. W. Bean, Esq. J.P.	10	0	0
Dr. Blease	10	0	0
James Dawson, Esq.	10	0	0
N. Fisher, Esq.	10	0	0
D. Shaw, Esq.	10	0	0
Miss Wise (Milverton)	10	0	0
G. Turner, Esq.	6	0	0
Rev. F. Edge	5	5	0
Mr. Ballard	5	0	0
Miss Bagnall	5	0	0
Mrs. Baylis & Son	5	0	0
W. Bell, Esq.	5	0	0
St. Cath. College, Cambridge	5	0	0
Miss Cooke	5	0	0
Rev. G. Cooke	5	0	0
Mr. James Green	5	0	0
Mrs. Murcott (Leamington)	5	0	0
J. Nickson, Esq.	5	0	0
J. Wilkes, Esq.	5	0	0
W. Woodhead, Esq.	5	0	0
Miss Julia Cooke	3	0	0
Mr. W. Fell	3	0	0
Mr. Flecknoe	3	0	0
Mr. Bennett	2	10	0
A. Bird, Esq.	2	2	0
Mrs. Cranstown	2	2	0
Mrs. Greaves	2	2	0
Mrs. T. Hyland	2	2	0
Cubbington Co-operative Soc'ty.	2	0	0
Messrs. Duggins and Sons	2	0	0
D. J. Flattley, Esq.	2	0	0
Mr. T. Gibbs	2	0	0
J. Keymer, Esq.	2	0	0
Mr. Marson	2	0	0
Mr. Penn	2	0	0
Mr. Whitmore	2	0	0
Rev. Maze Gregory	1	1	0
J. Pilling, Esq.	1	1	0
Mr. Poole	1	1	0

Miss Shepheard	1	1	0
The late Capt. Wise, R.N.	1	1	0
Mr. Bass	1	0	0
Mr. J. Bastock	1	0	0
S. Bird, Esq.	1	0	0
Miss C. Fell	1	0	0
Mrs Eliza Frankton	1	0	0
Mr Frankton	1	0	0
A Friend (per Col. Walker)	1	0	0
Mr Gardner	1	0	0
Miss Hensman	1	0	0
Mrs Hyland	1	0	0
Mr Johnson	1	0	0
The late Miss de Lancy	1	0	0
Mrs Lea	1	0	0
H. Pierce, Esq.	1	0	0
Mr Spicer	1	0	0
E.J. Walker, Esq.	1	0	0
Mr Wells	1	0	0
Miss Lucy Wheeler	1	0	0
Mr E. Duggins		10	0
Mrs Mary Frankton		10	0
Miss Frankton		10	0
Mrs Freer		10	0
Mr E. Bastock		5	0
Mr J. Brookes		5	0
Mr Davenport		5	0
Mr Elliott		5	0
Mrs W. Green		5	0
Mr King		5	0
Mr Peppitt		5	0
Miss Taylor		5	0
Mr Underwood		5	0
Mrs Williams		5	0
Mr Jas. Vincent		3	0
Mr Garner		2	6
Mr Gilbert		2	6
Mr Heycock		2	6
Mr Smith		2	6
	838	1	0

———†———

BY THE QUEEN

A Proclamation
FOR A GENERAL FAST

Whereas by the most Terrible and Dreadful Storms of Wind, with which it Pleased Almighty God to Afflict the greater part of this Our Kingdom on Friday and Saturday the Twenty sixth and Twenty seventh Days of November last some of Our Ships of War, and many Ships of Our Loving Subjects, have been Destroyed and Lost at Sea, and great number of Our Subjects serving on Board the same have perished and many Houses and other Buildings of Our Good Subjects have been either totally thrown down and Demolished, or very much Damaged and Defaced and thereby several Persons have been killed and Many Stacks of Corn and Hay thrown down and scattered abroad, to the Damage and Impoverishment of many others, especially the Poorer sort; and great numbers of Timber and other Trees have by the said storm been torn up by the Roots, in many parts of this Our Kingdom. A Calamity of this Sort so Dreadful and Astonishing, that the like hath not been seen or felt, in the Memory of any Person Living in this Our Kingdom and which Loudly Calls for the Deepest and most solemn Humiliation of us and Our People. Therefore out of a Deep and Pious sense of what We and Our People have suffered by the said Dreadful winds and storms (which we most humbly acknowledge to be a Token of the Divine Displeasure, and that it was the Infinite Mercy of God that We and All Our People were not thereby wholly destroyed) and putting our Trust in Almighty God, that upon Our Humiliation and Repentance, He will be Gracious to Us and Our Kingdom, and will yet Vouchsafe a Special Blessing to Us and Our People in the Just War wherein we are engaged. We have Resolved and (by and with the Advice of Our Privy Council) do hereby Command, that a General and Public Fast be observed throughout this Kingdom, in such manner as is herein after Directed and Prescribed that so that Both We and Our Subjects may humble Ourselves before Almighty God, and may in most Devout and Solemn Manner send up our prayers and Supplications to the Divine Majesty, to implore his Blessing and Favour, and the continuation of his Mercy, and the Protestant religion to us and Our Posterity and that it would please him to pardon the Crying Sins of this Nation which have drawn down this Sad and heavy Judgement on us and our people and to

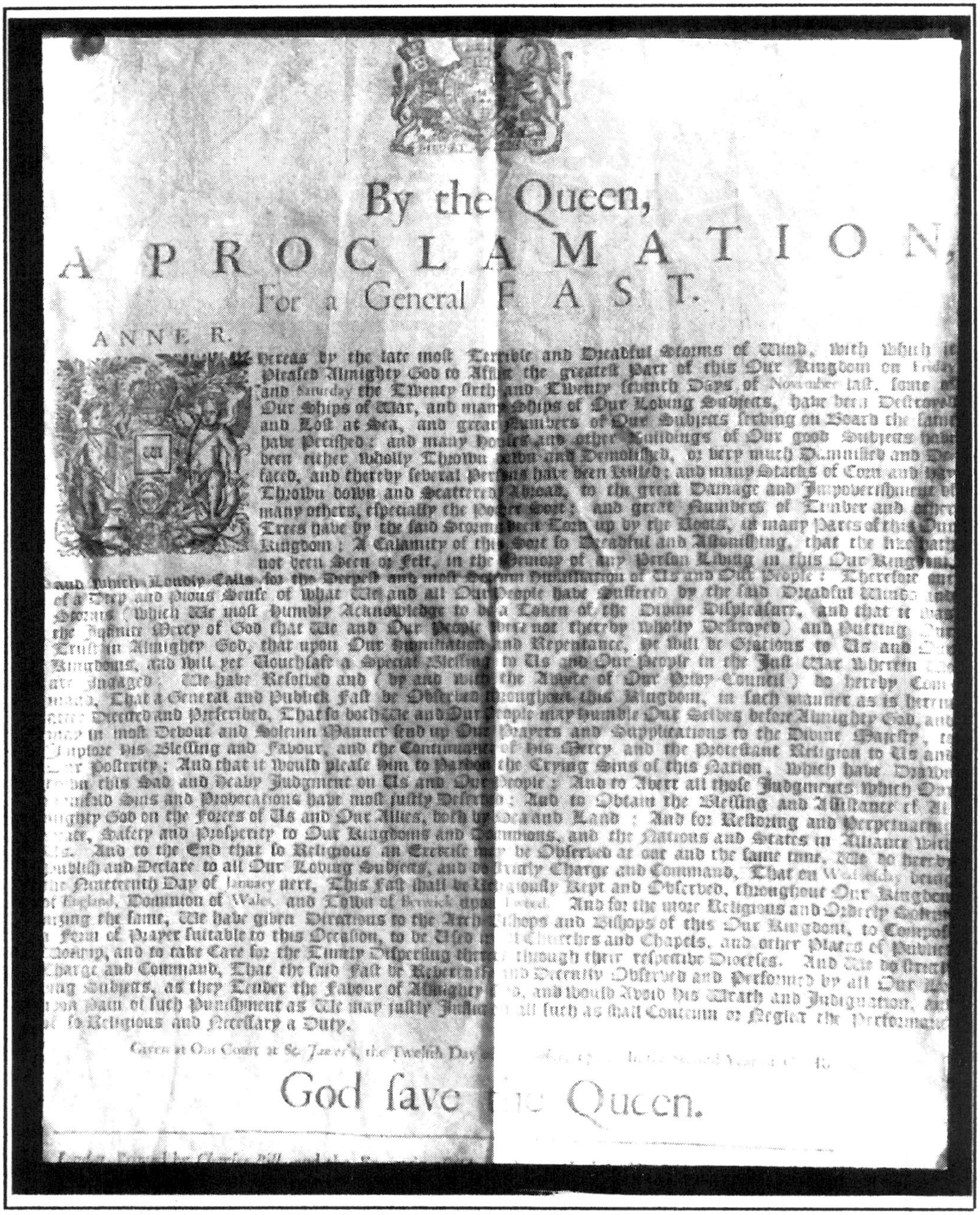

By the Queen,

A PROCLAMATION,

For a General FAST.

ANNE R.

Whereas by the late most Terrible and Dreadful Storms of Wind, with which it Pleased Almighty God to Afflict the greatest Part of this Our Kingdom on Friday and Saturday the Twenty sixth and Twenty seventh Days of November last, some of Our Ships of War, and many Ships of Our Loving Subjects, have been Destroyed and Lost at Sea, and great Numbers of Our Subjects serving on Board the same have Perished; and many Houses and other Buildings of Our good Subjects have been either wholly Thrown down and Demolished, or very much Damnified and Defaced, and thereby several Persons have been Killed; and many Stacks of Corn and Hay Thrown down and Scattered Abroad, to the great Damage and Impoverishment of many others, especially the Poorer Sort; and great Numbers of Timber and other Trees have by the said Storms been Torn up by the Roots, in many Parts of this Our Kingdom; A Calamity of this Sort so Dreadful and Astonishing, that the like hath not been Seen or Felt, in the Memory of any Person Living in this Our Kingdom, and which Loudly Calls for the Deepest and most Solemn Humiliation of Us and Our People: Therefore out of a Deep and Pious Sense of what We and all Our People have Suffered by the said Dreadful Winds and Storms (which We most humbly Acknowledge to be a Token of the Divine Displeasure, and that it was the Infinite Mercy of God that We and Our People were not thereby wholly Destroyed) and Putting Our Trust in Almighty God, that upon Our Humiliation and Repentance, he will be Gracious to Us and Our Kingdoms, and will yet Vouchsafe a Special Blessing to Us and Our People in the Just War wherein we are Engaged: We have Resolved and (by and with the Advice of Our Privy Council) do hereby Command, That a General and Publick Fast be Observed throughout this Kingdom, in such manner as is herein after Directed and Prescribed, That so both We and Our People may humble Our Selves before Almighty God, and may in most Devout and Solemn Manner send up Our Prayers and Supplications to the Divine Majesty, to Implore his Blessing and Favour, and the Continuance of his Mercy and the Protestant Religion to Us and Our Posterity; And that it would please him to Pardon the Crying Sins of this Nation, which have Drawn down this Sad and heavy Judgment on Us and Our People; And to Avert all those Judgments which Our manifold Sins and Provocations have most justly Deserved; And to Obtain the Blessing and Assistance of Almighty God on the Forces of Us and Our Allies, both by Sea and Land; And for Restoring and Perpetuating Peace, Safety and Prosperity to Our Kingdoms and Dominions, and the Nations and States in Alliance with Us. And to the End that so Religious an Exercise may be Observed at one and the same time, We do hereby Publish and Declare to all Our Loving Subjects, and do Strictly Charge and Command, That on Wednesday being the Nineteenth Day of January next, This Fast shall be Religiously Kept and Observed, throughout Our Kingdom of England, Dominion of Wales, and Town of Berwick upon Tweed. And for the more Religious and Orderly Solemnizing the same, We have given Directions to the Archbishops and Bishops of this Our Kingdom, to Compose a Form of Prayer suitable to this Occasion, to be Used in all Churches and Chapels, and other Places of Publick Worship, and to take Care for the Timely Dispersing thereof through their respective Dioceses. And We do Strictly Charge and Command, That the said Fast be Reverently and Decently Observed and Performed by all Our Loving Subjects, as they Tender the Favour of Almighty God, and would Avoid his Wrath and Indignation, and upon Pain of such Punishment as We may justly Inflict on all such as shall Contemn or Neglect the Performance of so Religious and Necessary a Duty.

Given at Our Court at St. James's, the Twelfth Day [illegible] Second Year of Our Reign.

God save the Queen.

London, Printed by Charles Bill, and [illegible]

The Proclamation for a General Fast

Avert all those Judgements which Our manifold sins and Provocations have most justly Deserved; And to Obtain the Blessing and Assistance of Almighty God on the Forces of Us and Our Allies, both by Sea and Land; And for Restoring and Perpetuating Peace, Safety and Prosperity to Our Kingdoms and Dominions and to implore his Blessing and Favour, and the continuation of his Mercy, and the Protestant religion to us and Our Posterity and that it would please him to pardon the Crying Sins of this Nation which have drawn down this Sad and heavy Judgement on us and our people and to Avert all those Judgements which Our manifold sins and Provocations have most justly Deserved; And to Obtain the Blessing and Assistance of Almighty God on the Forces of Us and Our Allies, both by Sea and Land; And for Restoring and

Perpetuating Peace, Safety and Prosperity to Our Kingdoms and Dominions and the Nations and States in Alliance with Us. And to the End that so Religious an Exercise may be Observed at one and the same time, We do hereby Publish and Declare to All Our Loving Subjects, and do strictly Charge and Command That on Wednesday being the nineteenth day of January next, This Fast shall be Religiously Kept and Observed, throughout Our Kingdom of England, Dominion of Wales, and Town of Berwick on Tweed and for the more Religious and Orderly Solemnizing the same, We have given Directions to the Archbishops and Bishops of this Our Kingdom to Compose a Form of Prayer, suitable to the Occasion, to be Used in all Churches and Chapels, and other Places of Publick Worship, and to take Care for the Timely Dispensing thereof through their respective Dioceses. And We do strictly Charge and Command, That the said Fast be Reverently and Devoutly Observed and Performed by all Our Loving Subjects as they Tender the favour of Almighty God and would Avoid His Wrath and Indignation, and upon Pain of such Punishment as We may justly Inflict on all such as shall Condemn or Neglect the Performance of so Religious and Necessary a Duty.

Given at Our Court of St. James, 12th day of December 1702, in the Second Year of Our Reign.

God Save the Queen.

——†——

A Fast Day in the Early Church was kept by observing a literal abstinence from food till evening, and then only a simple meal was eaten. There was no restriction on the kind of food eaten at this meal provided that, whatever it was, it was eaten sparingly.

The War referred to was that with France, declared on May the 4th, 1702. It culminated in the Peace of Utrecht, signed in 1713. Queen Anne died on August the first, 1714.

CHURCH ALES

There is no direct evidence that Church Ales were held in the village, but we have every reason to believe that they were. We had all the facilities — a malthouse and a brewhouse at the Vicarage. No doubt the forefathers of the fellow-villagers I knew in my early days would be most co-operative in supporting these early feasts.

The Churchwardens bought and received presents of malt and hops, which they brewed into a light, sweet beverage and sold to the company. Other gifts would be received, perhaps a sheep, a calf, a pig or geese. Here then were the ingredients of a right royal feast. During the banquet a collection was made and the results handed over to the Parish funds.

There were other holidays during the year, including the Wake, a festival to commemorate the dedication of the Church. The patronal festival of Cubbington Church is the nearest Sunday to September 19th. During the following week events were arranged for a general rejoicing. An old inhabitant told me that in the late 1800's competitions were held in the skittle alleys of the public houses, the ladies bowling for dress lengths which were given as prizes. The Statute Fairs at Warwick were a great attraction at other times in the year.

In some villages, Shrovetide was celebrated in a suitable manner. Harvest suppers were other occasions for pleasure and relaxation. There was plenty of gaiety in the village in those days. Later, these rural feasts disappeared. Their character degenerated, Puritans were disturbed and in some cases the feasts were prohibited.

METHODIST CHAPELS

The present one is now known as the Methodist Church.

There have been three Wesleyan Chapels in the village. The original, shown on the photograph as cottages, was situated in what was known as Chapel Yard. This building was used until 1843. The next Wesleyan place of worship was in the building now known as the Ledbrook Hall, the lower part of which was used both as a day school and Sunday School. This building was used from 1844 to 1888, when the present Methodist Church was built. In 1965 an excellent Church Hall was completed and opened. The Wesleyan Day School was opened on July 11th, 1863.

The first Weslyan Chapel, situated in North Close, later converted into three cottages

The second Weslyan Chapel & Day School now, the 'Ledbrook Hall'

Interior of Methodist Church before re-decoration

The Methodist Church

Laying the Foundation Stone of the Methodist Church Hall, 20th February, 1965

The Methodist Youth Club

METHODIST YOUTH CLUB

Youths who are not members of the Methodist Church are eligible for membership. One of its aims apart from the Club activities is 'Service to the Community'. This has taken the form of Christmas Parcel distribution to the needy, digging of gardens and house decorating for those who are unable to deal with these problems.

The athletic activities of the club consist of judo, weight lifting, basket ball, and the like. The annual pantomimes and Summer shows are wonderfully well produced and extremely well performed. The scenery and costumes are made by the members. The elderly of the parish are invited to the shows and the company pays visits to the local hospitals to entertain the inmates. The well equipped stage lighting system is due to their efforts in fund raising.

The club in its present form has been functioning for ten years.

Temporary Roman Catholic Church

THE GREAT HOUSE OF THE PARISH

It is difficult to say where, in remote days, this was situated.

The Manor House (not the Old Manor) was, during the 16th, 17th and 18th centuries, the most important house of the Parish. This house was demolished towards the end of the 18th century, and a farm house built on part of the site.

It appears that the building materials from the former Manor House may have been used for the erection of Cottages in New Street. At one time the Manor House was the residence of Anthony and Benedict Shuckburgh, Patrons of the Church, and Lords of the Manor of Cubbington. Later it passed to the Greswoldes (the senior branch of which family was located at Solihull).

It is difficult to realise what were the dimensions of the house. The timbered cottage at the entrance to the farm yard stood at the entrance to one approach of the mansion and there are indications that the main entrance probably began where now the Ledbrook Hall stands.

Upon a chimney of the farm house still remains a date in a kind of panel cut in stone — 1617.

A reference to the Old Manor House says:

The House was a large edifice built principally of timber, in panes with gable ends, having a large hall in which were two transom windows. A long wainscotted parlour, having folding doors, half glass, opening into the garden of nearly an acre, having a lofty stone wall on one side.An old manuscript also throws light on the subject:

The Pigeon house was a summer house in the Great Mansion of the Parish of the Greswolde's. The Manor House was taken down towards the end of the last century (18th) when a farm house was built on part of the site. One of the windows of this house contains the Arms of Shuckburgh with his quarterings. The door in the garden wall, opening into the farmyard, is the old hall door of the Mansion, curiously divided into twenty panels, with strong square-headed iron nails, and its curious iron long knocker, and a round hole through the door was, by tradition, to reconnoitre the visitor and watch the bailiffs, one of the family being reported to be much in debt.

A dreadful story is told about one of the owners who was, no doubt, a religious maniac.

'About the year 1635,' says Thomas, in his edition of Dugdale, 'Mr. Edward Greswolde, then living here, was so deeply possessed with these two fancies:

1. That we must not communicate with sinners
2. Nor have any human inventions in God's service,

so that to avoid the first (communicate with sinners) he shut up himself and children, in his house, having no meat but what was put in a hole or window, suffering no man to come in, and minister unto them, no, not when his children and himself, lay sick in great misery, inasmuch that the justices of the peace, in consideration of his case, gave order to break open his house, when they found him very sick in his bed and two of his children dead . . . and to avoid the other, number two (nor have any human inventions in God's service) he cut out the contents and titles of everything in his Bible, leaving nothing but the text itself.

THE DOVECOTE

This building was also the Summer House of the Great Mansion of the Parish.

The pigeons housed in the dovecote were used to provide a reserve of food and fresh meat in the winter, where otherwise the housewife had to rely on salted meat. Lack of feeding stuffs made the maintenance of any but breeding livestock quite impossible. The others were killed off and salted as soon as the grass gave out.

A secondary use for the birds lay in their reputable value for medicinal purposes. A medical writer of the 17th century refers to the dietary value of the doves as a preventive of plague, palsy and trembling, and to aid recuperation after illness. He mentions 'the blood of a cock pigeon' taken from under the right wing for curing eye troubles, and a mixture of the manure, salt and oil, as a cure for water on the knee.

Another contemporary medical writer quotes this recipe: 'of the powder of the dung of Pigeons, beaten and sifted, 2 oz; of Bear's Grease, 4 oz; and Pepper in a powder, 1 oz; Oil of Cummin, ½oz; mix for an ointment against Baldness'.

THE OLD MANOR

In the 1800's, this residence was known as 'The Cottage' and was the home of a retired Army Colonel.

The description of the building, written for the Victoria History of Warwickshire is as follows:

On the opposite corner to the South, is a large L-shaped house, of which the east limb and the east gable of the main front, facing on to the road from Offchurch, are of 16th century timber framing in square panels with brick nogging. The main front and an extension westwards are of ashlar with windows framed in a simple moulding but without mullions, perhaps of the end of the 17th century.

Since then, it has been discovered that the centre portion of the house dates back to about 1300 and that it was originally a Hall House with a single storey in this portion, with an open fire at ground level. The old parts of the roof structure are in good condition, due to the preserving effect of the smoke deposits.

The house has been much modified during its life by the addition of a very large fireplace and chimney, together with the installation of an upper floor in the central hall part with gable extensions.

The service end of the house has no trace of the original structure, and is half-timbered, while the living end was rebuilt in Stuart times with local sandstone.

The house is now the subject of a Preservation Order and has recently survived a threat of demolition to make room for the extension of a housing estate. During the last few years, it has been restored internally

Though there is no direct evidence, it is likely that this was the Manor House of Cubbington which was superseded in the 16th century by the Manor House referred to above.

The Manor House

The arms of the Shuckburgh family in a window of the Manor Farmhouse

Cottage entrance to manor House

The Farmhouse built on the site of the Manor House

The Dovecote

The Old Manor House — two views

A restored fireplace in the Old Manor House, 1999 photograph

The Grange

The following views are expressed by a Lecturer at Birmingham School of Architecture:

The Old Manor is thought to date back to about 1300 in its original form, but was extended by a timber-framed structure at a later date.

There are relatively few mediæval houses left of the 'open hall' structure, with one large, heavily timbered open living area with a fire set in the middle (special sliding shutters to windows helped to disperse smoke). It contains a particularly fine beamed structure and the moulded members are examples of exceptionally fine carpentry.

It is, in fact, reputed to be one of the oldest houses in the county — a century older than St. Mary's Hall, Coventry. It has, in architectural terms, a fine roof known as a 'Crown Post Roof'.

STONE HOUSE

This house appears to have been bought in the reign of Queen Elizabeth by Thomas Fawkoner, and entailed by him upon Eliza, his daughter, who was then married to George Bodyngton, and the heir of her body. This house has since been demolished.

THE GRANGE

This house and its grounds occupied the site now known as 'The Grange'. It was for a long time the home of the Wise family: the Revd. L. Wise, Vicar of Weston-under-Wetherley, lived there. Later Mrs Stow ran it as a very successful guest house.

THE WINDMILL

This stood at the top of the hill now known as 'Windmill Hill'. It used to be where there is now a farmyard facing Rugby Road. This link with the past was pulled down in 1870. The Windmill is shown on a map of Warwickshire dated 1789.

One reason assigned for its demolition was that the site was the scene of a fatal accident to the landlord's favourite dog.

The wheel was used to move the top of the mill round so that the wind would catch the sails.

A Windmill in Cubbington is mentioned in 1355 when the Prior of Kenilworth claimed that the Abbot of Stoneleigh should pay 4s. in lieu of the tithes thereupon, but it does not appear to be mentioned again in later records.

Church Farm House

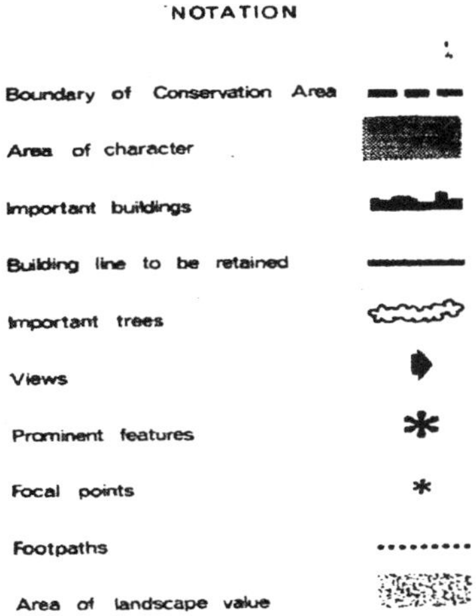

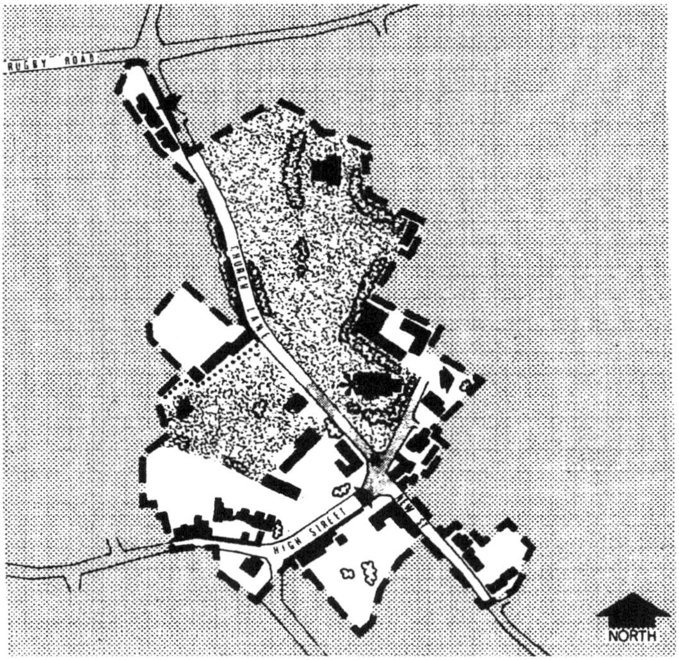

The published map of the Cubbington Conservation area.
The 'Area of Character' is that near the Church, where the streets are shown lightly shaded.

CONSERVATION

A Conservation Area is 'an area of special architectural or historic interest, the character or appearance of which it is desirable to preserve or enhance'.

It may be large or small, from a whole town centre to a small group of buildings. Open spaces or trees may also be significant and might contribute to the special character of an area. In order to define the Conservation Areas, it is necessary first to analyse the character of the town or area being examined. Designation is just a first step, but it enables the Planning Authority and the Minister of Housing and Local Government to acknowledge, immediately, the particular value of an area, by paying special attention to the character and appearance of it, when exercising any planning functions. The emphasis is on 'control' rather than 'prevention', to allow the area to remain alive and prosperous.

As can be seen from the accompanying plan, the old village has been designated a conservation area, so that we can continue to appreciate just what the neighbourhood must have looked like in years gone by. In any future development within the area, planners will have to consider whether their ideas will fit into the remnants of the past, and offer posterity a heritage as worthy as that which we enjoy now.

The Windmill

The old names of some of our streets are interesting, and in some cases are a clue as to what stood on the site

Jacob's lane became Regent Street later, and has now become Ledrook Road. There were almost as many steps in this street as there were on that Patriarch's Ladder, hence the name. The ventilated shuttering (bottom right) was part of a butcher's shop

Penn's Yard, now Penn's Close. An interesting feature of these back-to-back houses was that nearly all of them had cellars.

Penn's Close, once Penn's Yard, (compare picture above) 1999 photograph

Corner of Ledbrook Road and High Street. Note the Carrier's cart

Ledbrook Road — named after a well-known Cubbington family. The parishioners of seventy years ago (c.1900) were greatly indebted to a lady member of the family for a number of efforts she made for the benefit of her contemporaries (1999 photograph)

The lane which leads to Weston Mill. The mill has now been demolished

The old bridge at Weston Mill, the scene of a tragedy in which two sisters died. Their tombstone reads, 'In loving memory of Iris (Pickett) aged 9 who was accidentally drowned near Weston Mill.
Also Rose aged 15 who lost her life in a gallant attempt to save her sister on Good Friday, 1919

The Old Spring. This was situated opposite the front door of the Methodist Church on the other side of the road, and was the only supply of water to nearby property. A metal cover marks the site.

Cottage on Gallows Knob
(now known as
Mount Pleasant)

Note the draw-well
in the foreground.

The old name implies that some grim scenes were enacted at the spot, and if Cubbington possesses a ghost, it should haunt this neighbourhood The position of Gallows Knob is at the entrance to Mill Lane, on the right hand side. A bungalow is now built on the site.

Below

Malthouse Row, known as
Church Terrace.

This, evidently, was named from the proximity of a building used for making malt. We have already seen that the Vicarage of 1721 possessed a brewhouse, and, because at that period, a light kind of beer was the only beverage used by the majority of people, tea at that time being 16/2d a pound, one can see the advantage, even the necessity, of having a malt-house in the village

New Street

This street was evidently made at the same time that the Old Manor House was demolished, and the present farmhouse built on the site. The stone from the old house was used in the erection of the cottages in the street

New Street

Queen Street

Queen Street. Note the Public House — the New Inn — where the Post Office now stands

Ladycroft

Cottages at the lower end of Queen Street, now demolished.
Note the one pump supplying water from the well beneath to a number of cottages.

View up Queen Street towards the 'Queen's Head Public House on the right.
George Isham stands beside the car.

PUBLIC FOOTPATHS

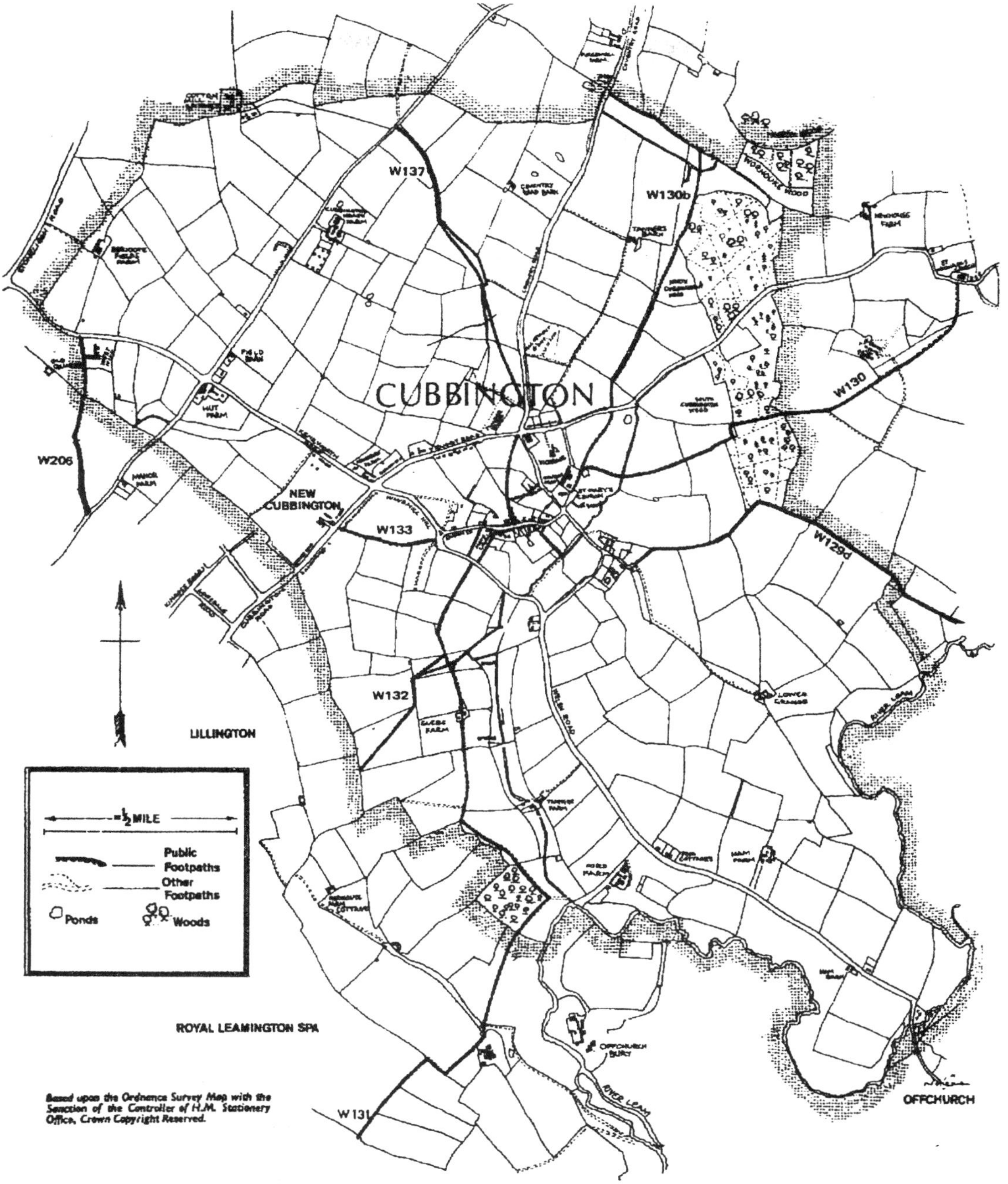

The numbers in the following notes are the same as those used in the Definitive Map issued by the Warwickshire County Council.
Kind permission has been given to use this map.
The following notes are on the most interesting footpaths.

W 129d

Starting point New Street, Cubbington. Destination either Weston Mill or Offchurch, opposite The Stag Hotel.

Continue down New Street, straight, do not turn right but follow 15ft. wide cart track. At the end of this track, cross the field directly in front of you. Cross to the hedge on the opposite side, by the side of the wood. Travel down this field and the following fields with the hedgerow on your left. Cross the end field, keeping slightly to the left, and you will arrive at a bridge across the river. Continue over the bridge practically in a straight line and you will eventually come to The Stag at Offchurch.

W 130

Starting from Cubbington, go up Church Hill in front of The King's Head, continue in front of Church Farm House; directly ahead is a field gate. Pass through this and immediately take a right turn. At the end of this field is a footbridge over a deep ditch. Continue with the boundary hedge on your right. Follow the path until you come to the wood, access gained by a stile. A good path leads through the wood, and, on emerging, continue with field hedgerows on your right. With Weston Hill farm on your left, you will emerge directly opposite Weston Church.

W 130b

Entrance to this footpath is from the Weston Road. Past the last houses of Cubbington and the succeeding field on the left-hand side of the road, is a stile. Cross into the field. Take a diagonal direction to the next hedge, and there is another stile. Cross this and continue with the hedgerow on the left for about two fields. Then continue to the boundary of the wood. Cross the next field to the opposite hedge. Cross into the next field and turn left with the hedgerow on the left and you will emerge on the Coventry Road about 100 yards from Furzen Hill Farm.

W 137

Entrance to this footpath at the Cubbington end is a stile on the lefthand side of the Coventry Road — the first stile adjacent to the last building on the left. Cross into this field in a diagonal direction, through two fields, into a third field with the hedgerow on the right. Cross three fields and you find yourself in Leicester Lane.

W 131 & W 132

The starting point is in Offchurch Road at a stile directly opposite North Close. The destination is Leamington, via Glebe Farm and Rangehills, or via Campion Hills. Cross the stile into the field, climb the hill and walk down the other side. Enter the second field. Here the paths diverge, one through Glebe Farm, the other to the right.

For the first route, leave Glebe Farm and carry straight on through two fields. Enter the third field and turn left to the boundary of the wood. Cross into the field and turn right. Cross the middle of two fields to Red House Farm on the left. Continue and you will emerge at Holly Walk, Leamington.

Alternatively, where the path diverges to the right at the bottom of the hill, cross to the hedgerow on the right. Cross the stile there, and follow the hedgerow on the left for one field. Turn right and you will emerge at Campion Hill.

OF CONSTABLES AND COUNCILLORS

LOCAL GOVERNMENT

One of the earliest areas for administrative purposes was the township or vill. In Saxon times this would not be very populous. Under Alfred the Great, the system of frankpledge was instituted under which all freemen in a vill were required to form themselves into groups of ten, known as tithings. Each tithing had its leader, known as tithingman or headborough. Members of each tithing were mutually responsible for each other's crimes, and if a crime were found to have been committed by one of them, the other nine were held responsible for bringing the offender to trial.

Tithings were grouped into hundreds — Cubbington was in Kenilworth Division of Knightlow Hundred. Knightlow Hundred contained the Domesday Hundreds of Mereton, Stanley and Bonelaw.

The Hundreds were grouped in turn into Counties.

The Kenilworth division of the Knightlow Hundred contained the villages of Ashow, Bishop's Tachbrook (Part of Tachbrook Mallory Hamlet), Bubbenhall, Cubbington, Harbury, Kenilworth, Leamington Priors, Leek Wootton, Lillington, Milverton, Offchurch, Radford Semele, Stoneleigh, Ufton and Whitnash.

In early days the Manor Court was the instrument of Village life. Meetings were held monthly or at longer intervals.

The Court was virtually controlled by the Lord of the Manor, with a Jury of Tenants, elected every year, and under the Chairmanship of the Steward.

Duties.

1. Keeping records of each tenancy.
2. Fixing and maintaining rules for good farm practice.
3. Maintaining the condition of the fields and the value of the estate.
4. Enforcing all fines and penalties and administering petty justice.
5. Annually appointing parish officials.
6. Providing a jury of tenants elected every year as part of Manor Court.

In the 14th Century, the Manor Court divided into two:

Court Baron dealt with all matters relating to the custom of the Manor.

Court Leet was concerned with petty justice. Court Leet was finally absorbed into Court of Quarter Sessions.

In the 16th Century the Church began to supplant the Manor as the arbiter of village affairs.

The Church affairs were administered by the Vestry, originally an assembly of all parishioners, presided over by the priest. The Annual Meeting of the Vestry was held directly after Easter and called Open Vestry, when an Executive Committee was appointed.

In 1601, Poor Law placed all responsibility for village affairs upon the shoulders of the Vestry. The Act charged the Churchwardens with the care of the poor, and a new official was appointed, called the Overseer.

Vestry functioned for 300 years until the Local Government Act, 1894, deprived it of its Civil Powers.

In 1894 Parish Councils were formed.

QUARTER SESSIONS

Justices of the Peace were appointed by the Crown. They met once a quarter to try criminal offences with the help of a Jury. They were made responsible for the supervision of vagrants, and had power to punish persons who defaulted in carrying out public duties. They also developed powers of administration. Their wide powers are best illustrated by extracts from the Warwick Sessions Order Book.

Administration.

April 7th, 1657. Enforcing the law on the inhabitants of Cubbington to allow the building of Old People's houses on the waste and common land in the village.

Trinity 1663. Offchurch Bridge. Suggested a stone bridge capable of accommodating all manner of traffic.

Easter 1674. Court orders overseers to pay Poor Relief.

Punishment for Defaulters.

1385. William Swan of Cubbington feloniously stole a horse worth 10/- from John Wython, outlawed on 18th September.

Trinity Sessions, 1632. Edward Ayleworth of Cubbington yeoman for shooting with a gun on the Sabbath Day and killing a pigeon forthwith.

Michaelmas Sessions, 1649. Henry Preist of Cubbington for taking in an inmate contrary to the Statute.

April 7th, 1657. Whereas the Court was this day informed on the behalf of Edward Walter an ancient inhabitant of Cubbington in this County that he being an aged shepherd and destitute of an habitation was licensed by the Lords of the Manor and most of the freeholders and inhabitants to have a poor cottage erected on the waste for the habitation of him and his wife, part of it being built, he is now interrupted that he cannot get it finished by which means the old man and his wife are without dwelling being enforced to live in a stable, the court declared that the erecting of such cottages for old people is warranted by Law and therefore doth order that the said Edward Walter may proceed to finish the said cottage for his habitation and the inhabitants are not to interrupt him but after the death of him and his wife the said cottage is to be demolished unless the lords and freeholders shall otherwise appoint but the materials are to (be) accounted to belong to the heirs or administrators of Edward Walter.

Sessions. April 12th, 1659. Thomas Greene may erect a cottage upon the Common at Cubbington. Cottage to be demolished after the death of he *(sic)* and his wife unless the inhabitants shall then see cause to the contrary.

Easter, 1661. Cubbington and Offchurch inhabitants presented for not repairing Offchurch Bridge.

Trinity, 1677. Maintenance order against the father of an illegitimate child.

Easter, 1682. Non-attendance at Church punished

Easter Sessions, 1685. Bridget Wilson of Cubbington, spinster, indicted for stealing and taking away of one pinner and one coif of the value of 6d. of the goods and chattels of Anne Welton. Confessed. Order to be flogged at Cubbington.

Minute. Bridget Wilson for stealing (as above) and having confessed the same is to be conveyed to the constable of Cubbington and there to be stripped naked from the waist upwards and there whipped until her body be bloody.

(Coif: A covering of the head worn by women; a close fitting cap of white lawn. Pinner: A variety of coif).

Easter 1688. Cubbington inhabitants presented for not repairing the highway.

Civil Responsibilities.

Epiphany Sessions 1661. Court informed Offchurch Bridge had formerly been and ought to be repaired at the charge of the inhabitants of Offchurch and Cubbington, is now in great decay.

The bridge being now only a horse bridge and made part of stones and part of wood as fit to be made a cart bridge and to be made all of stone.

Court ordered that the decays of the said bridge be referred to the consideration of Sir John Knightley and Sir John Shuckburgh baronets and Thomas Temple, squire, three of the Justices of the Peace of this County or any two of them, who are desired to call before them some of the chief inhabitants of both of the said towns, and also able workmen masons to their assistance and to take view of the decays of the said bridge and to estimate according to the best of their judgements how much money it will cost to make the said bridge a cart bridge all of stone and in good repair and to make a certificate under their hands or under the hands of two of them hereof to the Court at the next General Sessions of the Peace to be holden for this County Whereupon such further order shall be taken for the speedy repair of the said bridge as shall be meet.

General Sessions Trinity 1661. *[Sir John Shuckburgh had died and Sir John Knightley had been in London since the previous order.]*

This order hath not been pursued it is thereupon ordered by the Court that the said former order shall be revived and stand in force until the next Session and that Sir William Bromley Knight of the Bath be added to the said Sir John Knightley abd Nr. Temple in the room of Sir John Shuckburgh.

Trinity Sessions 1663. Inhabitants of Offchurch and Cubbington were presented for not repairing the bridge. Bridge lately broken down and driven away

Court decided that it would be very commodious for the County to have the said bridge (which was formerly a wooden bridge for the passage or horsemen and footmen only) at the rebuilding of the same made a stone bridge for all manner of carriages, the charge thereof will be too great for the said inhabitants of Offchurch and Cubbington aforesaid to bear (to whom the repairing of the said bridge doth of right appertain).

The above was referred to the Grand Jury at the next Assizes to consider.

1. Whether it be fit and convenient for the county that the said bridge at the rebuilding to be made a stone bridge for all manner of carriages.

2. How much it will cost. What proportion of the cost to be borne by the inhabitants of the whole county and what by the inhabitants of Offchurch and Cubbington.

Trinity Sessions 1664. Offchurch inhabitants. Cubbington inhabitants, presented for not repairing Offchurch Bridge.

(I cannot trace what the verdict of the Grand Jury at the Assizes was, but the bridge was built and, let us hope, to the satisfaction of everyone).

Easter Sessions 1674. On the petition of Elizabeth Lapworth of Cubbington, widow, showing that she is brought to extreme poverty and is lame and very aged and unable to gain her livelihood without a weekly allowance, the court orders the payment of 12d. weekly to the said Elizabeth by the overseers of the poor of Cubbington until further orders to the contrary.

It is recorded that this poor lady died and was buried in a woollen wrap, as required by Act of Parliament then.

Trinity Sessions 1677. On hearing the inhabitants of Cubbington, the court confirms the order of Sir Edward Boughton, baronet, and Sir William Bromley, K.B., two Justices of the Peace, for the payment of Edward Bosworth Woolston putative father of a female bastard child begotten on the body of Jane Willson of Cubbington, single woman, to the overseers of the poor of Cubbington of 2s a week to be paid monthly for the relief of the said child until she shall reach the age of eight years, when he is to pay the said overseers 5£ towards the putting out of the child to be an apprentice.

The court also confirms the order of the said Justices that Bosworth, who entered into recognisance with sureties before Sir William Bromley for his appearance at this session, should give a good security to one of the said overseers to perform the said order and that the said Jane should keep the child until she reaches the age of eight years. The Court also orders Bosworth to be committed to the Court's gaol for want of sureties to obey the order of the two Justices, there to remain until he finds good sureties for his performance thereof.

Easter 1682. Richard Westley of Cubbington, presented for not coming to Church to hear divine service. Fined.

FIXING OF WAGES

In April 1684, the Justices of Warwick met, as was their custom under the Act of Elizabeth, to fix wages for the year, with special regard to the prices of victuals and clothes. Wheat at that time was 42s. 0½d. a quarter, a high price considering the value of money at that date.

Common Labourers, except in harvest time, were to have 8d. a day. The Ordinary Artisan was to have 1s. a day. The Mower of Grass and Corn was to have 1s. a day. The Haymaker, 8d. a day; if a woman, 4d. a day.

The above were the wages paid in the summer. In winter, they were one penny lower.

The hours of labour were also defined:

Between March and September, from 5am. to between 7pm. and 8pm. from which the fair allowance of two and a half hours was made for meals, (i.e.) half an hour for breakfast, one hour for dinner and one for drinking. Between the middle of May and the middle of August, an extra half hour was allowed for sleep. From the middle of September to the middle of March, work was to be from daybreak to dark, and the workman was to forfeit a penny an hour for absence. Those giving higher wages than the above were to be imprisoned for 10 days and fined £5, and those taking more were to be imprisoned for 21 days. These wages were considerably lower than those fixed for Essex, for example:

Wages 1768 - 1771.

Harvest and Haytime: 1s. a day and board
During Winter: 8d. a day and board
Reaping (piece work): 4/6 to 5/- an acre
Mowing Corn: 1/6
Digging: 6d a rood

Women in harvest and haytime received 6d. a day and beer.

The regulating of wages, which ceased in most counties during the early part of the century, was continued by the Warwickshire Justices at their Easter Sessions until 1779.

PRICE OF PROVISIONS

Wheat bread cost 1/- for 11 lbs.
Cheese 2½d. per lb.
Butter 8d. per lb.
Beef 2½d. per lb.
Mutton 2d. per lb.
Milk ½d. per pint
Coals 12s. 0d. per ton
A labourer paid for his cottage 30s. to 50s. per year
Masons and carpenters were paid 1/8d per day
Oak timber from 1/- to 2/- per cubic foot
Elm 1/- to 1/6 per cubic foot

ISSUE OF COLLECTING BRIEFS

These briefs were a form of alms-giving for the relief of towns or villages suffering under such calamities as fire or the failure of the harvests. The Brief was issued by the Lord Chancellor, but it was the business of Quarter Sessions to assess on reliable evidence the sums required and to draw up the necessary petition. There are two Warwickshire briefs of fairly late date: one of 1766 for the rebuilding of St. Nicholas' Church, Warwick; and one in 1768 for the relief of the inhabitants of Brailes and Sutton-under-Brailes whose crops had been destroyed by a violent hailstorm.

A similar device was the issue by Quarter Sessions of Letters of Request of Licence, allowing persons who had suffered some heavy loss, through no fault of their own, to beg relief throughout the County without being liable to be taken up as vagrants. Thus, at the Midsummer Sessions of 1775, John Mills, a farmer and waggoner of Stockingford, whose house and furniture had been destroyed by fire, was granted a licence 'to solicit throughout the County for six weeks the charity of well-disposed persons'. Letters of request were not issued until an estimate of the damage suffered, attested by reliable witnesses and signed by the Minister and Churchwardens of the applicant's parish, had first been delivered into Court.

The System today.

At the present time justice is administered locally within each of the districts into which England and Wales are divided for the purpose. It is applied through Petty Sessions held by local Justices of the Peace able to hear minor offences, and through the Quarter Sessions, held quarterly, as the name implies, which may be attended by all the local Justices to hear the more serious offences. The gravest misdemeanours are heard by a High Court Judge at the Assizes, held periodically. Civil disputes are examined by a qualified County Court judge; the more serious of these disputes can be heard at the Assizes. Very minor cases may be settled by the local Justices.

The running costs of the County Court are met by the Central Government; that is to say that the County Authority does not have to bear the cost of such courts, although it is obliged to contribute towards Assizes and Sessions.

OVERSEERS OF THE POOR

In April 1684, the Justices of Warwick met, as was their custom under this Act.

In the appointment of Thomas Boddington and Thomas Gibbs as Overseers the following points are worth noting:

1. The penalties for not carrying out their duties.
2. Meeting once a month.
3. Providing work for children and adults.
4. Providing work for physically handicapped.
5. Placing of children as apprentices.
6. Raising of money by taxation.
7. Dealing with unlawful settlers.
8. Keeping Poor Book.
9. Listing people receiving relief. Names to be read over at Vestry Meeting.
10. Seeing that poor persons receiving relief wear badge on shoulder of right sleeve. Letter P. followed by letter C. (for Cubbington) cut in red on blue cloth.

11. Providing accommodation, if necessary in conjunction with neighbouring parishes, of a suitable building for lodging, maintaining or employing the poor.

Finally, the Act of 1834 removed the administration of the Poor Law from the parish altogether. Parishes were combined into unions to which workhouses were allotted. The unions were administered by locally-elected Guardians under the centralised control of the Poor Law Commissioners in London.

DUTIES OF OVERSEER AND APPOINTMENT

To Wit. To Thomas Boddington and Thos. Gibbs substantial Householders of the Parish of Cubbington in the Hundred of Knightlow.

By virtue of several Statues in that case made and provided, we whose hands and seals are hereto set, His Majesty's Justices of the Peace (whereof) one is of the Quorum of and for the said County dwelling in or near the said Parish of................................ Do hereby nominate and appoint you Overseers of the Poor of the said Parish for one year next ensuing the Date hereof or until other Overseers are appointed in your stead and who for the time being, under the Penalty of forfeiting Twenty shillings each, are to meet once in every Month in your Church upon the Sunday afternoon to confer together and consider of and take Order (with consent of the Justices) for setting to work the children of all such within your said Parish as shall not be thought able to keep and maintain them, and also for setting to work all such Persons, Married or Unmarried, having no means to maintain themselves, and using no Trade to get their living by, and also for the raising of a convenient Stock of Hemp, Flax, Wool Thread, Iron and other stuff for those purposes, and also for the providing of necessary Relief for such Persons as are Lame, Old, Blind, Poor or unable to work within your said Parish......

And for the placing out as apprentices all such children within your said Parish as are fit to be put for, whose Parents are not able to keep and maintain them. To which end you are to raise (by Taxation of every Inhabitant, Parson and other, and of every Occupier of Houses, Lands, Tithes Impropriate, Coal Mines or saleable Underwoods within your Parish) such sums of Money as shall be allow'd by us, or any two Justices of the Peace of this County dwelling in or near your said Parish. Stat. 43. Eliz. Cap. 2 and 13C 14 Car. II Cap. 12

And for your better and more effectually executing the said Office of Overseers. We do hereby make known to you as follows to wit:

That you together with the Churchwardens of your Parish with the Consent of two Justices of the Peace of this County may bind Apprentices any such poor Children as aforesaid: if a Man-Child until he attain his Age of four and twenty years, and if a Woman-Child until she attain her age of one and twenty years or the time of her Marriage.

And the Persons to whom they are bound are obliged to receive and provide for them and to execute one Part of the Indentures, whereby they are bound under the Penalty of forfeiting Ten Pounds to the Poor of your Parish and you together with the Churchwardens of your Parish by the Leave of the Lord of the Manor, may build on any Waste or Common within your Parish by Stat. 43. Eliz. Cap. 2 and 8 and 9. Will. iii. Cap 30.

You together with the Churchwardens of your Parish with the Consent of two Justices may set up any Trade only for the settling on Work and Relief of your Poor. By Stat. 3 Car. 1 Cap. 5.

If any Person coming to settle in your Parish and not being a Parishioner thereof, shall deliver to, or leave at the House of your Abode, or of any Churchwarden of your Parish, a Notice of the House of such Person's abode, and number of his or her family, you are to cause the same to be read publicly immediately after Divine Service in your Church, on the next Lord's Day, and to register such Notice in the Book kept for Registering your Poor's Accounts, otherwise you forfeit Forty Shillings, by Stat. 3 and 4 Will. and Mar. Cap. 11.

And by the same Statute you forfeit Five Pounds if you refuse to receive any Person that shall be removed from any other Parish or Place to your Parish by Warrant under the Hands and Seals of two Justices of the Peace.

You are to take care that there be kept in your Parish, a Book, or Books wherein the Names of Persons of your Parish who receive Collection, Pay or Relief, shall be registered with the Day and Year when they were admitted and the Occasion which brought them under that Necessity.

And yearly in Easter Week (or as often as shall be thought convenient) your Parishioners shall meet in Vestry, before whom the book shall be produced, and all Persons receiving Collection or Relief shall be called over, and the Reason for their taking relief examined, and a new List made of such as they shall think fit to receive Collection or Relief and no other Persons to be allowed Collection at the charge of your Parish, but by Order under the Hand of some Justice of the Peace residing in or near your Parish, or by order of Quarter Sessions (except in Cases of Pestilential Disease, Plague or Small Pox) and also upon any sudden and emergent occasions and if any Justice of the Peace shall order relief for any Persons as aforesaid you are to enter in said books such Person's name as one who is to receive Collection as long as the Cause of such Relief continues and you are to pay no Weekly or other Payments under the Pretence of Extraordinaries to any Poor Person whatsoever whose name is not Registered as aforesaid (unless by such Order or except as aforesaid) and if you charge any paid money contrary hereto, you forfeit Five Pounds to the Poor of your Parish by Stat. 3 and 4 Will. and Mar. Cap. II and of Geo. I Cap. 7 and in consequence thereof you are not to bring to the Account of your Parish any monies given to Soldiers or Sailors, although they have proper passes or Certificates (for these are to be relieved by the Treasurer of the respective Counties through which they pass by Stat. 43 Eliz. Cap. 3 and not by the Parish Officers) nor any monies given to any other Persons travelling with the Passes or pretended Passes, nor to any Persons begging for Losses by Fire or on any other Pretence whatever under the said Penalty of Five Pounds.

Every such Person whose Name shall be registered as aforesaid, together with his Wife and children cohabiting in the same house (such child only excepted as shall be by you permitted to live at Home to attend on impotent Parent) must wear upon the shoulder, of the right sleeve of his or her uppermost Garment such Badge as is herein after mentioned (that is to say) a large Roman 'P' with the first letter of the name of the Parish, cut in red or blue cloth and if you relieve any such poor Persons who shall not at all times wear such Badge as aforesaid you forfeit Twenty Shillings for every such offence. Stat. 8 and 9. Will. 3 Cap. 30.

You and the Churchwardens of your Parish with the Consent of your Parishioners or Inhabitants in Vestry may purchase or hire a House or Houses in your Parish, and contract with Persons for the Lodging, Maintaining and Employing all such Poor of your Parish as shall deserve Relief and if any poor Person shall refuse to be lodged in such House he or she shall be put out of the books and not be entitled to Relief and with the Consent of one Justice of the Peace your Parish may join with any adjacent Parish in purchasing or hiring a House for the purpose aforesaid and you may contract with the Churchwardens and Overseers of any other Parish for the Lodging, Maintaining or Employing of any of your Poor. Stat. 9 Geo. I Cap. 7.

On any poor Persons coming to inhabit in your Parish not having a lawful settlement there nor bringing with them any Certificate of their being settled elsewhere, nor giving Security for the Discharge of your Parish you ought to make complaint thereof to some two Justices of the Peace of this County in order to the Examination and Removal of such Persons to the Peace of his or her last legal settlement.

Given under our Hands and Seals this 6th day of April in the 22nd Year of the Reign of our Sovereign Lord George the Second by the Grace of God King of Great Britain etc., and in the Year of our Lord 1749.

Payment made by the Overseers:

Barleston. Oct. 5th, 1811

Gentlemen I wright to you informing you that Wm. Oraham A parisioner of yours as Made appycation for Releife to me wich I thought it My Duty to informe you before I do Give him Releife As wee Must be Under the Nessesity of a Removal from our parish the Man is A hardworking Man And has Six

Small Children all under 10 years of age And I Verily beleive the Man is in Grait Distress At this time As Every thing is so Excessive Deare that is required for the Suport of his family he thinks he Cold do if you wold be So Kind as to give him A Small Matter to ward his Rent and Coles wich I hope you will be so kind and pervent farther trouble.

Edwd. Cuthbert Overseer
J. Fox Churchwarden

Direct for Wm Oraham
Barleston Near Makt
Bosworth Leicestershire.

Payment made by the Overseers of the Poor of the Parish of Bedworth in the County of Warwick:

By order of the Rev G. Beresford and the late Rev. H. Bromfield to the family of J. Hammersley now serving in the Militia of the said County as a substitute for Edw. Pritchett of the Parish of Cubbington in the County aforesaid.

1804. His wife from July 10th, to October 2nd. 12 weeks at 2 shillings per week — £1.4.0. 7th November, 1804
Settled John Hartup.

THE MILITIA

The Militia consisted of bodies raised by the several counties, in number varying according to the population and other circumstances, the number or 'quota' to be provided by each shire being fixed by the government. Since 1803 the law has been that the quota may if necessary be raised by compulsory enlistment, a ballot being taken among the men between 18 and 35, but as sufficient numbers may he obtained by voluntary enlistment, a 'Militia Ballot Suspension Act' was passed annually.

The Militia were bound to assemble for 28 days in every year for training and may at any time be embodied for compulsory service within the kingdom but cannot be sent abroad except as volunteers and then only by Consent of Parliament

SETTLEMENT ACT, 1662

Under this Act no man was permitted to settle anywhere, other than his own birthplace, unless he could prove substantial means of support.

SETTLEMENT ORDER ON JOHN RUSSELBY.
1754
Warwickshire.

To the Churchwardens and Overseers
of the Poor of the Parish of Cubbington
in the County of Warwick and to the
Churchwardens and Overseers of the Poor
of the Parish of Baginton in the said County:

Whereas Complaint has been made by you, the Churchwardens and Overseers of the Poor of the said Parish of Cubington unto us, whose Hands and Seals are hereunto set, two of His Majesty's Justices of the Peace (whereof one is of the Quorum) for the County aforesaid.

That John Russelby and Elizabeth His Wife lately intruded Themselves unto your said Parish of Cubington there to inhabit as your Parishioners contrary to the Laws relating to the Settlement of the Poor, and are there likely to become chargeable. We, upon this Examination and Enquiry made into the Premises, as well upon the Oath of the said John Russelby as otherwise, do adjudge the same to be true, and that the Place of the last legal Settlement of the said John Russelby and his wife is the Parish of Baginton aforesaid.

These are therefore, in His Majesty's Name, to require you, the said Churchwardens and Overseers of the Poor of the said Parish of Cubington, or some of you, forthwith to remove and convey the said John Russelby and his wife from your said Parish of Cubington to the said Parish of Baginton and then deliver to the Churchwardens or Overseers of the Poor there, or some, or one of them, together with this our Warrant, or Order, or a true copy thereof; and likewise to require you, the Churchwardens and Overseers of the Poor of the said Parish of Baginton forthwith to receive the said John Russelby and Elizabeth his wife into your said Parish of Baginton and provide for them as your own Parishioners.

Given under our Hands and Seals the fourteenth day of December in the Year of our Lord, One Thousand Seven Hundred and fifty four.

Edw. Jackson
Thos. Neale

County of Warwick. To the Church-wardens and Overseers of the Poor of the Parish of Bedworth in the said County, and to the Church wardens and Overseers of the Poor in the Parish of Cubbington in the said County and to each and every of them.

UPON the complaint of the Church wardens and Overseers of the Poor of the Parish of Bedworth aforesaid, in the said County of Warwick unto us, whose names are hereunto set and seals affixed, being two of his Majesty's Justices of the Peace in and for the said County of Warwick and one of us of the Quorum: That George Flint, Maria his wife and their 3 children Namely William aged 7 years John aged 5 years and Anne aged 4 months, have come to inhabit in the said Parish of Bedworth not having gained a legal settlement there, nor produced any certificate owning themselves to be settled elsewhere, and that the said George Flint, Maria his wife and their said three children are actually chargeable to the said Parish of Bedworth.

We the said Justices upon due proof made thereof, as well upon the examination of the said George Flint upon Oath, as otherwise, and likewise upon due consideration had of the premises, do adjudge the same to be true; and we do likewise adjudge, that the lawful settlement of them the said George Flint, Maria his wife and their said 3 children is in the said Parish of Cubbington in the said County of Warwick.

We do therefore require you, the said Church wardens and Overseers of the Poor of the said Parish of Bedworth or some, or one of you, to convey the said George Flint, Maria his wife and their said 3 children from and out of your said Parish of Bedworth to the said Parish of Cubbington and them to deliver to the Churchwardens and Overseers of the Poor there, or to some or one of them, together with this our Order, or a true copy thereof. And we do also hereby require you, the said Churchwardens and Overseers of the Poor of the said Parish of Cubbington to receive and provide for them, as inhabitants of your Parish.

Given under our hands and seals, the 17th day of January in the year of our Lord, One Thousand Eight Hundred and Seventeen.

Wade

Boswell

APPRENTICE INDENTURE 1774

THIS INDENTURE made the Ninth Day of October in the Fourteenth Year of the Reign of our Sovereign Lord George the Third by the Grace of God, of Great-Britain, France and Ireland, King, Defender of the Faith, and so forth; and in the Year of our Lord One thousand seven hundred and Seventy Four Witnesseth. That John Smith and Joseph Hiorns Church-Wardens of the Parish of Cubbington in the County of Warwick And Benjamin Gibbins and John Sabin Overseers of the Poor of the said Parish, by and with the consent of his Majesty's Justices of the Peace for the said County whose Names are hereunto subscribed, have put and placed, and by these presents do put and place Mary Carter a poor Child of the said Parish, Apprentice to Caleb Gibbins of Cubbington aforesaid, Husbandman with him to dwell and serve from the Day of the Date of these Presents, until the full end and Term of Five Years according to the Statute in that Case made and provided. During all which Term the said Apprentice her said Master faithfully shall serve in all lawful Business, according to her Power, Wit and Ability; and honestly, orderly and obediently, in all Things demean and behave herself towards her said Master and his, during the said Term. And the said Caleb Gibbins for himself, his Executors and Administrators doth Covenant and Grant to and with the said Churchwardens and Overseers, and every of them, their and every of their Executors and Administrators, and their and every of their Successors, for the Time being, by these Presents, That the said Mary Carter the said Apprentice in the Art of Husbandry, shall Teach and Instruct, or cause to be taught and Instructed in the best way that he can. And at the Expiration of her Apprenticeship shall pay the said Mary Carter two Pounds two Shillings, And shall and will, during all the Term aforesaid, find, provide and allow, unto the said Apprentice, meet, competent and sufficient Meat, Drink and Apparel, Lodging, Washing, and all other Things necessary and fit for an Apprentice. And also shall and will provide for the said Apprentice, that she be not any way a Charge to the said Parish, or Parishioners of the same; but of and from all Charge shall and will save the said Parish and Parishioners harmless and indemnified during the said Term. IN WITNESS whereof, the Parties abovesaid to these present Indentures interchangeably have put their hands and Seals the Day and Year above-written.

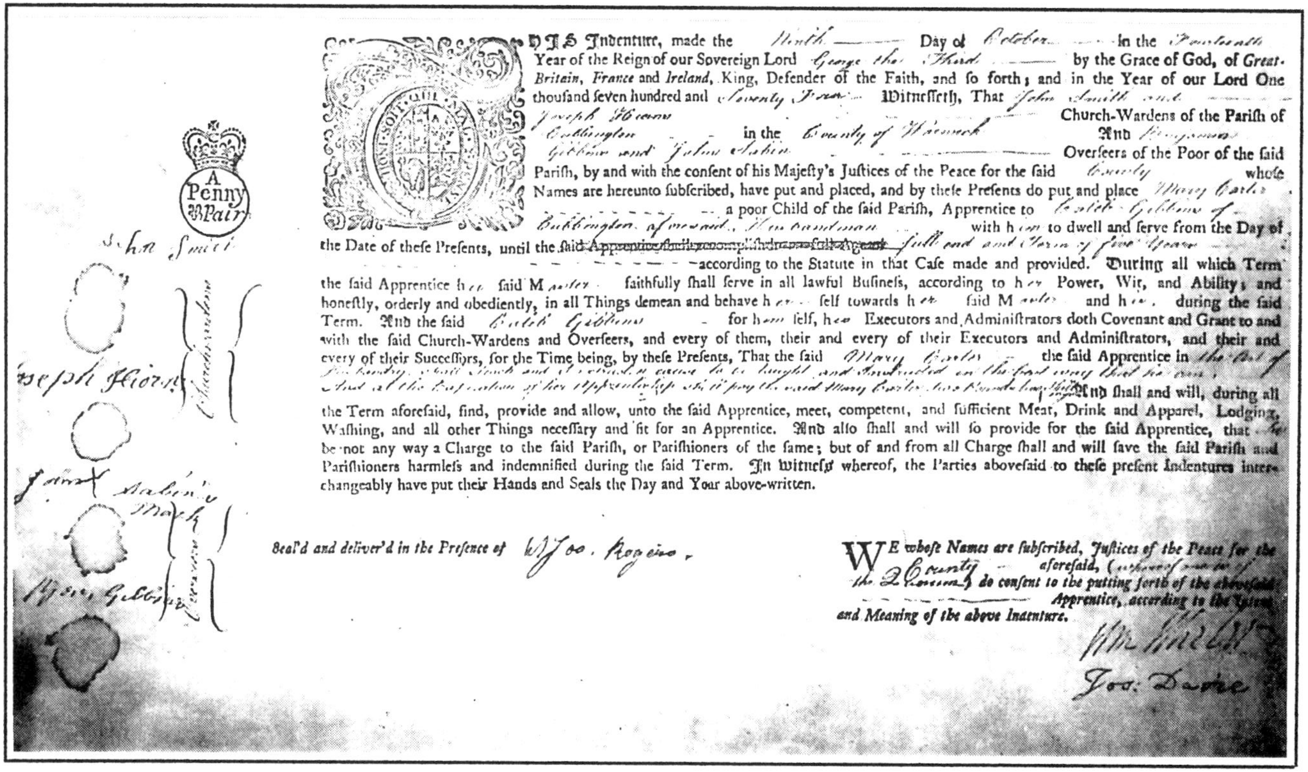
THIS Indenture, made the Ninth Day of October in the Fourteenth Year of the Reign of our Sovereign Lord George the Third by the Grace of God, of Great-Britain, France and Ireland, King, Defender of the Faith, and so forth; and in the Year of our Lord One thousand seven hundred and Seventy Four Witnesseth, That John Smith and Joseph Hiorns Church-Wardens of the Parish of Bubbington in the County of Warwick And Benjamin Gibbins and John Aston Overseers of the Poor of the said Parish, by and with the consent of his Majesty's Justices of the Peace for the said County whose Names are hereunto subscribed, have put and placed, and by these Presents do put and place Mary Carter a poor Child of the said Parish, Apprentice to Caleb Gibbins of Bubbington aforesaid with him to dwell and serve from the Day of the Date of these Presents, until the full end and Term of five Years according to the Statute in that Case made and provided. During all which Term the said Apprentice her said Master faithfully shall serve in all lawful Business, according to her Power, Wit, and Ability; and honestly, orderly and obediently, in all Things demean and behave herself towards her said Master and his during the said Term. And the said Caleb Gibbins for himself, his Executors and Administrators doth Covenant and Grant to and with the said Church-Wardens and Overseers, and every of them, their and every of their Executors and Administrators, and their and every of their Successors, for the Time being, by these Presents, That the said Mary Carter the said Apprentice in ... And shall and will, during all the Term aforesaid, find, provide and allow, unto the said Apprentice, meet, competent, and sufficient Meat, Drink and Apparel, Lodging, Washing, and all other Things necessary and fit for an Apprentice. And also shall and will so provide for the said Apprentice, that she be not any way a Charge to the said Parish, or Parishioners of the same; but of and from all Charge shall and will save the said Parish and Parishioners harmless and indemnified during the said Term. In Witness whereof, the Parties abovesaid to these present Indentures interchangeably have put their Hands and Seals the Day and Year above-written.

Seal'd and deliver'd in the Presence of W. Jos. Rogers

WE whose Names are subscribed, Justices of the Peace for the County aforesaid, do consent to the putting forth of the abovesaid Apprentice, according to the Intent and Meaning of the above Indenture.

Jos. Davie

An Apprentice Indenture of 1774

Seal'd and deliver'd in the Presence of W. Jos. Rogers.

We whose Names are subscribed, Justices of the Peace for the County aforesaid, (whereof one is of the Quorum) do consent to the putting forth of the above-said Apprentice, according to the Intent and Meaning of the above Indenture.

Wm. Whilet
Jos. Davie

John Smith Churchwardens
Joseph Hiorns
John + Sabin's Mark
Ben. Gibbins Overseers

HIGHWAYS

Since Cubbington's inhabitants were regularly presented at Warwick Quarter Sessions for 'not repairing the King's Highway', it would be appropriate to look at the village's responsibilities in this respect. An Act of Parliament of 1555 held every parish liable in maintaining its own roads, and this Act was in force for some 300 years. It required every parishioner of substance to contribute to road work, a horse and cart and two men for four days in the year — others were to work themselves. Later, the period was extended to six days.

Roads became extremely bad so the Turnpike Trusts were established to improve main roads and make those who used them subscribe towards their upkeep. Parish labour remained obligatory and paupers were often put to this sort of work.

The 1835 Highway Act made an end of compulsory work and substituted Highway rates. Finally, turnpikes disappeared and the Act of 1862 grouped parishes together into Highway districts and heavily subsidised the rates. Finally, all rural highways matters were transferred to the County and Rural District Councils.

During the enforcement of the 1555 Act, Surveyors were appointed to maintain the quality and correct usage of public highways. This gave them the status of traffic police and road repairers, as can be seen from the following transcripts of the official appointments.

APPOINTMENT OF BENJAMIN GIBBINS AND JOHN HINDE AS SURVEYORS OF THE HIGHWAYS OF CUBBINGTON, 1761. THE CHARGE:

YOU, the within-named Surveyors, are to take notice, that by an Act of Parliament made in the Thirtieth Year of the Reign of his present Majesty King George the Second, among other Things, it is enacted, for preventing Obstructions in all the public Highways of this Kingdom, That if any Person after the 24th Day of June 1757, shall set, place, Or leave any empty Waggon, Cart, or any other Carriage on any public Highway within this Kingdom, so as in any manner to interrupt or hinder the free Passage of any other Carriage, or of His Majesty's Subjects, except only during such reasonable Time as such Waggon, Cart or Carriage shall be loading or unloading:- Or if the Driver of any Waggon, Cart, Dray or other Carriage on any public Highway, shall ride upon any such Carriage, not having some other Person on Foot or on Horseback to guide the same (such Carriages as are respectively drawn by one Horse only, or by two Horses abreast, and are conducted by some Person holding the Reins of each horse or Horses excepted) or if the Driver of any Carriage whatsoever on any of the said Highways, shall by Negligence or wilful Misbehaviour cause any Hurt or Damage to any Person passing or being upon such Highway or shall by Negligence or Wilful Misbehaviour prevent, hinder, or interrupt the free Passage of any other Carriage, or of His Majesty's Subjects on the said Highways, or if the Driver of any empty or unloaded Waggon, Cart or other Carriage, shall refuse or neglect to turn aside, and make Way for any Coach, Chariot, Chaise, loaded Waggon, Cart or other loaded Carriage. Every Person so offending and being convicted of such Offence, either by his own Confession or by the Oath of one or more credible Witness or Witnesses before any Justice of the Peace for the County, Riding, Division, City or Place where such Offence shall be committed, shall for every such Offence forfeit and pay any Sum not exceeding Twenty Shillings, to be levied by Distress and Sale of the Offender's Goods and Chattels, by Warrant under the Hands and Seal of any such Justice of the Peace; and for want of sufficient Distress, such Justice is empowered and required to commit such Offender to the House of

Correction, or some other Prison, of the County, Riding, Division, City or Place in which the Offence shall have been committed, or the Offender shall have been apprehended, there to remove and be kept to hard Labour for any Time not exceeding one Calendar month.

And if any Person shall see any of the Offences, intended by the said Act to be redressed, committed, shall and may by Authority of the said Act, and without any Warrant, apprehend such Offenders, and deliver them to a Constable, or other Peace-Officer in the County, City or Place where the Offence be committed or Offender apprehended, in order to be conveyed before some Justice of the Peace, there to be dealt with according to the Law.

And in case such Offender shall refuse to discover his Name and place of Abode to such Justice before whom he shall be brought, such Person so refusing shall be immediately delivered over to a Constable or other Peace-Officer, and shall by him be conveyed to the Common-Goal *(sic)* or House of Correction of the County or Place where the Offence shall be committed, there to remain until he shall declare his Name and Place of Abode to the said Justice or to some other Justice of the said County and Place.

And that all Penalties and Forfeitures for Offences against this Act shall be applied one Moiety to the Informer and the other Moiety to the Surveyor or Surveyors of the Highways in the Parish where such Offence shall be committed and to be applied in the Repair of the Highways within such respective Parish.

THE APPOINTMENT:

To Wit. At a Special Sessions held at Dunchurch for the Hundred of Knightlow in the County of Warwick the 15th day of January the First Year of the Reign of Our Sovereign Lord George 3rd King of Great Britain and so forth by the authority of His Majesty's Justices of the Peace of the said County.

By virtue of an Act of Parliament made in the Third and Fourth Year of the reign of our late Sovereign Lord and Lady King William and Queen Mary and in the year of our Lord 1691, Entitled:

An Act for the better Repairing and Amending to Highways and setting the Rates of Carriage of Goods.

We the said Justices do Nominate and Appoint you Benjamin Gibbins and John Hinde of the Parish of Cubbington as in the County aforesaid to be Surveyors of the Highways in your said Parish and so to continue for one year next ensuing the Date hereof, and until you have given an Account according to the Direction of the said Act: and do require you, to take upon you, and duly Execute the said Office, under the Penalty of Five Pounds to be Levied upon you. And the said Act requiring that it should be declared to you, what you are obliged to do by Virtue of that or any former law. We do hereby make known to you That within fourteen days after Notice shall be given you of this your Nomination and Appointment to the Office of Surveyors of the Highways, and so from time to time every four months during your Continuance in the said Office (and oftener if need be) you are to take View of all the Roads, common Highways, Water Courses, Hedges, Bushes, Trees, Ditches, Drains and Gutters in or near Adjoining the Highways within your Parish, and also all Bridges, Causeys and Pavements which are to be repaired at the Common Charge of Your Parish and to make a Presentment upon Oath, to some Justice of the Peace of the Division wherein your Parish lieth, (if any such be resident there) and if there be none resident in the said Division, then to some other Justice of the Peace in the said County, in what state and condition the same are respectively and if you shall neglect your Duty therein, you incur the Penalty of Five Pounds which the said Act requires to be levied upon you.

[Here follows a summary of the Rules:]

1. To give notice of any Faults or Annoyances in the said Highways etc., with respect to bushes and trees overhanging, to the Owners of the land adjoining who are to remedy the fault within ten days under Penalty of five shillings for every offence, and you are from time to time to give notice in the Parish Church after Divine Service or Sermon ended and if the faults are not remedied after thirty days after notice, then Surveyors to deal with the trouble themselves.

2. Ditches to be kept clean. In default fine of 10s. for every default.
3. Inhabitants of the Parish are Six days in every year before the Feast of the Nativity of St. John Baptist (June 24th) or at farthest before the Feast of St. Luke (October 18th) to endeavour themselves to amend the Highways. The Surveyor to appoint the days. Owners of horses and oxen to find one Wain or Cart furnished after the custom of the country with Oxen or horses, or other cattle and all other Necessaries meet to carry things convenient for mending the Ways and also two able bodied men with the same on pain of forfeiture of ten shillings. And every Householder, cottager and labourer of your Parish able to Labour and being no hired person by the year, must themselves or by one sufficient labourer for each of them upon every the said day, Work and Labour in the Amendments of the said Highways on the pain of forfeiture of One Shilling and Sixpence for every one of them making default, and for every man and horse making default Three shillings. And every person shall have and bring with them, such shovels, spades, Picks, Mattocks and other tools and Instruments as they do make their own Ditches and Fences, and such as are necessary for the said Work. And all the said persons and Carriages are to do and keep their work, as they shall be appointed by you eight hours in every day that you shall employ them.
4. And you are required to make all Cart Ways and other Ways within your Parish used for Draught Carriage leading to any Market Town, to be full eight feet wide at the least, and as near as may be, even and level, and all Horse Causeys within your Parish three feet wide at the least.
5. Water to be turned into ditches and ditches cleaned out.
6. And for the better repairing of your Highways, you may without Licence of the Owner or Owners thereof, take or cause to be taken and carried away, any Rubbish or broken stones of any Quarry within your Parish and in default thereof to dig for gravel or sand (not on gardens, orchards or meadows) of any Person or Persons in your Parish on lands adjoining the Highway needing Repair and Likewise to gather stones lying upon any land. You are not to dig more than one foot in any one enclosed ground and the pit not to be more than 10 yards over the breadth and length. Pits to be filled in after use. And you are to take notice, that by an Act made in the 26th Year of King George the Second (1752/3) Encouragement is given to all Persons to use Broad Wheels, in order to preserve all the Highways of the Kingdom in good repair; therefore it is enacted, that immediately after passing the same Act, it shall and may be lawful for any Waggon or other four-wheel Carriage, having the Fellies of the Wheels thereof of the Breadth or Gage of nine inches or upwards, to travel, pass, or be driven on any Highways with any Number of Horses or Beasts not exceeding eight, or for any Cart or any two-wheel Carriage, having like wheels with any number of Horses or beasts of Draught not exceeding five, without being subject to any Penalties for causing the same to travel or be drawn by a greater number of Horses or Beasts of Draught than we are now allowed by law.
Nevertheless it is provided by an Act made in the 30th. year of his said Majesty's Reign, it shall not be lawful, for such Waggon, etc., so to pass, unless the same be drawn by Horses or Beasts of Draught in pairs, but if there is an odd horse, it shall be lawful for such odd horse to draw such waggon, together with the other Horses or Beasts of Draught drawing in Pairs aforesaid, provided they do not in the whole exceed the Number of Horses or Beasts of Draught allowed by Law. And it is also enacted, that it shall not be lawful for any Waggon or Wain having the Fellies of the wheels thereof of less Breadth than nine inches to pass upon any Turnpike Road, or through any Turnpike Gate or Barr, if the same be drawn by Horses or Beasts of Draught in pairs, and not by oxen.
And it is likewise enacted that no Waggon, having the Fellies of the wheels thereof of the breadth of Nine inches at the Bottom, shall pass any Turnpike Road, which shall be wider than Five Feet Six inches from the Middle of the Fellies of the Wheels on one side to the middle of the Fellies of the Wheels on the other side of each Waggon and the Surveyors or Gate Keepers of such Turnpike Roads are authorised and required to measure such Waggons and if any Master or Driver shall hinder or refuse, it shall not be lawful for any such Waggon to pass along any such Turnpike Road.

No Waggon travelling for Hire or not for Hire, or in any other manner whatsoever, shall go or be drawn with more than six Horses, either at length or in pairs, or sideways. And no Cart travelling for Hire, or not for Hire, shall go, or be drawn with more than three Horses, under Penalties and Forfeitures of losing all the Horses above three on a Cart, together with the Feers, Bridles, Halters, and Accoutrements to the sole use and benefit of such Person who shall seize or distrain the same. And all Persons who shall offend against the Statutes in the Cases made, shall for every such offence, (being convicted within three days after such Offence committed) forfeit and be liable to all Penalties in the several Statutes for that Portion contained to be levied and applied in such manner as are therein mentioned. And all Horses, with the Geers, Bridles, etc., so forfeited shall, for the space of three Days after such Offence, be liable to such Seizures, and for the use of such Persons as they would have been, had they been seized in the ACT during the Commission of such Offence.

The Person making such Seizure shall deliver the Horses or other Things so seizen or distrained, to the Constable, or other Parish Officer of the same next, or adjacent Town or Parish where such Distress is made, (who is required safely to keep the same) till proof shall be made upon Oath by the Person so distraining, before some Justice of the Peace, of the Offence committed. And the Justice, before whom such Proof is made, is to issue his Precept to the Constable or other Parish Officer, immediately to deliver the Horses or other Things, so forfeited, to the Seizor for his sole Use paying such reasonable charges for keeping and securing the same, as the said Justice shall allow.

No travelling Waggon having the Wheels bound with Streaks or Tire, of a less breadth than two inches and an half when worn or being set in with Rose-headed Nails shall go or be drawn with more than three Horses on Forfeiture of all Horses above three, with all the Geers and Accoutrements etc. to be seized and applied in manner as aforesaid.

If any Person shall hinder, or attempt to hinder, the Seizure or Distress from any Forfeitures in this Act, or shall refuse the same, or use any violence to the Persons concerned in making such Seizure on Oath, by one or more Witnesses, before a Justice of the Peace for the County or Place, where such Offence shall be done, such Person shall be committed to the Common Gaol, for three months without Bail, and shall also forfeit the sum of Ten Pounds, to be levied on his Goods and Chattels by Vertue of a Warrant from such Justice. And if the said Penalty be not paid in three days then the goods to be sold, and the Overplus to be returned, deducting the Charges.

This Act is not to extend to Waggons or Carts employed in Husbandry or manuring of Land, or in carrying of Cheese, Butter, Hay, Straw, Corn unthrashed, Coals, Chalk or any one Tree or Piece of Timber, or any one Stone or Block of Marble, Caravans and Covered Carriages of Noblemen and Gentlemen for their own private use, or Timber, Ammunition or Artillery for His Majesty's Service.

You are on the 26th Day of December next, to call together and meet the Constable, Headborough, Tything Man, Churchwardens and Inhabitants of your Parish and together with the Major part of them so assembled, make out a list of the Names of a Competent Number of the said Inhabitants who have an Estate in Land, Tenements or Hereditaments in their Own Right or their Wives, of the Value of Ten pounds by the Year, or a Personal Estate of the Value of One Hundred Pounds, or are occupiers or Tenants of Houses, Lands or Hereditaments of the Yearly Value of Thirty Pounds (if any such there be) and if there be no such in your Parish, then the said list to be of the most Sufficient Inhabitants of your Parish, and to return such list unto two or more Justices of the Peace of your Division of the County at a Special Sessions which the Law requires to be held for that purpose on the third day of January then next following or within fifteen days thereafter of the time and place of the holding of such Sessions you will have Publick Notice given by the Justices according to the Direction of the Statute and you together with the Constable, Headborough, Tything Man or some of them within six days after the said Justices have by their warrant at the last Sessions nominated out of said list, Person or Persons, to be Surveyor or Surveyors of the Highways within your Parish, are to give the said Persons Notice of their Nomination by serving him or them with the said Warrant or by leaving the same at his or their Houses Or usual place of abode.

And you are to take Notice that before you can go out of or be dismissed from your said office you must at some Special Sessions give an account upon Oath of all Money that hath come to your hands, which ought to be employed in the Amending of the Highways and how you have disposed of the same. And if any Money shall be in your hands you must deliver it to the Surveyors that shall immediately succeed you or else *(sc. you will be held responsible)* for the value of what shall be judged by the Justices to remain in your hands.

And lastly you are to observe that if you neglect your duty in any of the duties herein mentioned (except where you incur the several Penalties above mentioned) you will for every such Offence incur the penalty of Five pounds to be levied by distress on you and therefore we do strictly charge and require you from time to time, and at all times, whilst you continue in the said Office, well and duly to execute the same at your Peril as witness our Hands and Seals this 15th Day of January in the First Year of the Reign of Our Sovereign Lord George the Third by the Grace of God, Great Britain, France and Ireland, King, Defender of the Faith and in the Year of Our Lord 1761.

TOLLS 1725

Tolls as set out in Turnpike Acts and applied by Turnpike Trusts:

For every coach, berlin, chariot, chaise or chair drawn by 6 horses or more	1s. 0d.
As above but only 4 or 5 horses	6d.
Drawn by fewer than 4 horses	3d.
For every waggon, wain, cart or carriage drawn by 5 or more horses or oxen	8d.
4 horses or oxen	6d.
3 horses or oxen	4d.
2 horses or oxen	3d.
1 horse or ox	2d.
For every horse, mule or ass laden or unladen and not drawing a vehicle	1d.

For every drove of oxen or meat cattle, 10d. per score and so on, in proportion, for any greater or lesser number.

For every drove of hogs, calves, sheep or lambs, the sum of 5d. per score, and so on in proportion, for any greater or lesser number.

(A berlin was an old fashioned four-wheeled covered carriage with a seat behind covered with a hood. A chaise was an open carriage for one or more persons).

In the Leamington Spa Courier of Saturday, October 24th, 1829 appeared this advertisement showing the method of collecting Toll Monies at the Toll-gates mentioned. A similar procedure would have been followed at the Toll-gates in this Parish.

Site of the Turnpike Gate, junction of the Kenilworth Road and Rugby Road

TURNPIKE TOLLS TO LET

Annual Meeting of Trustees of the Turnpike Road leading from Birmingham through Warwick to Warmington in the County of Warwick and so on to the utmost limits of the said county on Edgehill will be held at Eleven o'clock in the forenoon at the Mermaid Inn in Knowle at which meeting the intended Application to Parliament for a renewal of the Act and adding the Branch Road from Oakley Wood to Leaminton as approved at the meeting at Birmingham, will be submitted for consideration, and the Tolls payable at the Gates on the said Road, viz,

Sparkbrook Gate, Acock's Green Gate, Wroxall Gate, Wedgnock Lane Gate, Warwick Bridge Gate, Oakley Wood Gate, Burton Dassett Gate and Shotteswell Gate will be let by Auction to the best bidder either together or separately as the Trustees present shall think proper in such conditions as will be then produced. The Tolls arising from the said Gates were let last year for the following sums.

Sparkbrook Gate	£1155
Acock's Green Gate	£442
Wroxall and Wedgnock Lane	£650
Warwick Bridge, Oakley Wood, Burton Dassett and Shotteswell Gates	£543

[The Turnpike Road from Warwick to Rugby passed through Cubbington.]

TRANSPORT

Transport in the early days consisted mainly of movement in the village. Imports were few, and the roads mere tracks. Baggage horses would be used. We have seen that, in 1663, the inhabitants of Offchurch and Cubbington were presented at the Quarter Sessions for not repairing Offchurch Bridge. The bridge at that time was made of wood, and intended for the passage of horsemen and footmen only; it was not wide or strong enough for vehicles. One assumes that to go from Cubbington to Offchurch with a vehicle, the ford would need to be negotiated. Eventually the present bridge was built.

In the appointment of the Surveyors of Cubbington dated 1761 we found a real Highway Code of that period as well as details of maintenance, and so on. Cartways to all market towns must be at least 8' wide. An Act of Parliament passed in 1757 dealt with obstructions on the cartways. Empty wagons must not be left on the highways. The penalty was a fine of 20s. for each offence. Regulations are mentioned in that Act with respect to the number of horses and draught animals to be used.

Later, in the Enclosure Award of 1768, the Commissioners stated that the highways in the parish were to be at least 60 feet wide, and so transport became easier. In the following pages I have told of the problems of transport as late as 1886.

An advertisement in the Leamington Spa Courier shows the availability of Transport for places further afield.

FROM COPP'S COACH OFFICE CLEMENTS STREET, LEAMINGTON

By the Following Fast Four-Inside Mails and Post Coaches

Miles	
90	LONDON ROYAL EXPRESS every morning at eight.
90	LONDON CROWN PRINCE every morning at quarter past Nine.
122	LIVERPOOL EXPRESS every morning at quarter past Three.
122	LIVERPOOL MAIL every afternoon at Three.
121	LIVERPOOL ROCKET every evening at quarter before Five.
104	MANCHESTER (Light Coach) every Morning at a quarter past Three.
104	MANCHESTER MAIL every afternoon at Three.
67	SHREWBURY AND HOLYHEAD PRINCE OF WALES every morning at Nine, except Thursday at Seven.
88	BRISTOL ROYAL PILOT every Monday, Wednesday and Friday morning at Eight.
88	BRISTOL TALLY HO! every Tuesday, Thursday and Saturday Morning at Half-past Eleven.
88	BATH (POST COACH) every Monday, Wednesday and Friday Mornings at Eight.
88	BATH TALLY HO! every Tuesday, Thursday and Saturday Mornings at Half-past Eleven.
54	GLOS'TER (POST COACH) every Monday, Wednesday and Friday Mornings at Eight.
54	GLOS'TER (POST COACH) every Tuesday, Thursday and Saturday Mornings at Half-past Eleven.
44	CHELTENHAM PILOT every Monday, Wednesday and Friday Mornings at Eight.
44	CHELTENHAM TALLY HO! every Tuesday, Thursday and Saturday Mornings at Half-past Eleven.

47 OXFORD REGULATOR through Banbury, every Morning, (Sunday excepted) at Half-past Eleven.

39 WOODSTOCK (POST COACH) through Banbury every Morning (Sunday excepted) at Half-past Eleven.

22 BIRMINGHAM EXPRESS every Morning at a Quarter past Three.

22 BIRMINGHAM TELEGRAPH every Morning at Nine except Thursday at Seven.

22 BIRMINGHAM REGULATOR every afternoon (except Sunday) at Three.

22 BIRMINGHAM AMICABLE every afternoon except Monday, at a Quarter before Five.

22 BIRMINGHAM CROWN PRINCE every Evening at Quarter past Five.

63 STAMFORD and LEICESTER ROYAL MAIL every Morning at Eight.

39 LEICESTER REGULATOR through Rugby every morning (except Sunday) at Half-past Eleven.

36 LEICESTER ALEXANDER every afternoon at Three.

36 LEICESTER TALLY HO! every Monday, Wednesday evenings at a Quarter past Four.

12 COVENTRY (LIGHT COACH) every morning at Eight.

10 COVENTRY TALLY HO! every Monday, Wednesday and Friday at a Quarter past Four.

WAGGONS

WAGGONS to LONDON (Golby's) every Thursday and Sunday mornings.

WAGGONS to BIRMINGHAM (Golby's) every Monday and Friday evenings.

WAGGONS to CHELTENHAM, BATH and BRISTOL every Monday and Thursday evenings.

NORTHAMPTON and DAVENTRY. CARRIER every Tuesday and Friday mornings.

The advent of the Railway made transport much easier for longer journeys. I remember in the 1900's as a small boy, frequently visiting my Aunt in London, taking advantage of the half-day excursions. I went up on one excursion and after my stay returned by another. I think that the fare was five shillings.

The coming of the motor buses revolutionized local transport. At this time there are 52 buses every weekday except Saturdays, when there are 55, going from Cubbington to Leamington. On Sundays there are 16. There are about 5 buses each day to Coventry and Rugby.

At the end of the last century, the occupations of the men folk were varied. Quite a number worked in Leamington, others worked on the farms in the parish. In those days the farm labourers were specialists in their particular work. A waggoner looked after the horses and any work in which they were used, a cowman looked after the cows, a shepherd cared for the sheep, and so on. These men walked to their work.

The workers in Leamington comprised a number of brewery workers; others worked at the nurseries or brickyards. Most of these walked but some had bicycles. The first machines were penny-farthings, then came solid tyres, then cushion tyres and finally, pneumatic tyres. The majority of villagers going to Leamington for shopping, went on foot. A Carrier's cart went to Leamington two or three times a week, and to Coventry on Fridays.

Many households took in washing from the gentry in Leamington. The Carrier would fetch the soiled linen on Monday and deliver the clean linen on Thursday or Saturday. The vehicle was available for passengers.

On Fridays the opportunity was eagerly seized to travel to Coventry via Stoneleigh, where other passengers were picked up. In those days, a pleasure to which I looked forward, was to go with my father, during the school holidays, to Coventry, where he visited wholesalers who supplied hardware goods and so on, and Banks and James, Tobacconists, to pay his quarterly bill. On these occasions we had a meal in a restaurant known as the Mayor's Parlour. To reach this room, it was necessary to climb quite a long flight of steps. We also visited the market, where Glenn's (the sweet firm) had a tempting stall. I have an idea that the carrier's horse was stabled at a Coventry public house called 'The Three Tuns' where the passengers assembled for the return journey. This, like the outward journey, was done more or less at a leisurely pace, a short trot every now and then. No-one was in a hurry, so there was no need to persuade the horse to travel any faster.

To go to Leamington for pleasure meant, in the majority of cases, walking. The Theatre in Regent Grove was always an attraction. I remember, when a very young boy, accompanying my sister, with friends, to see a play called 'The Lights of London', a story illustrating the great differences, very often tragic, between the glamour of the show pieces of the City and the poverty in other parts. I was greatly impressed by a very realistic scene of a poorly clad waif, shivering in the cold, and, to add to the discomfort, in the falling snow.

After the show came the walk home, but before this it was usual to visit a butcher's shop in Warwick Street (these shops remained open very late, especially on Saturday nights). This shop sold hot saveloys. These were bought and when, on the outskirts of the town, they were readily eaten, they were most welcome on a cold night. The street lamps ended at Lillington and the rest of the journey to Cubbington was on an unlit road and comparatively lonely. Home was finally reached, where warm drinks were quickly available; in return, an excited description of what we had seen was given. I mentioned the late hour at which the butchers' shops closed in the town. At this time there were no refrigerators and it was necessary, especially in late spring and summer, to sell off all the meat on a Saturday night. Butchers used to stand in front of their shops and call out their wares and prices to the passer-by. Many of the poorer people would wait until this time to buy their week-end joint. Two farm labourers who had large families used to make this trip together, every Saturday night. Each carried on his back a basket made of plaited rushes. These were made by a one-legged man, and almost all the workmen used them to carry their sandwiches. I have no doubt that some hard bargaining was done with the butcher. The customer knew that he must sell, as the hour drew near to closing time.

The shortage of transport and communication facilities was most keenly felt in dealing with emergency calls for the doctor. There were two visiting doctors to the village. One, who lived at Leamington, was known as the Club doctor, and he was the Medical Officer of the Oddfellows' Friendly Society. He had a surgery in the village, as did the other doctor, who lived at Kenilworth. He was the Poor Law doctor. Each of these doctors had private patients. They visited their village surgeries, which were generally the sitting rooms of cottages, on definite days of the week. The Club doctor from Leamington paid his visits on foot.

Communication in times of emergency was difficult. This was experienced in February, 1914, when my cousin needed attention for his wife at the birth of her first baby. About 1.30 a.m. I was asked to go to Kenilworth to call the doctor. My only means of transport was a bicycle, lit by an oil lamp. I travelled as fast as I could, gave my message and returned home. The doctor arrived at the patient's home before I did. I was then asked to go into Leamington with a note asking for the specialist to come as soon as possible. An operation took place but both the mother and baby died.

Both visiting doctors made up their prescriptions in their respective surgeries but if a special prescription was needed it meant a visit to either the Kenilworth or Leamington doctor's home, in some cases, on foot. Kenilworth is five or six miles from Cubbington.

CUBBINGTON REGISTRAR'S EXPERIENCE

Extract from a diary compiled by my uncle, Mr. Thomas Whitmore, Registrar of Births and Deaths for the District, who also had a Bakery business in High Street.

August 16th, 1886.

Having received notification to attend at several places for Registration purposes, made arrangements in consequence. Having completed nearly all business in Leamington, left boy to finish and take home horse and cart. Borrowed tricycle from Bro. B. Davis (a Coventry Rotary) and made best of my way to Radford (calling on a friend in High St. and there registered death of Mr. Pope, Fosse Farm) — proceeding thence, I made my way along 'Fosse Way' en route for Red House Farm, Tachbrook (near Warwick), via Harward's House. Sudden showers at intervals rendered the roads smeary, making the driving very heavy while on Fosse, but Harward's House at length reached, I turned to the right along the Banbury Turnpike where progression was much easier although, owing, I suppose, to being on strange ground and in solitude, the way seemed long. At last, however, I reached what (by consulting a map) I thought was my destination (a house which lay two fields to the left of the road) but on making enquiries there, they knew nothing of anyone by the name I required, there remained, therefore, nothing but to regain the road (which I did) and extend my search. My next venture was a large farmhouse on the right, where, luckily, I found a youth who gave me the information I sought. Once more on to the High road and proceeding some distance along it, came at last to the house I wanted. Having transacted the business required, I again started Warwick way. By this time it was growing dark, so I lighted my lamp, but no sooner had I continued my journey than out it went. Several attempts to re-light it were ineffectual, at last I gave up in despair. The remainder of the way was very hilly, being for the most part bordered by woods and spinneys which rendered it dark in places. Leaving the town, I found seats placed at intervals for the convenience of wearied travellers, but instead of being occupied by persons of the ilk, they were mostly claimed by votaries of Cupid.

A charming little maid
Who sets the heart all of awhirl
With thoughts of sweetest bliss,
and Nice Young Men
Who give the hand a squeeze
And talk all sorts of pleasant things
Beneath the moonlit trees.

The long-looked-for lights of the town burst upon my view and right glad was I to see them. Crossing the Avon by the Castle Bridge, I entered Warwick, turning down Smith Street, and made my way towards home, which I reached quite used up about 9.45 p.m.

He had tricycled nineteen miles.

The entrance to Hill Farm.
The Pound was situated on the verge a few yards beyond the tree in the centre out of sight round the corner

THE PINDER

This man was responsible for the care of the animals which had been placed in the pound. Chambers' Dictionary describes a 'pinder' as 'one who pins or fastens' and 'pound' as 'an enclosure in which strayed animals are confined'. The village pound was a fenced enclosure divided into two compartments and situated on the grass verge on the lower side of the entrance to Hill Farm.

When animals were found straying, they were driven to the pound and the gate fastened when they were in. The pinder was then informed, who would come down, lock the gate and feed the animals until they were claimed, when the owner had to pay the cost of the food and service. In my early days the pinder was a bent, short man with bushy eyebrows. He had the reputation of being able to charm warts, and, I think, successfully. The last animals I saw in the pound were four horses.

A neighbourly squabble revolved round this place, involving Mr. North (who, I presume, lived at the top of North Close) and a Mrs. B... Mr. North found some of his pigs locked in the pound. He suspected (and we may assume with some justification) that they were deliberately driven into the pound by Mrs. B... and with a little imagination we can see Mrs B... opening the gate of Mr. North's field to allow the animals to escape, then hurriedly driving them a few yards up the road to the pound. She would then hurry to tell the pinder who, of course, would come and lock them in.

This accomplished, she would relax with the knowledge that she had scored over Mr. North.

It was not long before Mr. North found where his pigs were and also would be told who had put them there. He did no more but to go to the pound, withdraw the staple and release his animals. This act caused the Parish Authority to censure him and the following is a copy of the apology which Mr. North wrote to the Local Authority.

Mr. North's Acknowledgement for Pound Breach. 4th October 1825.

I, James North, am sorry for having drawn the Staple of the Parish Pound at Cubbington and taken my pigs away inasmuch it might appear to be a resistance of the Parish Authority, but I did the above in a moment of anger occasioned by the abuse and misconduct to me of Sarah B.... — and by no means with a view to insult the Parish Officers.

Signed, James North.

As we have already said, the Cubbington Pinder had a reputation for charming warts.

An air of mystery surrounds their cure. People who have suffered from the malady tell me the following recipe is a certain cure:

Rub the warts with a piece of meat, and then bury the meat without telling anyone what you have done. The meat will, of course, decay, but as it does, so will the warts disappear.

House erected for a school. The old Village 'Lock-up' occupied the left-hand part of the building.

THE CONSTABLE

A Parish Constable was appointed every year by the Justice of the Peace, and, until 1842, no property qualification was required. He was, of course, responsible for the maintenance of law and order and therefore had the power to arrest offenders and put them in the Parish Lock-up. He also had charge of the Stocks, Whipping-post and Ducking Stool. Among his other duties were the checking of Ale-house licences and the removal of Settlement cases.

His expenses were met by a special Rate.

THE ENCLOSURE AWARD 1768

Before studying the Cubbington Enclosure Award of 1768, it may help us to understand it if we can find the reason for the request of these awards and the willingness with which they were granted.

The feudal system, as described on other pages, with its orders of Society and its three-field system of farming, worked well enough for about 250 years. At its best, it offered absolute security and tolerable conditions of life. At its worst, it was rigid and repressive. Indeed, this system of rigidity contributed to its decline, for the system was unable to absorb profound economic change.

The bondmen who suffered under the multitude of services they had to perform offered the most serious objections. Soon, however, many of the villeins secured the right to find substitutes for work on the demesne. Then the entire obligation was commuted for a money rent which was used by the lord to hire labour for the performance of the work. By the early 1300's commutation of services was common and although the lord retained the right to revert to the old system there was rarely any going back. Another change was put on hand by the lord himself, and it was not a popular one. Where labour was scarce, he took to letting off the demesne in one or more separate farms, receiving a rent in exchange, and consequently there was a tendency towards yet another innovation — Enclosure.

Not only did the lord begin to enclose the demesne where possible but he also extended it by taking in part of the common waste. This aroused strong opposition, for it deprived the peasants of an important part of their living — the right to turn small stock out to forage and also the right to gather fuel and house timber.

In 1236, the Statute of Merton forbade these ventures. In 1348 the Black Death reduced the population by a third, possibly even a half. The price of labour rose. Sheep farmers required less labour and this encouraged the larger landowners to commercialise their estates and enclose demesne and common land.

In some parts of Warwickshire, hamlets and whole villages disappeared to make room for the sheep farms. Although the wholesale enclosure had been restrained, the enclosing movement steadily continued and took the form of mutual arrangements between village farmers who wished to consolidate their holdings. By this time it was beginning to be realised that enclosure was indispensable to any improvement in farming technique.

Population began to increase and consequently the demand for more food. The old order of village farming was essentially a system of subsistence inherited from an age that set traditions above efficiency.

To meet the needs of the new situation, agriculture had to undergo a drastic change. Enclosure was the first step.

Between 1760 and 1793 there were 1,355 Enclosure Acts. Between 1793 and 1815, 1,934 Acts were passed. In the latter period there were two distinct stages. First, the open fields were taken in with a view to improving the output of existing cultivation. Then the commons and wastes were appropriated in order to bring new land into cultivation, a more drastic step with greater social repercussions. This can readily be understood from the manner in which a private Enclosure Act was obtained.

In the first place, the leading landowners and farmers in a parish met together and decided to enclose. Possibly they settled their differences beforehand and made all necessary arrangements in private. In the early days no public statement of their intention was required but after 1774 notice of a scheme had to be posted on the Church door for three Sundays during August and September. Next they applied to Parliament for permission to enclose and a Bill was brought in, to which objections might be heard in Committee. Unless there was serious opposition from a big landowner, little notice was taken of complaints, certainly not of the petitions sent in by the small farmers and peasants, assuming that the latter had been able to present their case in a proper manner at all. Three-quarters of those interested had to give their consent before the Bill could be passed, but since this proportion was calculated by property and not numerically, there was rarely any difficulty. The Act then nominated three Commissioners (often neighbouring gentry) to investigate the claims and allocate the land and also to decide such matters as liability for fencing and access to the new farms.

In many cases land was given to the Lord of the Manor and to the tithe holder, possibly a piece of ground was allotted to the poor, otherwise every holder of land, provided his title was satisfactory, received his share. For many, the problem was to establish the validity of their title. Copyholders particularly suffered owing to the disappearance of the Manor Rolls, likewise the great majority who enjoyed customary and common rights, of which there was no written record. Such rights stood little chance with the Commissioners. In other cases the properties allotted were too distant or inconvenient or unproductive to be of value to a villager who could not pay either for the fencing or the legal costs incurred. In such a case a poor man had no alternative but to sell out to his more prosperous neighbour and this happened in by far the majority of parishes. In some cases the Lord converted unfree tenure into a freehold of a sort, whereby the villein became a copyholder paying a money rent for his land, the title of which was a copy of the Manor Court Rolls.

CUBBINGTON AWARD 1768

Commissioners Appointed:

Rev. Henry Homer of Birdingbury
John Newcome of Brinklow
John Brothers of Wyken
Thomas Aston of Tachbrook

This last named gentleman was unable to fulfil his duties and William Man of Wolston was appointed in his place. The land was surveyed by George Salmon of Long Itchington.

Area of Open and Common Fields, Common Meadows, and Commonable Lands was 1,893 acres, 2 roods, 32 perches.

Expenses incurred in Surveying etc. . . . £984. 3. 6.

There follows a list of the names of the people to whom the land was allocated. The list not only gives the area, but also the amount of money each recipient was asked to pay to defray the expenses of surveying, a key to the Enclosure Map. This is an example of the legal phrasing used in the Enclosure Award.

To the Lord, or Lords, Lady or Ladies of the Manor, or Manors, Lordship or Lordships Manor or Manors Lordship or Lordships of Cubbington aforesaid in lieu of his, title or interest of and in the Soil of the Lands and grounds by the said to be enclosed. All that lot, plot, piece or parcel of land or Ground lying in Gratus hill field containing by statute measure five acres three roods and thirty seven perches including the ditches but exclusive of all roads as the same is now set out.

This was followed by a very detailed description and account of ownership of the mentioned, and this was done in every instance.

	Acres	Roods	Perches	Paid £. s. d.
Lord of the Manor	5	3	37	2. 1. 10½
Lord Leigh	375	1	14	219. 12. 1¼
John Dodson (Vicar)	122	1	17	- - -
Joseph Blissett	168	1	26	90. 0. 9
Elizabeth Wise	385	3	8	227. 1. 10½
Thomas Wightwick Knightley	96	0	12	47. 12. 2½
William Murcott	197	0	30	116. 17. 1¾
William Charnley	108	2	38	20. 10. 1½
John Preston	4	1	32	22. 17. 2½
Katherine Russell	4	0	4	23. 7. 5¾
John Boddington	114	2	8	64. 14. 2¼
Ann Parsons	67	2	28	42. 16. 9½
Joseph Russell	57	0	59	28. 4. 9¾
Mary Umbers	15	3	3	6. 13. 0
Master & Fellows of St. Catherine the Virgin, Cambridge University	36	1	16	22. 6. 8
George Warner	18	3	6	12. 2. 3½
Thomas Sotherne's Charity	22	3	31	14. 0. 11½
Sarah Elkington	20	2	2	14. 11. 11¼
Elizabeth Butcher	6	0	23	3. 3. 1¼
James Ladbrook	4	1	15	2. 7. 1
John Barber	4	1	2	2. 7. 1
Churchwardens	-	3	15	14. 9½
Freeholders	3	Stone Quarry		
				984. 3. 5¾

THE HIGHWAYS OF CUBBINGTON

In the olden days Cubbington must have possessed ample and spacious highways.

The Enclosure Act of 1768 directed also that the Commissioners should: ascertain, set out, and appoint both public and private roads through the new enclosures or allotments with the assizes and breadths thereof, so as such public roads and highways shall be and remain 60 ft. broad at the least between the ditches (except bridle and footways) which said public roads and highways should at all times be repaired, and kept in repair by and at the expense of all the inhabitants of Cubbington in such manner as before the passing of the Act was so accustomed.

In the following year, the Award under the Act was made, and the Commissioners: did order, set out, and appoint the roads, and ordered them to be and remain for ever thereafter of the breadth of 60 ft. in every part thereof as the same was then marked out and staked.

It is believed that all these were ancient roads, and that no new roads were set out.

From time to time there were encroachments upon the grass verges and gardens made, when second hedges on the edges of the road were planted. Most of these wayside gardens were claimed by the Lord of the Manor, the Countess of Aylesford, who lived at Offchurch Bury. Rents for them were paid to her agent.

The Offchurch estate was eventually sold to Lord Manton and the rents of the wayside gardens paid to him. Some time later he decided to sell these gardens by public auction. Quite a number of the people who rented them bought them.

In 1928 the Local Authority stepped in and said the gardens were encroachments and they must be thrown open to the road. This was done with the exception of the gardens along the Rugby Road which had already been taken over by the Rural District Council. I have a photograph of the hedges bordering the road being pulled up by a traction engine. These hedges were down the Coventry Road but the hedges along the other roads were dealt with in the same manner.

Lord Manton, however, acted very fairly and gave the money back to those people who had bought the gardens.

So in 1929, with the exceptions mentioned, the roads reverted to the widths of 1768, namely 60 feet between the ditches.

THE QUARRY AND CLOSE

Extract from Enclosure Award 1768

And we, the said Commissioners, parties thereto, do, accordingly to the directions of the said Act hereby set out allot and appoint the old or present Stone Quarry in the said Common Fields and all that lot, plot, piece or parcel of land or ground adjoining thereto containing by Statute measure three acres as the same is now set out and bounded in the North West, North East, and South East by the largest Allotment to the said Edward Lord Leigh, for his common field lands on the South West by the said Old Stone Quarry and the Allotment to the said John Boddington to be for ever hereafter used and enjoyed as a common Stone Quarry for digging and getting of Stone by the several Freeholders and Landowners within the Parish of Cubbington aforesaid for their several buildings and repairs, as well within the Parish of Cubbington as in the other Lands and Estates of the said several Freeholders and Landowners in other parts of the said County of Warwick, and likewise for such other purposes and under such restrictions and regulations for the good and advantage of the same Parish as the said proprietors or the major part of them in number and value shall from time to time by writing under their hands direct and appoint, with liberty nevertheless for such of the said proprietors whose lot or lots shall happen to be contiguous thereto, at any time or times to get marle thereout for his, her, or their own use or uses, the hedges, ditches, mounds and fences of which said Allotment made for a Stone Quarry as aforesaid on the North West and North East next the largest Allotment to the said Edward Lord Leigh for his common field lands shall be made and for ever hereafter maintained and kept in repair by and at the expense of all and every the said proprietors and of the said Impropriator according to their several interests in the said open and commonable fields, common meadows and other commonable lands so intended to be enclosed except the said John Dodson and his successors, Vicars, as aforesaid.

Traction engine operating in Coventry Road pulling up the hedges of the roadside gardens, which were illegal enclosures. This operation took place on all the Cubbington roads, except part of Rugby Road.

The Quarry, Leicester Lane

THE QUARRY

Stone from the quarry was sold to builders who were not freeholders in the Parish, and also the remainder of the field was let. This money was invested and Trustees were appointed to supervise its use. An annual meeting was held at the time of the Easter Church Vestry meeting. When the Church business was concluded, the Freeholders' meeting was held directly afterwards.

Often, the Vicar, who had presided at the Vestry meeting, was chosen as Chairman for the Freeholders' meeting. It was customary at this meeting to allocate any moneys available to some project in the Village which would benefit the whole village and not sectarian interests.

Here are two extracts from the Minute Book.

June 1st, 1893

At a meeting of the freeholders held this day the sum of Twenty Pounds from the Quarry Fund was unanimously voted for the purpose of entertaining the inhabitants of this Parish of 60 years of age and upwards on the occasion of the Marriage of the Duke of York and Princess Mary. B. M. Bean. Chairman.

July 25th, 1893

At a meeting of the Freeholders of the Parish (specially called) it was decided that the money now on hand of the Quarry Fund, viz £70 or thereabouts be devoted to the relaying of the footpaths throughout the village so far as the said sum will allow. The work to be done in blue bricks, and under the direction of Mr. Penn.

B. M. Bean. Chairman.

The Trust is now registered with the Charity Commissioners as Charity No. 246309.

THE QUARRY AS A REFUSE TIP

A meeting of the Freeholders and Landowners was held at the Ledbrook Institute, Cubbington, on Tuesday the 6th, December, 1949 at 8.20 p.m.

The Clerk of the Warwick Rural District Council attended by invitation, to discuss the terms of the proposed lease to the Council for use as a refuse tip of part of the field in Leicester Lane, Cubbington — the old stone quarry.

The Clerk read to the meeting the draft lease prepared by him, as amended, as the result of previous suggestions by freeholders. The question of leasing of the whole or part of the field to the District Council and the terms, were discussed and it was decided that the following terms be accepted:

1. That the whole of the field to be leased to the Warwick Rural District Council for use as a refuse tip for a period of 14 years with an option by the Council for a further 7 years, at an annual rent of £30 (thirty pounds).

2. That a right of entry to the field be reserved to the freeholders or other persons entitled for the purpose of extracting stone therefrom.

3. That the Council may, at their own expense, construct any access required to the land. and any service road on the land and use the land as a refuse tip, the Council to keep the land and leave it at the end of the tenancy in a reasonably tidy and clean condition and to take steps for the control of vermin.

4. That the Freeholders Trustees be requested to grant a lease on these terms.

The voting was not unanimous, the author voting against.

The Quarry has since been leased to the County Council.

SOUTHERNE'S CHARITY

By Will, in the first year of King Charles 1 1625 Thomas Sotherne of Starton in the Parish of Stoneley, Husbandman, bequeathed land he had recently bought of Robert Standfield, with all appurtenances thereto belonging to certain Feoffees to pay the sum of Four Pounds yearly for and towards the repair of the footbridges, Starton leading to the Church of Stoneley, and unto and amongst the poorest people, and neediest inhabitants of Stoneley, Starton and Cubbington as followeth.

That is to say, Thirty Shillings to the poor of Stoneley, and towards the maintenance of Hudson's Bridges, and Twenty Shillings yearly to the poor of Starton, and to the repair of Starton Footbridges, leading to the Church of Stoneley, and the full residue of the said Four Pounds to the poor of Cubbington. The Feoffees not doing "spoyl or wast" in any timber trees or otherwise.

The Feoffees may not lease for more than twenty-one years. On the death of any Feoffee the survivors to choose unto them another good, and honest person of the Towns and places where the other so deceased did inhabit, the number of Feoffees always remaining four in number. The remuneration of each Feoffee to be two shillings yearly, to be paid twelve pennies apiece on the Feast of the Blessed Virgin Mary and St. Michael the Archangel.

Sotherne's Charity.

The above Charity will be distributed at the Ledbrook Institute, Cubbington, on Tuesday, the 20th December, 1955, between the hours of 3-30 and 4-30p.m.

Will any person entitled to the Gift who cannot attend through illness, kindly send a representative.

E. R. Draper
G. F. Peppitt Trustees of Sotherne's Charity.
K. E. Plank

13th December, 1955.

If any trouble, suit or contentions shall happen the Feoffees shall 'recompense and save themselves harmless and set themselves clear', out of the Estate.

A Clause says:

I give and bequeath to every one of my God-children two shillings apiece. My Will is that if any four of my God-children be able to carry me to Church at the time of my Burial that they do so, and then I give to every one of them four twelve pennies apiece more.

The two cottages belonging to this Charity were built in the year 1799, at a cost of £65. 17. 2d.

According to an old Directory of 1874, by the Award of the Commissioners for enclosing the common fields of Cubbington dated 12th February 1768, some exchanges were made in the property for this Charity which in 1874 consisted of two small houses and outbuildings, two parcels of old enclosure containing about 2 acres, and three fields of new enclosure, containing about 21 acres, let at the yearly rent of £50.

The rent is paid to the trustees, and by them to the different parishes, agreeable to the division by the donor of the £4, being about three-eighths to the trustees of Cubbington, and the rest divided between the parishes of Stoneleigh and Stareton.

The cottages and land have now been sold and the money invested and controlled by the Charity Commissioners. The registered number of the charity known as the Charity of Thomas Sotherne is 256502.

The notice, a copy of one displayed in 1955, shows the method of distributing the share coming to Cubbington. The average amount is £35 for this village and the number of applicants at the last distribution was 66.

WINDOW TAX

This was first imposed in 1695, the Act 6 and 7 Wilm. III c 18.

It was frequently re-imposed notwithstanding its injurious effect in offering an obstacle to good ventilation. When it was extended in 1766 to houses having seven windows and over, the number of such houses decreased by nearly two-thirds.

In 1798 it was extended to houses with six windows. It was reduced in 1823 and repealed and the house tax substituted for it in July 1851.

PARISH OF CUBBINGTON

We, the .... hereby certify, that we have carefully examined the Assessments of the Duties on Windows or Lights, for the year ending 5th April 18— and the Allegations therein made by the Assessors of the said Parish touching the Persons therein stated to be Poor and not having more than Six Windows in their respective Dwellings, and from the Result thereof, are satisfied that the several Persons hereinafter mentioned being in number the Provisions of the Act of 43 Geo. III Cap 161 to be exempted by Reason of their Poverty, and are wholly unable to pay the Duties assessed upon them.

Dated this Day of 1819

Signed

1819

NAME		NO. OF WINDOWS
Batten	Wm.	3
Bicknell	Mark	3
Barber	Wm.	2
Bailess	Wm.	3
Brooks	John	3
Bascott	Thos.	2
Brooks	Jos.	3
Boys	Wm.	3
Barber	Sarah	2
Ballard	Thos.	5
Bruce	John	3
Barber	Jas.	2
Boys	Robt.	2
Ball	Wm.	3
Benitt	Richd.	4
Checkley	Wm.	5
Clemons	John	2
Chater	Thomas	3
Cotterill	Mich.	3
Checkley	Wm.	3
Dingley	John	3
Dowlar	Saml.	3
Douty	Thomas	2
Dingley	Wm.	3
Draper	Thos.	5
Everton	Rich.	5
Flint	Eliza	3
Fell	Jos.	3
Fell	Thos.	3
Fell	Jos.	3
Green	Edward	3
Gibbs	Richard Jnr.	3
Grant	John	2
Garner	John	3
Gibbs.	C. (Weaver)	4
Green	John	3
Gibbs	Geo.	3
Gibbs	Wm.	2
Green	John	4
Heritage	Wm.	3
Hogins	John	4
Holt	J.	3

Hogkins	Thos.	2	
Heath	Francis	3	
Haycock	John	3	
Judd	Thos.	5	
Judd	John Senr.	2	
Judd	John Junr.	2	
Judd	Wm.	2	
Keen	George	3	
Ledbrook	Rich.	5	
Lee	Matt.	3	
Lewiss	Wm.	2	
Ledbrook	W.	5	
Ludgate	Saml.	5	
Lieirman	John	3	
Mills	Rich.	4	
Mander	John	3	
Mills	Geo.	3	
Morris	Jas.	4	
Muddiman	Wm.	5	
Murcott	John	3	
Murcott	John	5	
Murcott	Wm.	4	
North	Wil.	3	
Palmer	Jos.	3	
Penn	Saml.	3	
Palmer	John	3	
Penn	John	3	
Parker	Rich.	3	
Savage	John	2	
Schelcher	Thos.	3	
Schelcher	John	4	
Stiles	Jos.	2	
Thomas	George	3	
Turner	Saml.	3	
Turner	John	4	
Turner	Wm.	3	
Thornitt	C.	2	
Taylor	Jos.	5	
Turner	Wm.	2	Empty
Taylor	Saml.	5	
Townsend	Wm.	3	
Vincent	Richd.	4	
Whitmore	Jos.	5	
Walker	Edward	3	
Whitehead	G.	4	
Ward	Jas.	3	
Wills	W.	3	
Wright	Charles	2	
Watson	Jos.	5	
Whitehead	W.	3	
Webb	Richard (School)	6	
Barrott	Joshua	3	

HEARTH TAX

Hearth money was an unpopular tax of two shillings on every hearth in all house paying to Church and poor. It was first imposed by parliament in 1662. King William promised to repeal it — 'that badge of slavery collected by the hated chimney men'.

This was done in 1689.

Hearth Tax Return for Cubbington 1663.

No. of Houses	No. of Hearths
1 with 8 hearths	8
3 with 5 hearths each	15
3 with 4 hearths each	12
7 with 3 hearths each	21
8 with 2 hearths each	16
18 with 1 hearth each	18
15 not liable, 1 hearth each	—
55	90

POPULATION

A.D.	1086	88
	1665	257 (188 Ratepayers) 69 cottages
	1730	280
	1801	440
	1811	544 (281 Males, 263 Females)
	1821	614
	1831	677
	1841	830
	1851	885
	1861	964
	1871	995
	1881	980
	1891	1074
	1901	1164
	1911	1144
	1921	1170
	1931	1264
	1941	—
	1951	1479
	1961	3553
	1971	4400 (Estimated)

1969 — No. of Council Houses including 23 Old People's dwellings: 216
Total number of Houses in Parish: 1,470.

It is interesting to note that the population in

1801 was	Leamington 315	Cubbington 440
1811	do. 543	do. 544
1821	do. 2183	do. 614

POPULATION
ON MAY 27th, 1811

112 houses inhabited. One empty. 115 Families.

Males	281
Females	544
Families by Trade	31
Families employed in Agriculture	81
Not employed as above (other families)	3

This survey is given in detail and from it we can extract the following:

Families	Children	Families	Children
One	9	Twenty	3
One	7	Seventeen	2
Four	6	Twenty-six	1
Five	5		
Eight	4		

Twenty-four families employed 47 servants:

Families	Servants (male)	(female)
One	6	3
One	5	1
One	4	1
One	4	2
Three	3	2
Two	3	—
One	2	1
One	2	—
Four	1	1
Two	2	2
Two	1	—
Five	—	1
Twenty-four	33	14

POPULATION ON MAY 28th and 29th, 1821 ascertained by J.B. Murcott, J. Smith & Sons and Thos. Smith.

Males		Females	
Age under 5	47	Age under 5	57
5 - 10	40	5 - 10	41
10 - 15	42	10 - 15	24
15 - 20	22	15 - 20	16
20 - 30	50	20 - 30	49
30 - 40	38	30 - 40	35
40 - 50	24	40 - 50	28
50 - 60	24	50 - 60	20
60 - 70	22	60 - 70	20
70 - 80	4	70 - 80	8
80 - 90	1	80 - 90	2
90 - 100	—	90-100	—
	314		300

Inhabited houses	132
Number of families	157
Houses now building	1
Houses uninhabited	—
Families employed in Agriculture	107
Families employed in Trade	44
Families not employed in Trade or Agriculture	6
No. of males	314
No. of females	300

1968:

Number of men employed in Agriculture — about 20

THE PARISH

The Parish was at the outset an ecclesiastical area. This area for church administration tended to fall in with the area of the Manor or the township.

To provide money for the upkeep of the local church, the whole body of parishioners made a practice of meeting in the vestry to decide ways and means. The parishioners elected Churchwardens, which office dates from the 13th century; the Churchwarden had the ownership of the Church furniture. A rate of contribution towards Church maintenance was agreed and levied by the Vestry.

Parish Councils were formed in 1894, and every Rural Parish must now have a Parish Meeting. Today the following factors decide whether or not a parish shall have a Council:

1. Councils existing on the 1st June, 1934 and not since dissolved, continue to exist.
2. In the case of a parish without a Council, the County Council must, by order, establish a Parish Council if the parish has 300 inhabitants or more, or if the Parish Meeting of a parish with a population of between two and three hundred so resolves.
3. The County Council may establish a Parish Council in a parish with fewer than 200 inhabitants if the Parish Meeting so resolves.

The Parish Council is the administrative authority.

The Parish Meeting is needed to give certain consents to the Parish Council. It also has the power of conferring 'adoptive' functions on the Parish Council. It consists of all the Local Government Electors of the parish. Thus, it is

A meeting of Cubbington Parish Council observed by senior scholars from the local school
No bright robes or tricom hats here, but nonetheless the Council, with its limited powers
is able to give more consideration to the general welfare of the individual
than anywhere else in local government

able, especially in financial matters, to limit the activities of the Council.

A Parish Meeting may be convened by

1. Six electors for the Parish.
2. The Chairman of the Parish Council.
3. Any two Parish Councillors.

The Parish Council, which in Cubbington consists of twelve members, is obliged to meet annually on May the 20th or within 14 days of that date, and on three other occasions during the year.

Parish Meetings must assemble annually between the first of March and the first of April and at other times determined by the Council. The money required to meet the expenses of the Council are charged separately in the Parish.

The rateable value of Cubbington on the 1st of April, 1968 was £143,728 when the population was a little over 4,300. The Rate is limited inasmuch as expenditure must not exceed the product of a 4d. rate without the consent of a Parish Meeting, unless the Minister permits a higher rate by order, and it must not exceed an 8d. rate with the Meeting's consent, again unless the Minister permits more.

The Council is empowered to provide Allotments, Public Lighting and Rights of Way.

If the Parish Council represents to a Rural District Council that a Right of Way has been unlawfully stopped up, the R.D.C. is duty-bound to take action. Amongst the other things the Council may provide are Wash-houses, or, as in the Village, a public Laundrette, litter bins, (as long as it arranges to empty them!), seats. shelters, recreation grounds and similar open spaces, and burial grounds. If the Parish adopts the Burial Acts of 1852—1906 it becomes the Burial Authority, makes the charges, settles the fees and so on.

QUALIFICATIONS TO PARTICIPATE IN LOCAL GOVERNMENT

To qualify as an elector, a person must have his name included on the Register of Electors, which comes into force annually on February the 16th. Everybody is entitled to be registered if on the 10th of October of the previous year he was:

1. of full age,
2. a British Subject or a citizen of the Republic of Ireland,
3. a resident in the parish, and
4. occupying as tenant or owner rateable land or premises worth £10 a year or more.

Candidates for election must:

1. be an elector,
2. own or lease land in the parish and
3. have resided in the parish or within three miles of it for twelve months before the election or since March the 25th of the year before it.

On the other hand, a candidate is disqualified if

1. he holds a paid office under the Council,
2. he becomes a bankrupt or composes with his creditors (until five years after an ordinary discharge),
3. he has been surcharged with £500 or more in the last five years or since election or
4. has been convicted during the last five years in the United Kingdom, the Channel Islands or the Isle of Man and sentenced to not less than three month's imprisonment without the option of a fine.

RURAL DISTRICT COUNCILS

Rural District Councils were instituted in 1894. Hitherto the countryside had been governed by the Justices of the Peace and by the Vestries together with a number of independent bodies charged with special duties — poor law, highways, sanitary questions and so on. Most of these duties were now transferred to the Local Government Authority.

Cubbington is one of 34 Parishes sending representatives to Warwick Rural District Council. It elects two members to serve on the Council.

The area of the Warwick Rural District is 55,896 acres. Estimated population in the middle of 1964 was 28,886.

WARWICK RURAL DISTRICT

	Area in Acres	Seats in WRDC.	Pop: 1961	Electors 1967	Rateable Value 1/4/67	Estimated Penny Rate 1968/69 £
Ashow	1079	1	152	81	3512	14
Baddesley Clinton	1362	1	186	115	5071	20
Baginton	1626	1	914	485	115716	459
Barford	1684	1	838	727	41707	186
Beausale with Honiley	2004	1	268	146	4866	20
Blackdown with Old Milverton	687	-	133	82	7678	34
Bubbenhall	1265	1	294	202	9111	46
Budbrooke	2979	1	705	440	17189	138
Bushwood with Lapworth	482	-	20	20	598	2
Cubbington	2112	2	3553	2886	139704	572
Eathorpe	531	1	111	83	3288	14
Guy's Cliffe with Leek Wootton	12	-	2	1	306	1
Haseley	1201	1	223	149	7315	31
Hatton	1311	1	1835	323	36679	146
Honiley with Beausale	655	-	64	32	2032	8
Hunningham	1261	1	182	124	5227	20
Lapworth with Bushwood	4606	2	1234	1124	58669	254
Leek Wootton with Guy's Cliffe	2677	1	671	473	29415	138
Norton Lindsay	621	1	204	196	8983	39
Offchurch	2286	1	288	191	9165	34
Old Milverton with Blackdown	744	1	272	161	24375	113
Radford Semele	2123	1	1273	1009	57049	247
Rowington	3817	2	790	678	30244	119
Sherbourne	1043	1	143	88	3682	24
Shrewley	1268	1	653	519	21124	93
Stoneleigh	6072	2	5409	871	115800	467
Tachbrook	3575	1	801	729	28965	141
Wappenbury with Weston-under-Wetherley	953	-	72	47	1923	8
Wasperton	1646	1	141	104	4550	20
Weston-under-Wetherley with Wappenbury	1361	1	429	133	8591	46
Whitnash	1198	2	4486	3376	138395	619
Wroxall	1651	1	144	93	7591	95
Gas Hereditament	-	-	-	-	-	1582
Electricity Hereditaments	-	-	-	-	-	19549

—†—

The Rateable Value of Warwick Rural District in 1967-1968 was £999,651.

The Rural District Council is responsible for Public Health, building Council Houses, the licensing of private contracts, refuse collection and disposal, certain health matters and collection of rates for Parish Councils, the Rural District Council and the County Council for parishes in its area.

The Rural District Council is divided into three Electoral Divisions for the County Council:

Cubbington Electoral Division :

The Parishes of Ashow, Baginton, Blackdown, Bubbenhall, Cubbington, Guy's Cliffe, Leek Wootton, Old Milverton and Stoneleigh.

Rowington Electoral Division :

The Parishes of Baddesley Clinton, Beausale, Budbrooke, Bushwood, Haseley, Hatton, Honiley, Lapworth, Norton Lindsay, Rowington, Shrewley and Wroxall.

Whitnash Electoral Division :

The Parishes of Barford, Tachbrook, Eathorpe, Hunningham, Offchurch, Radford Semele, Sherbourne, Wappenbury, Wasperton, Weston-under-Wetherley, Whitnash.

COUNTY COUNCILS

These were instituted in 1888.

The Administrative County of Warwickshire includes the following areas:

	Area 1966 Acres	Est Pop 1966
Boroughs		
Leamington Spa	2875	44700
Nuneaton	11757	61800
Rugby	7010	55800
Stratford-on-Avon	6000	18250
Sutton Coldfield	13691	80510
Warwick	5057	17330
Urban Districts		
Bedworth	7820	37100
Kenilworth	5967	19950
Rural Districts		
Alcester	37374	19530
Atherstone	34574	34400
Meriden	66228	61230
Rugby	80939	25670
Shipston on Stour	53339	9400
Southam	62527	17700
Stratford on Avon	86464	28500
Warwick	55986	25010

Rateable Value 1968: £23,047,089

There are 71 Electoral Divisions.
71 Councillors & 23 Aldermen.
Councillors are elected by the electorate;
Aldermen are elected by the Councillors.

The duties of Warwickshire County Council include administering Education, Public Health, Local Health Services, Services for the aged, infirm and handicapped, care of deprived children, Fire Services, Maintenance of Highways and Bridges, and the Police (in conjunction with the City of Coventry).

SANITATION

The drainage system of the village until 1953 when the public sewerage was completed, consisted of a large brick culvert, between three and four feet in diameter, which came from near the Post Office, down High Street and New Street to the Pingle Brook, and, from the Post Office, the other way down Queen Street to the Pingle Brook near Mr. Thwaites' factory. The drains from the cottages or groups of cottages were outside the houses and led into the culvert.

Very few houses had sinks inside. The washing was done in a communal wash house available for groups of households. A time-table was arranged amongst the households when this building could be used.

The toilets were bucket toilets. The public water supply was not completed until 1936. In some cases toilets were quite a distance from the houses, situated down the gardens and sometimes one toilet was shared by several families. The responsibility of emptying these buckets rested with the tenants. A brick-built enclosure known as the ashpit was used, as the ashes from the fire grates were deposited therein, together with the contents of the lavatory buckets.

The responsibility of emptying the ashpits rested with the landlord, who sought the help of local farmers to do this, the contents finding their way on to the farm lands as manure. Eventually a vehicle was used to collect the contents of the buckets. In 1953, water closets were added to the properties. The old culvert still functions to carry storm water.

The present system carries the sewerage to a small pumping station near Mr. Thwaites' factory, from where it is pumped to the Leamington sewer at New Cubbington.

The Public Water Supply to Cubbington was completed in 1956, and when the Public Sewerage system was completed early in 1953, building operations proceeded at a great pace.

In 1950, Broadway was started. This estate had its own sewage disposal system until 1953 when it was connected to the public system. Price Road, Cross Lane, Stonehouse Close, Windmill Hill, Queen Street, Ledbrook Road, Offchurch Road and The Grange followed in quick succession, and on January 30th, 1969 the statistics read as follows:

Estimated Population Mid-1967	4316
Council houses including 23 Old Age Pensioners' dwellings	216
Total number of houses in the Parish	1470
Income from a 1d. rate 1968-69	£572
Rateable Value April 1st, 1968	£143728
Estimated no. employed in agriculture	20

View along Queen Street towards Methodist Church before the Club was built

Queen Street from the Methodist Church, looking towards High Street
Two views of the same stretch of street

SCHOOLDAYS

THE SCHOOL

The earliest document relating to any school at Cubbington dates only to the year 1780, when a 'Messuage or dwelling house was erected for the purpose of a school'.

In 1820 the Rev. George Leigh Cooke became Vicar, and with his advent great educational progress began to be made. Mr. Cooke, the grandson of Dr. Theophilus Cooke, who for more than fifty years was Master of Balliol College, Oxford, was himself also a man of scholarly attainments, having been at one time Tutor in Corpus Christi College, Oxford. He was frequently Examiner in 'the Schools' and occupied the Chair of the Sedleian Professor of Natural Philosophy from 1810 to 1853.

Amongst eminent men who had the benefit of Mr. Cooke's instruction may be mentioned the famous Dr. Arnold of Rugby, the Rev. John Keble, and Sir John Coleridge.

Mr. Cooke was distinctly a pioneer in the cause of education in rural parishes. To him we are indebted for our excellent school buildings (1846), for, having obtained the site generously given by Chandos, Lord Leigh, Mr. Cooke personally contributed £535 towards the total cost of £907. The Committee of Council of Education contributed £220, the National Society £70, and general subscribers £182. The cloakroom and porch were added later at a cost of £200.

ENDOWMENTS

Extract from the Will of John Glover 1799.

In the name of God, I, John Glover of Cubbington, in the County of Warwick, Taylor, being sick and weak in body, but of sound and disposing mind, memory and understanding, Prais'd be God for the same, do therefore make and ordain and publish this my last Will and Testament in manner and form following (That is to say) first I give and bequeath unto my friends, William Murcott, of Bubbenhall, Gentleman, and to Thomas Webb, of Lillington, Yeoman, the sum of Two Hundred and Fifty Pounds, to pay the interest therefrom yearly unto such Person or Persons as shall be appointed by the Minister and Churchwardens of Cubbington to teach and instruct twenty children of the poor Parishioners of Cubbington to read and write the English language.

By a Will, proved at Lichfield, April 21st. 1775, Hannah Murcott, of Bubbenhall, bequeathed One Hundred Pounds for establishing a School in the Parish of Cubbington for the teaching of poor children to read.

The house on Church Hill, near the present school, was once used for educational purposes.

[The Methodists also had a Day School, in the basement of The Ledbrook Hall, once a Methodist Chapel.]

The successive Managers who, as the School was a Church of England School, were usually the Vicar and Churchwardens, were very much aware of their responsibilities by providing those extras which made such a difference to the well-being of the scholars. A roomy shelter in the playground, for use in bad weather, was erected, as well as Parallel bars, Horizontal bars and a Giant Stride. This consisted of a substantial pole, from the top of which hung about a dozen ropes, each with a loop at the end. The children put an arm through this loop and ran round. The top of the pole revolved, so, gaining speed, the children were carried with giant strides in a circular direction, culminating in a swing.

The School, 1846. Note the absence of Lobby and Cloakroom

EXTRACTS FROM THE SCHOOL LOG BOOK

1862 *Some away sowing wheat for farmers. Many boys digging parents' potatoes.*

1863 *July 11th. Wesleyan School opened.*

Nov 2nd. Children began paying fire money.

1864 *Small-pox rumours in the village.*

1866 *May 11th. Children informed of payments to be made for schooling.*

July 17th. Miss Boddington attended and spoke to two children respecting the length of their hair.

1867 *Nov 29th. Day spent in exercising and singing, too dark for lessons.*

1869 *Nov 22nd. Mr. S . . . sent written message to Vicar that children who paid 3d. per week, in his opinion, should be exempt from sweeping the school. Vicar, believing such class distinction injurious, determined to adhere to the rule. Mr. S . . . intimated his compliance and the girl continued her share of duties.*

1869 *Nov 26th. Drawing on paper for first time.*

1872 *June 7th. Volunteers (military in Stoneleigh Park) attendance thin.*

June 10th. Labourers' strike and parade through streets – lessened attendance.

1875 *Agnes G . . . and Emma owe for a copy book and exercise book since December. Agnes sent back, was cheeky – left for Chapel School, and Emma.*

1885 *Two boys appointed to make and attend to fires during the winter – 6d. a week each.*

The School after the additions

Early School photograph showing addition of second door

Besides the Headmaster, the staff at the School mainly comprised pupil teachers. As the name implies, these were both pupils and teachers. If a scholar decided to become a teacher, he continued at the same school; the Headmaster acted as tutor. At Cubbington School, the pupil-teachers attended at school several mornings each week at seven o'clock in the morning (please note!). A rota system was arranged whereby a teacher was given the duty of lighting the fire in sufficient time for it to be burning brightly by the time the Headmaster arrived at 7am. The teacher was also responsible for filling the oil lamps in the room. The fire had already been laid by the boys appointed for this work, at 6d. a week each. Great anxiety was felt by the teacher on duty as to whether the fire-lighting would be successful. Various means were used to ensure that the fire was burning brightly at the appropriate time. My father was the village carpenter, so my sister, during her period of duty, would go to these lessons armed with a substantial bundle of dry fire-wood, to supplement the wood already laid. Other members of the staff used to take candle-ends, and sometimes, in a last desperate effort to make the fire burn, the contents of an oil lamp were poured on to the coals. This action had dire repercussions. Occasionally, the lamp from which the oil had been taken would gradually dim, until the final 'pop' would signal the end of the light. This, of course, would arouse the interest of the Headmaster: "Who is on duty this week?" A faltering reply from the teacher. "Then please take another week's duty."

Homework was given to the candidates. This was to be done in the evenings, and if pupil teachers were seen too frequently at village functions, a careful scrutiny was made of their homework.

This instruction continued for several years, until the young teachers entered for the Scholarship Examination. If successful in passing this, they became Uncertified Teachers.

In 1885 a Headmaster was appointed who was a strict disciplinarian, and periodic conflicts arose between parents and the Head. A parent, nick-named 'Blarney Nell', a lady quickly aroused and then particularly aggressive, featured in two incidents. Her son Tom, who had been punished for playing truant or some other misdemeanour, had been 'kept in' during the dinner hour. The boy's mother, learning of this, came to the school, burst open the door at the entrance and calling out 'Tom' told him to come out of school. The Headmaster, without a word, clasped the lady round the waist and carried her outside, where a noisy altercation took place.

The same lady, on another occasion, took her complaint to the Vicar, as School Manager, and asked him to come and help to resolve the difficulty with the Head. The interview happened in the playground and after a turbulent argument the lady, who had her umbrella exclaimed, "Hold my umbrella, Vicar, and I'll fight him!" The Vicar, unthinkingly, took the umbrella, but, I am glad to say, no blows were struck, as the unfortunate man intervened in time. All the same, I have no doubt that the lady would have been a tough opponent, not with the uppercut, left hook or jabs of the male pugilist, but as in her contests with feminine opponents, by hair pulling. Most of her encounters ended in this way.

The school under this Headmaster, Mr. Rowbottom, reached a high standard of efficiency, and a report stated: "The School stands high amongst the best in the County".

In the photograph of the original school building, neither porch nor lobby is shown. It is difficult to imagine what happened to the children's outdoor clothing when they arrived at school on a wet day. Were they hung on pegs in the classroom?

Eventually a porch or cloakroom was added in 1893.

The organisation of the school has varied from time to time. We find the house on Church Hill still used for educational purposes long after the new school was built. In the school Log Book is an entry dated 1865 in which Her Majesty's Inspector of Schools writes:

> *In another school room about 60 yards off, I inspected an Infant School and found 49 boys and 52 girls.*

Again in 1867, another report by an HMI reads:

> *Infants' now a school for babies as it should be, only 3 over 5 years.*

As the years went by, a classroom was added in 1893 and the children were all accommodated in the one building. The Infants' and Upper Schools, although in one building, were run as two separate departments, a Head Teacher for each. The Infants occupied one large room, the Upper department the other large room and classroom.

The lighting of the school in the early days, especially in the winter months, seems to have been a problem. In 1867 on two occasions, one in November, the other in December, the teachers abandoned writing and reading lessons on account of the bad light. On November 29th the entry in the Log Book reads:

> *Day spent in exercising and singing, too dark except for oral lessons.*

On December 10th the entry reads:

> *Children sent home 3.30 p.m. Too dark to see.*

I don't know if they had artificial lighting, but if so, it would be oil lamps, as gas did not arrive until 1906.

The parents of children attending school were expected to pay. We have an entry in the Log Book for October 5th, 1865:

> *Alteration in charge for Infants — 2d. for 1st child, 1d. for every other.*

These were weekly payments.

On November 3rd, 1863, children began to pay Fire money. There does not appear to have been a school cleaner: the older children were expected to sweep the schools after school hours. A protest was made in 1869 that children who paid 3d. per week for their schooling should be exempt from sweeping the schools. (Evidently the charge for schooling was graded according to the parents' ability to pay). The Vicar, to whom the protest had been addressed, believed that such class distinction would be injurious, and was determined to adhere to the rule. The protestor intimated his compliance and so all was well. In 1885, two boys were appointed to make and attend to fires during the winter months, for which they received 6d. per week.

Writing was done on slates for some time. We find an entry in the Log Book for November 26th, 1869:

Drawing on paper for 1st time.

As late as 1895, slates were in common use instead of paper. When the slate pencil became too short to hold, it was placed in a metal pencil holder. Occasionally the pupils were expected to take the pencils home and have them sharpened. One way of doing this was to rub them on a sandstone wall. The grooves made by this process can still be seen on the walls of the old houses.

A wet sponge was not always available to clean the slates after use, so the boys found an alternative method, sometimes drying them with the cuffs of their jacket sleeves.

We noticed, when the school was built in 1846, a donation of £70 was received from the National Society. This Society was formed in 1811 to provide voluntary elementary schools on strictly Anglican principles. The British Society was formed in 1814. This was non-denominational, and was supported by Non-Conformists.

In 1870, an Act was passed which recognised that a national system of education should be provided for every child of school age. This Act allowed a dual system of control. Voluntary schools were allowed to continue and State elementary schools provided. The State schools were organised under School Boards and supported by the rates.

In 1902, School Boards were abolished and rural elementary education handed over to the County Council. The County Council was given powers to establish Secondary Schools to which both pupils from Voluntary and County Schools could gain admission by scholarships at the age of 11 years.

In 1918 the Fisher Act fixed the school leaving age at 14 and provided a more advanced and practical curriculum for the older pupils.

In 1926 as a consequence of the Hadow Report, many elementary schools were organised as senior or central (i.e. centrally-placed) schools for children between the ages of 11 and 14, and infant and junior schools for children between 5 and 11. The school leaving age was raised to 15.

In 1944 a further Education Act was passed. Publicly provided education was envisaged in this Act as a single process subdivided into three parts, primary, secondary and further. At the age of 11 every child proceeds to one of three types of secondary education: grammar, technical or modern.

The dual system of Church and State is retained, but the managers of the Church or aided schools are now liable to bear half the cost of improvements and repairs and these are so high that the Managers of Church Schools are unable to afford them. The result has been the transfer of Church Schools to the County Education Committee. These are now known as Controlled Schools.

Cubbington School was granted aided status on the 13th May, 1954. This was revoked on the 18th June, 1957, when Cubbington School became 'Controlled'. Generally speaking when the School was an aided school, the Managers were responsible for the outside of the building, while the Authority was responsible for the maintenance of the inside of the premises. Now that the school is 'Controlled' the Authority is completely responsible for the premises.

The Cubbington School Managers are appointed as follows:

(a) Two by the County Council.

(b) Two by the Cubbington Parish Council.

(c) Two Foundation Managers, the Vicar of Cubbington being Ex-Officio and the second being appointed by the Diocesan Education Committee.

When Cubbington School became a Controlled School, plans were made by the County Education Authority to build a new school at the rear of the old one. While still retaining the old buildings, the new buildings were erected.

New school building, showing old school behind. Photo 1999

The swimming bath before it was roofed

Part of the Roman Catholic School

THE PARENT TEACHER ASSOCIATION

As the name implies, this is an organisation made up of Teachers and Parents.

What a wonderful asset to a school is a good P.T. Association — the main object being the welfare of the children. The Cubbington Parent Teachers' Association has been highly successful.

Social efforts are held so that parents may get to know the staff.

Money-making efforts are arranged in order to provide equipment which is not readily provided by the Local Authority. One of the latest efforts has been the provision of a swimming bath for the children.

OUR LADY AND ST. TERESA'S R.C. SCHOOL

This school was opened in September, 1961. Situated on one of the highest points in the parish it overlooks hundreds of acres of the mid-Warwickshire countryside.

At the time of opening, the school consisted of five classrooms with 226 on roll. It was therefore necessary to commence with a class in the Hall. By September, 1963, two further classrooms were added and, in April, 1967, one more, making a total of eight. The number on the roll is about 300.

AGRICULTURE

We are grateful to Mr. Victor V Bonham-Carter for his kind permission to quote the following from his book, The English Village, (Penguin Books, Ltd. 1952). It portrays admirably the general development of English agriculture and it is against this background that the reader should view Cubbington's own development.

In the early days of the manor, money was a rarity for the peasant, since by means of barter and personal labour he had been able, to a large extent, to dispense with it altogether.

However, as time went on, cash became more essential both for the payment of feudal dues and for the conversion of services into rent. Likewise, it was needed by the larger tenant and freehold farmers, and by the landlord, to buy materials and hire the labour which had previously been obtained by the feudal system.

This was the primary cause of the tremendous development in sheep farming between 1350 and 1550, for sheep and pasture required less expenditure than arable farming and they showed far higher returns. Eventually sheep became so popular that the profit motive entirely replaced what had at first been merely an expedient to save labour and make ends meet. This encouraged the larger land-holders to commercialize their estates and enclose demesne and in some cases, common land on an even larger scale.

In Warwickshire, hamlets and whole villages were swept away to make room for sheep farms. The fact was that wool paid.

At first, the raw material had been exported in large quantities to Flanders for manufacture. After the accession of Edward III in 1327, this policy was altered. With the aid of Flemish immigrants a native clothmaking industry was established that by the sixteenth century had secured first place in export trade and in due course absorbed almost the entire output of home-grown wool.

Late in the sixteenth century, the impetus of the wool trade was reduced. For the first time for two hundred years, the population began to rise and food became a matter of great concern. The demand for corn gradually improved and the price of wheat rose from less than 5/- a quarter in 1500 to nearly 40/- in 1600.

In addition, parliament took more effective steps, both to penalize sheep enclosures and to subsidize the arable farmer. Mixed farming regained its balance and corn benefited from the fact that the land, after a century of grass, responded miraculously. The long rest, and the treading and digging of the sheep restored heart to the soil, and yields practically doubled. How then, fared the villager at this time, say, in the year 1600?

At the bottom of the scale stood the landless labourer who lived almost entirely on his wages. If housed by his employer, he was probably better off than if he lived out. He was sure of food and lodging, was accepted by the household and earned £2 to £3 per year.

A skilled man, such as a stockman or waggoner, earned a little more and had privileges besides. Wages were fixed, not by the farmers, but by the Justices of the Peace in each county.

The labourer with little or no land was the first to suffer and it was he who formed the bulk of the beggars who roamed the countryside. Nevertheless, the labourer without land was still in the minority and it was not until the Great Enclosures of the late eighteenth and early nineteenth centuries that there appeared a large, permanent and depressed class of landless countrymen.

We have noted that Enclosure of the Common Land deprived the peasants of an important part of their living — the right to turn small stock out to forage, and also the right to gather fuel and house timber. As a result, there gradually arose a large class of labourers utterly dependent on their wages for a living. The average rate did not exceed one shilling and sixpence a day, thus, it was not possible to make ends meet on anything but a starvation scale. The countryside was soon divided into two main classes, the employers and employed.

There were advantages in Enclosure. Farming became an industry and once the land was fenced and re-allocated, progress was made all round. Production expanded by the introduction of primitive machinery and fertilizers, and by the improvement of crops and stock and the increase of technical knowledge.

Transport was made easier by the use of better roads, canals and, later, railways. Food was distributed more readily. The returns were profitable and capital was invested in the industry. Until 1815, the profits yielded by the new farming were sufficient to benefit all classes, even assuming a higher cost of living and the loss of common land.

If proper wages had been paid to the labourers, the problem of poverty would have been partly solved. Enclosures increased work in the long run, but at first they threw a lot of labour on the market at once and the farmers took advantage of this to keep wages low. In every parish there were unemployed and in 1814 prices fell and so the numbers increased. Without any means of support, a man fell into pauperism and had to be kept on the rates.

In order to reduce unemployment and the rates, the parish officers hired out pauper labour on advantageous terms, and this principle was taken a stage further by the Speenhamland system.

This system supplemented wages from the rates by a sliding scale of allowances, based on the price of bread and on the size of a man's family. The effects were disastrous. The farmers now had no call whatever to pay proper wages, knowing that the balance would be met by public assistance. The labourers found that they were almost as well-off, work or no work. Demoralization was inevitable. In many parishes, more than half of the working men were on Poor Law relief.

A writer of the age, Arthur Young, vividly describes the condition of the time, 1793. Of the misery around him he wrote:

> *Go to an ale house kitchen of an old inclosed country, and there you will see the origin of poverty and the Poor Rates. For whom are they to be sober? For whom are they to save? For the parish? If I am diligent, shall I have leave to built a cottage? If I am sober, shall I have land for a cow? If I am frugal, shall I have half an acre for potatoes? You offer me no motives, you have nothing but a parish officer and the workhouse. Bring me another pot.*

Arthur Young, 1741—1820, was the first Secretary to the Board of Agriculture founded in 1793. He instituted a nation-wide enquiry into the state of agriculture county by county.

He was a keen advocate of Enclosure on economic grounds, but he was shocked by the social changes and urged that sufficient land should always be set aside to enable every man to keep a cow and a garden.

The condition of country life between 1815 and 1837 was the most grim in the history of village life. Not only was there upheaval in the practice of farming, but also the Industrial Revolution had undermined the only other source of income available to the countryman..

Factory manufacture was steadily displacing handicrafts. The smith, the saddler, the thatcher, the wheelwright, the carpenter, the mason, tailor and shoemaker were the craftsmen who survived.

During the twenty years preceding Waterloo the cost of living had doubled, while the expenditure on poor relief had risen from less than £2 million in 1785 to nearly £8 million in 1817.

At the height of the boom, previous to 1815, land reached record prices. Farmers heavily mortgaged their property and stock to raise the ready cash. However, prices began to fall in 1813, but, two years later, the end of the war hastened their decline.

Arable farming suffered first, and wheat prices dropped from 126/- a quarter in 1812 to 44/- in 1822, with a similar fall in the value of livestock.

National expenditure, which was £20 million in 1792, rose to £106 million in 1815.

Taxation was high and as a result, bankruptcies forced sales, and orders to quit were the order of the day in the countryside, and, either, rents had to be reduced or land abandoned, as it was, in many places. Rural unemployment was aggravated by the de-mobilization of men in the armed services, and the misery of persistent poverty brought many to desperation.

Tension was increased by the behaviour of the authorities, who now, being frightened, repressed all misdemeanours from petty theft to serious crime, with extreme brutality.

Poaching was the only alternative for countrymen with large families and this developed into serious warfare between the poacher and the owner of the land. Although the poacher knew that if captured, death or transportation was the penalty, necessity drove him to continue.

Riots broke out in 1830 in Kent and spread to Hampshire, Berkshire, Wiltshire, Dorset, Gloucestershire and East Anglia. A rise in wages to two shillings or half-a-crown a day was demanded and in some districts there was a good deal of sympathy for the men.

The Government took quite a different view and Lord Melbourne, the Home Secretary. sent troops to quell the disorders, and Special Commissioners to try the offenders.

Sentences were heavy. Although only one man lost his life in the riots and he was a rioter, 450 men and boys were transported to Australia, nine were executed and scores of others imprisoned.

We must relate the experience of the six labourers of Tolpuddle in Dorset, who tried to form an Agricultural Labourers' Union, as a more effective way of securing a living wage. These men were transported to Australia. Similar unrecorded cases occurred. The injustice of the Tolpuddle trial aroused public opinion at last, secured a free pardon for the men, and eventually brought them home again. Parliament also began a series of reforms which recognised the changed condition of the countryside and laid the foundations of recovery.

The Reform Bill of 1832 redistributed the franchise, and awarded restricted representation in Parliament to the middle classes in the industrial and county towns and to the farmers in the countryside.

The Poor Law of 1834 ended out-relief and reintroduced the workhouse as a test for the receipt of public assistance.

The effects of this were far-reaching. The cost to the Exchequer was reduced by half within seven years and the parish was relieved of its heaviest burden. One result of this was that, as the farmer could no longer rely on parish subsidies, he was now compelled to pay a higher wage. Nevertheless, wages rose only a little — in 1837, the average weekly payment was less than 10/6, an increase of 8d. since 1824. The farmworker, although no longer a pauper, had, still, barely enough food to enable him to work and showed small improvement on the worst days of Enclosure.

Another important piece of legislation was the Tithe Commutation Act of 1836, that abolished tithing in kind, and substituted a money rent based on the average price of corn over seven years. Later in the century, the owner was compelled to bear this charge, not the occupier of the land.

The period between 1832 and 1853 was one of preparation. Parliamentary action has been described already, but much was done by agriculturists themselves. In 1840, The Royal Agricultural Society of England, with Queen Victoria as its Patron, received its Charter. The Society has fostered invention and research and has provided a national Show (at neighbouring Stoneleigh) of world-wide reputation that has stimulated progress in every branch of farming.

There soon followed other important foundations — for example, the Agricultural College at Cirencester and the Experimental Station at Rothamsted, with which are associated the names of Sir John Lawes and Sir Henry Gilbert. These two men scientifically investigated the value of manures; they also studied crop rotation and the properties of cattle foods. Similar progress was made in geology, botany and in all branches of animal study, and in engineering as applied to the land. Steam was now being introduced as a motive power for ploughing and threshing, and new or improved implements and labour-saving machinery, such as cultivators, rollers, drills, reapers, mowing machines, horse rakes, elevators, turnip and chaff cutters and many others all began to appear.

Technically there was renewed progress. Economically, farm prices were rising in response to the demands of the towns and the growing population. By taxing foreign corn, the Corn Laws continued to protect the arable farmers and in 1839, wheat stood as high as 70/- a quarter.

Opposition to the Corn Laws was growing, and an Anti-Corn Law League led by Cobden had a large middle-class following in the towns.

In agitating for repeal, the townsmen argued that the free import of foreign corn would provide cheaper food for the working classes, would encourage the sale of British manufactures abroad, and would discourage the setting up of foreign industry.

The opposition thought otherwise. Agriculture would be ruined and farm labourers would lose their employment. Free trade was on the way, and the Irish potato famine of 1845, necessitating urgent supplies of corn to prevent starvation, forced the hand of the Conservative Prime Minister, Sir Robert Peel. The Corn Laws were repealed and import duty was reduced in stages to 1/- a quarter by 1849. Later, it was abolished altogether.

Between 1848 and 1852 prices fell and there was a mild panic when wheat dropped to 38/- a quarter. Later, a marked improvement was shown. Between 1853 and 1874, British agriculture enjoyed an era of prosperity and progress, due, in part, to a succession of circumstances.

When the Crimean War was over, England was at peace, while much of the rest of Europe and America was disturbed. Russian trade was suffering from the consequences of the War; America, still undeveloped, was torn by the Civil War of 1861–5; Germany was involved in a series of campaigns with Denmark in 1853, with Austria in 1866, and with France in 1870–1. Each of these events stimulated British exports and diverted the import of foreign food, with the result that home agriculture experienced little competition and prospered exceedingly. It was a wonderful age.

Inventions and improvements came into their own, livestock breeding flourished and the general level of farming rose quickly.

Some landowners offered allotments as well. Allotments, as the name implies, had appeared in some areas at the time of the Great Enclosures as compensation for loss of holdings in the open fields. (There is no evidence that that happened in Cubbington). Some farmers opposed allotments on the ground that the labourer might reserve his best efforts for his own ground.

With all this prosperity, one might have thought that the labourer was going to receive his just reward. In fact, although profits and rents rose sharply between 1853 and 1862, wages still lagged a long way behind. In 1860, the average nominal rate was a little over 11/6d. a week, and in 1870, 12/2d, very little more than in the depression days of 1830.

In winter and in slack times, a man earned less and this meant that he had to depend upon the labour of his wife and children in order to make ends meet. In the Eastern Counties there developed a system known as Gang Labour, which consisted of the employment by farmers of troops of men, women and children who had no home, but wandered about, doing field work under the direction of gang-masters. Public opinion was aroused and the practice became controlled by the Gangs Act of 1868 and then, by various Education Acts. After 1870, all children up to the age of fourteen were sent to school, none to be employed on the land without permission.

In 1874, trade in Britain experienced a depression. Farming first felt the bleak wind through a series of bad harvests. The summer of 1879 was the wettest season on record, but the rise in the price of grain was forestalled by a flood of cheap American corn grown upon the virgin soils of the broken prairies, with the result that the bottom fell out of corn production. A further blow was to follow. Hitherto, the prices of fat cattle, pigs and sheep remained firm, but with the advent of refrigeration, even that market was lost. From 1890 onwards, dead meat from America, Argentina, New Zealand, and Australia poured into the country. Cheese, butter and wool were also heavily imported.

Industry in Britain had developed to such a degree that it now depended for its export of vast quantities of manufactured goods. In the eyes of the manufacturer, these could best be exchanged for raw materials and for cheap food. In this way, foreign food kept the export trade alive, and industry had an interest in the depression of home agriculture.

Between 1871 and 1901, the corn area of the country declined by nearly three million acres and the stubble fell back to grass.

Far worse, the people began, rapidly, to leave the land. Agricultural labourers decreased by 300,000 in thirty years.

Agriculture at this time, held a low place in the national economy.

By some, this tragedy was attributed to the influence of Free Trade. It was also stated that only two kinds of farmers could make a living, the wealthy man able to use capital to convert land, plant and stock to grass husbandry, and the small man who employed no labour but that of himself and his family. The farm labourer's wages had risen to 14/- a week, but there was a great temptation to leave a dying industry and seek employment in the towns. Protection would seem to be the solution to this depression but the country was wedded to Free Trade and cheap food.

Rider Haggard, in his survey of twenty-seven English counties, urged the President of the Board of Agriculture to operate by Credit Banks, co-operative marketing and State subsidies for rural housing. He also suggested a special transport service to compete with the railways and carry agricultural goods at cheap rates.

It was clear that the only way to make a living on the farm was to sell liquid milk, develop market gardening and fruit crops and multiply pigs and poultry fed on cheap imported grain. The social laws introduced at this time affected the countryside greatly. The franchise was extended to agricultural labourers in 1884. The Education Acts compelled children to attend school between the ages of five and fourteen. The work of the agricultural unions was a source of change.

Between 1871 and 1875, the Trades Union and various amending Acts were passed, legalising the status of Unions and establishing their right to bargain on behalf of their members.

The Old Age Pensions Act of 1909 assured him a pittance on retirement and the National Health Insurance Act of 1911 assisted him in times of sickness.

In 1916, intensive U-Boat warfare caused a desperate shortage of food and County Executive Committees were set up. In 1917 the Corn Production Act was passed, which empowered the Board of Agriculture to enforce the ploughing up of pasture and the intensive cultivation of arable land for a period of six years. In return, guaranteed prices for corn were secured by the farmers. This dual policy of compulsion and incentive obtained much of the extra food required. Central and District Wages Boards were formed, which regulated the hours of work and fixed a minimum wage. After this, wages rose quickly and by 1921 they were little short of 50/- a week.

In 1920, the Agriculture Act was passed, which superseded the Corn Production Act, withdrew State control over cultivation, continued the guarantee of grain prices, retained the Wages Boards and adjusted the relations of landlord and tenant, particularly in regard to the payment of compensation for disturbance.

World prices, however, began to fall and all the guarantees were thrown overboard. In 1921, the Agriculture Act, after eight months' life, was repealed. As a result, arable farming went to pieces and the land reverted to grass. Wages, no longer under the care of the Wages Board, dropped sharply, and by 1923, were down to 30/- a week or less, and the number of farm workers in England and Wales declined from 612,000 in 1921 to 511,000 in 1939.

In due course, however, a measure of protection for agriculture was introduced. In 1924, Wages Boards were brought back, with the result that by the beginning of the Second World War basic rates had risen to 35/- for a 50-hour week.

Sugar beet and wheat were subsidized. Marketing Boards were set up, some soon discarded, others, such as the Milk Marketing Board, to be retained. However, at the time of the Second World War, fundamental changes were forced upon the whole structure of the nation's trade, to the betterment of agriculture.

LOCAL AGRICULTURE

In the preceding pages we have watched the vicissitudes of agriculture nationally, through the centuries. We now see how local farming fitted into this pattern. Fluctuations of prosperity and depression were felt in Cubbington as in other parts of the kingdom. The sufferings of unemployment and poverty were as well known here as elsewhere. The low wages of the labourers and long hours of work which were official, fixed by the Justices of the Peace, are enumerated within these pages.

The attempt of the Cubbington labourers to call attention to their plight is also told. About the year 1902, it was stated that only two kinds of farmers could make a living, (1) the big man with capital and (2) the small farmer who employed no labour except that of his family. Probably Cubbington was fortunate, as most of the land was owned by wealthy landlords, the Boddingtons, the Murcotts, the Leighs, the Ledbrooks. Some of them lived in the farmhouse attached to the land and in other cases the land was let to tenant farmers. In 1817 we find thirteen owners and occupiers of farm lands in the parish.

In the early 1900's changes began to take place. Some of the old families had died out and the ownership of the land was inherited by people who let out their inheritance to tenant farmers. At this point we see the tendency for people in business to invest their capital in farming and to place a bailiff in the farmhouse. The owner of one of the largest hotels in Leamington also owned Church Farm and the owner of the Cubbington Saw Mills farmed a small acreage. Also, we find that two of our farmers, through lack of capital, failed and had to give up.

What of the farms themselves? In the early 1900's we had ten farms in the parish, with five farmyards in the centre of the village. On one side of the yard would be the buildings to house the cows, horses, calves and pigs with a much larger building known as the Barn. This building was sufficiently tall and with an entrance large enough to admit a wagon fully loaded with hay or corn. The yard outside would contain ricks of hay and corn in their respective seasons.

Roaming about the farmyard and in the adjoining fields would be the poultry, each flock led by a proud self-esteemed cockerel. In the daytime, when the children were in school, the silence of the village was broken by the crowing of the cockerels answering each other over the immediate neighbourhood, sometimes as many as eight or nine challenging calls.

What happy memories are revived in me by describing this truly free-range method of poultry keeping. I stayed at a farm in a neighbouring village for some weeks, and what a delight at the end of the day to help with the egg collection. Nests were found in the most unexpected places and the excitement reached its peak when a nest was found with nine or ten eggs in it. The corn harvest was carried from the fields and made into neatly built stacks or ricks. These were built on wooden beams raised about two feet from the ground by stone pillars called staddles. Frequently these are found used as ornaments in the gardens of villas. The ricks, when finally built, were thatched with straw, neatly finished off, with the edges carefully trimmed, and sometimes straw plaiting adorned the work. What a pride the thatcher took in this exercise. After the corn had been carried home, the gleaners came along. Their work is described later.

Farm labourers were specialists. The waggoner was responsible for the horses and for the transport vehicles. He had an assistant or a young boy fresh from school, known as the plough boy, and one of his duties was to lead the forehorse, when ploughing had reached the headland, round to the position of the return journey of the plough. This was the position to which I hoped to aspire when I was quite young. The other duties would be connected with the feeding of the horses, chaff cutting and so on.

With the harvest over, the ploughing started. This work generally ended fairly early in the afternoon in the winter months. For one thing, the horses were tired and the waggoner had food and bedding-down to deal with. The ploughboy, on his way home, would occasionally need to leave the coulter at the blacksmith's to be sharpened and would often ask that it be ready for the next morning. The blacksmith worked to a very late hour.

The cowman, at an early hour, would be milking. Our milk was delivered to us, direct from the farm, at about 7am., the retailer, with yoke on his shoulder, carrying two milk buckets full of milk uncooled and quite unprocessed. One bucket would be left at his home, with the other he visited his customers. The milk was warm when it arrived at our house and after being measured was poured into the jug. Some of the customers went to the milkman's house for their supply. There were several poor people in the village at this time and the farmer at Ford Farm, about a mile and a half or more down the Offchurch road, had skim milk for sale after making butter. Some children, after school, used to trudge a mile and a half there and back for this milk. I remember thinking, that if those children were helping their mums by fetching the milk, why shouldn't I help mine? After persuading my mother to allow me to go, I trudged along with the others, carrying a jug with a metal lid. What a glow of satisfaction I had when I returned!

At some time in the winter months, the farmer would decide to thresh his corn. The man owning the machine would be notified and the day fixed. The illustration shows what is known as a portable engine driving the threshing machine, or drum, as we used to call it. The name 'portable' is given to the engine because it was capable of being moved, but not under its own steam. You will notice the shafts, between which one horse stood, with about five more in front of him, the engine taking about six horses to pull it. The farmer who needed the threshing machine was responsible for fetching it from its previous employment to his own farm. The next farmer who needed the machine would do likewise. The farmer also provided the coal for the engine. This particular machine was owned by the man in the photograph who was driving the engine. He was a Cubbington man and lived in one of the cottages at the lower end of New Street. The sheaves, one at a time, were passed from the rick to the machine. One of the two men on top of the machine cut the binding and the other fed the sheaf gently into the thresher. Inside, the sheaves were shaken, releasing the grains, and these passed through a grading section, which divided the corn into two or three grades and delivered it into sacks, suspended below the apertures. If the rick had been standing for some time, there would certainly be mice, and in many cases, rats, inside. The rats would remain in the rick as long as they could, travelling down to the bottom. The farmer, if he thought there may be a number of rats, would surround the bottom of the rick with wire netting, so as to hinder their escape, thus enabling them to be dealt with in no uncertain manner. Mice were a different proposition. I remember visiting a farm yard in New Street when threshing was in progress, and on leaving was accompanied by a school chum who had been there with me. After going some distance up the road, our conversation was interrupted by a shriek from my friend. He realised that a mouse was crawling round his neck on the inside of his coat. He quickly put his hand down his back and caught it and threw it on the ground. The poor wee beastie ran away to live another day. The mouse had evidently run up his trouser leg and had almost reached the summit of its endeavours when it was caught. The labourers working on the rick tied string round the bottom of their trousers.

A second user of steam power on the farm was a heavy plough called the cultivator. This was operated by two heavy traction engines. One engine would be positioned on one side of the field, the second on the other. The cultivator would be attached to each engine by a wire cable capable of being wound on a drum on each engine. This plough or cultivator would be drawn across the field by the cable, the engines remaining stationary. On reaching the other side, the engine would give a signal with its whistle. This meant that the engine on the opposite side of the field would draw the plough back. The engines, after operations, would move forward slightly.

The transport of animals from farm to market and from market to other destinations, was undertaken, as late as the early 1900s, by a man called a drover. He directed the animals along the road from one place to another. With what skill the job was done — no movement or shout which would excite the animals. They gently moved along the roads, occasionally munching the grass on the roadside verges as they went. Animals were moved great distances in this way. The Welsh Road, which the Offchurch Road is sometimes called, was named thus, because it was used by the Welsh farmers to bring their animals to the large Midland markets. In places in the locality, between Offchurch and Kenilworth, there were ponds in fields beside the road, and there the verges were cut back so that the animals could get to the water to drink.

What a revolution has occurred during the last twenty or thirty years, with the advent of tractors, multiple ploughs, combine harvesters and many other power-drawn machines. The milking machine and the milking parlour, the housing of the cows in winter in large buildings with the opportunity for the cows to help themselves from the silage, the battery hens and other poultry, the housing and feeding of cattle and pigs for market, are all, it seems to me,

Threshing (see text for description)

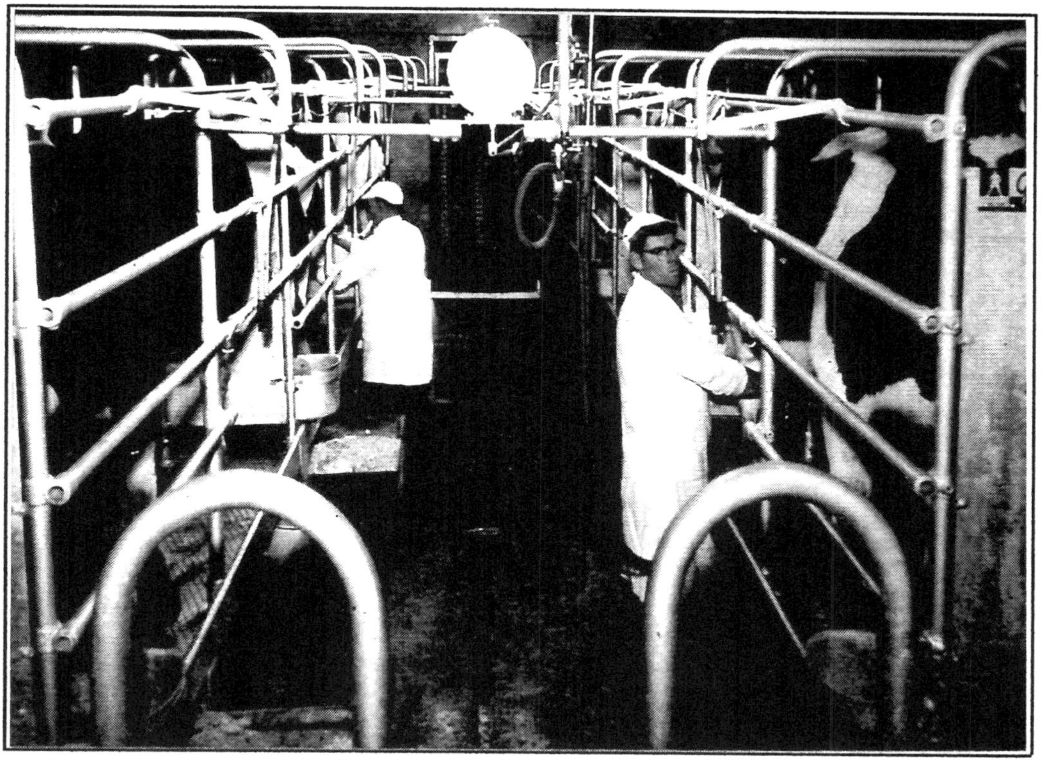

Milking Parlour

further aspects of the twentieth century's obsession with mass-production.

The 'milking parlour' is an appropriate name, when the system is compared with the method used years ago — animals tethered in a long row in a building known as the cowshed, straw loosely scattered on the floor, hay racks and feeding troughs placed conveniently for each animal. The cowman with his pail and three-legged milking stool visited each animal in turn. There was nothing to prevent dust from entering the pail.

The cowman wore a cap, and he usually rested his head against the animal's side as he worked. Naturally, the cap became very greasy after continuous use. It was said of one of our cowmen that when he thought it wise to have another cap, he would then throw the old one to the sheep dog who began to eat it.

You now realise the advantages of milking as shown in the 'milking parlour'. The cows are milked by machine, the milk passes, without coming into contact with the atmosphere, into a refrigerated tank in which it is kept at 40°F

In the background is a board with the numbers 1-50. By the numbers are the names of the cows and the amount of milk each one gives. The volume of milk from individual cows is passed automatically into a measuring glass container before passing into the tank.

The photograph was taken at Glebe Farm by the Leamington Spa Courier.

FARMING TODAY

In 1947 the Agriculture Act established County Agricultural Committees. Each Committee has twelve members, appointed by the Minister of Agriculture. These members are drawn from all sections of the agricultural industry. Their main task is to promote the development of agriculture in their counties.

Committee members are consulted on grant and subsidy applications when there is a doubt about eligibility, and the Committee itself advises on cases in which applications are made against official decisions.

Comprehensive information on acreage, production of crops, numbers of livestock, agricultural workers, agricultural holdings, some agricultural machinery and prices of agricultural produce, store stock, feeding stuffs and fertilizers, is given in 'Agricultural Statistics, England and Wales' published annually by H.M. Stationery Office.

These notes are taken from the 1968-69 'At the Farmers' Service; Training Facilities' issued by the Ministry of Agriculture, Fisheries and Food, and reproduced here by kind permission.

AGRICULTURAL, HORTICULTURAL AND FORESTRY INDUSTRY TRAINING BOARD

The Board is a statutory body, set up by the Ministry of Labour under the Industrial Training Act, 1964.

The purpose of the Board is to ensure an adequate supply of properly trained men and women at all levels of the industry, to secure an improvement in the quality and efficiency of training and to share the cost of training more evenly between employers.

The Board is responsible for raising a levy on employers and for paying grants to employers who release workers for training approved by the Board, or who provide facilities for training.

Full and sandwich courses in agriculture and horticulture are provided at Universities and at Agricultural Colleges. Awards for these courses are offered by local Education Authorities in their areas.

Wages and Conditions of Service

Orders made by the Agricultural Wages Board under the Agricultural Wages Act, 1968, prescribe minimum wage rates and holidays with pay, for all persons employed in agriculture and define and value benefits (e.g. a cottage which may be provided by an employer in part-payment of wages at the minimum rates).

Permits of exemption, authorizing payment of specific lower minimum rates for individual workers who are physically or mentally handicapped, may be granted by Local Agricultural Wages Committees.

Houses and Cottages

Local Authorities (except County and County Borough Councils may, in certain circumstances, make grants of up to £10 per annum for 40 years, for the building of a house reserved for members of the agricultural population. Application for grant should be made before building begins and work should not start until approval has been given.

Grants are also given for 'Improvement of Existing Houses and Cottages'.

Investment Grants

The following investment incentives are available for agriculture (including horticulture) in respect of expenditure incurred on or after 17th January, 1966.

A grant of 10%, increasing to 12½% during the period, from 1st January, 1967 to 31st December, 1968, on investment in farm buildings and other fixed equipment, new fixed plant and new fixed machinery for the purpose of an agricultural (including horticultural) business, or long-term improvements to the land comprised in such a business. Only businesses where labour requirements amount to at least 250 man-days will qualify and there is a minimum expenditure limit of £100 per claim.

A Standard man-day is 8 hours' manual work for an adult worker under average conditions.

A grant of 10%, increasing to 15% during the period from 1st January, 1967 to 31st December, 1968, is available on new tractors and self-propelled harvesters licensed under the Vehicles (Excise) Act, 1962, as agricultural machines, paying duty at an annual rate of £5.0.0. The grant for tractors purchased for cash will be paid in two equal instalments, one year and two years respectively, after the date of purchase and for harvesters in a single payment, twelve months after the date of purchase.

Lime

Farmers can obtain a contribution towards the cost of liming land for the improvement or maintenance of soil fertility.

Loans
Improvements to Land and Buildings, 1968

The Agricultural Mortgage Corporation Ltd. and the Lands Improvement Company, are empowered to grant loans to landowners, to carry out improvements to agricultural land and buildings. The amount of the loan is charged on the land improved in the form of a terminal rent-charge, which is payable half-yearly for a period not exceeding 40 years.

Ploughing

A grant of £12 per acre is available during the year ending 31st May, 1969, for bringing into cultivation land which has been continuously under grass since before 1st July, 1956 and for which the cost of the ploughing and other operations is substantially higher than normal.

Water Supply

Grants towards the cost of farm water supplies are available to owners and occupiers of agricultural land. The water supply can be in respect of fields, farm buildings, or for spray irrigation, and, in certain circumstances, farm houses and cottages, provided the cost is reasonable and the benefit to agriculture is adequate. A flat rate of 40% of the approved cost (i.e. costs which are approved as suitable for grant-aid before work commences) of fixed, permanent and normally external works is offered, on schemes using a private source of water, and 25% for a scheme using a public source.

Grants for Livestock:
Beef Cow Subsidy

A subsidy at the rate of £9 a head is payable on cows maintained throughout 1968 in regular herds, kept permanently for breeding calves for beef.

Bulls

Grants are paid towards the cost of an approved bull when the owner makes the services available for neighbours' cows.

Calf Subsidy

Subsidy is payable either for steer and heifer calves of beef type (Stage A) or for steers and heifers of any breed which have been slaughtered for beef. (Stage B)

Stage A
To qualify at Stage A, calves must have been born in the United Kingdom, they must have been properly reared and be suitable for further rearing for beef production or if heifer calves for use for breeding for beef production, and in each case, if slaughtered either immediately or after further rearing and fattening, be likely to yield reasonably good quality beef. Application must always be made early enough for animals to be inspected and certified before they have cut their first permanent incisor tooth. Heifer calves of the Jersey, Guernsey, Freisian and Ayrshire breeds and of crosses by these breeds are not eligible. The rates of subsidy are £8 and £10. 5s. per head, respectively, for heifers and steers born before 1st January,1967, and £9 and £11.5s. per head for those born after that date.

Stage B
To qualify at stage B the carcass must be presented at an approved deadweight centre at the same time as it is presented for certification for a fatstock guarantee payment and must be of a standard eligible for such payment. The animal or carcass must not have been imported and not have been certified previously for the calf subsidy. Subject to these conditions, the carcasses of fat cattle of any age or sex are eligible for Stage B payment. The rates for Stage B subsidy are £8 for heifers and £10. 5s. for steers, regardless of the dates of birth of individual animals presented. These rates will be increased in due course to £9 and £11. 6s., respectively, for heifers and steers, when it is judged that the generality of animals presented were born after 1st January, 1967.

Annual Review and Determination of Guarantees.

Under the Agriculture Acts, 1947 and 1957, the Government provides price guarantees for cereals, fatstock, milk, eggs, potatoes, wool and sugar-beet. Guaranteed prices for these products are determined each March in the light of the Annual Review of the economic position of the agricultural industry. Details of the guaranteed prices are given in a White Paper published each year. The Agriculture Act 1957 gave statutory effect to long-term assurances that set minimum limits to the price determination that may be made after an Annual Review.

The guarantee for milk, eggs, potatoes and wool are implemented through the marketing boards for these products. The guarantee for sugar-beet is implemented through the British Sugar Corporation and the guarantees for cereals and fatstock are implemented through deficiency payment schemes operated by the Ministry.

FARM MEN WIN RISE!

This is the title of an extract, taken from a daily newspaper dated November 20th, 1968:

Britain's 383,000 farm workers have won a 17s. a week rise – which brings the minimum for men to £12.8s.

But there will be no cut in the 44-hour working week and leaders of the Farm Workers' Union are bitterly disappointed.

The award is an increase of 7.4%. As it exceeds 3½%, it will have to be considered by Mrs. Barbara Castle's Employment Ministry, who may refer it to the Prices and Incomes Board.

The rise, from February 3rd next year, may help to stem the drift from the land. Last year 35,000 farm workers left for higher paid jobs in factories.

The National Union of Agricultural Workers had asked for an increase of £4. 9s. a week, to bring the minimum to £16. 0s., and a four-hour cut in the working week.

SCHOOL LOG BOOK:

June 10th, 1872. Labourers' strike and parade through the streets, lessened attendance.

Thus reads an entry in the Cubbington School Log Book: is the strike a sequel to a meeting held in Leamington on May 29th, 1872, the culmination of months of early Union activity? Between 1871 and 1875 the Trades Union and various amending Acts were passed, legalizing the status of Unions and establishing their rights to bargain on behalf of their members.

In February, 1872, Joseph Arch was asked to found a local Trade Union of farm-workers at Wellesbourne in Warwickshire. Arch was born in Barford. A liberal and a Methodist lay preacher, he was a man of intelligence. He was a skilled workman and a contractor for hedge-laying and field work. This brought him economic security. He was neither dependent on wages nor on the whim of one master for a living.

A thousand people attended the first meeting. At the second meeting a Committee was elected and Secretary appointed to organise a Union.

On May 29th at a conference of delegates from all the local unions held at Leamington it was decided to set up the National Agricultural Labourers' Union.

This was the first Trade Union for farm workers. The entrance fee was 6d., the contribution, 2d. A year later the membership rose to 71,835 with 982 branches opened over every English county except six.

Joseph Arch was Chairman of this Union. In 1874 membership was 150,000 but trouble was at hand, for in 1873, a number of farmers in the Eastern Counties had threatened Union men with dismissal, and in the following year the process was repeated on a wider scale. By April, 6,000 men had been locked out in Suffolk and North Essex for refusing to leave their Union. The farmers solved their difficulties employing 'black-leg labour' but the Union men had to depend on strike pay for their living. The Unions asked help from the towns and large sums of money were collected. In July the Unions stopped strike pay and advised the men to work elsewhere. Soon the depression in agriculture caused wages to fall and Union membership declined. The national figure dropped from 55,000 in 1877 to 4,250 in 1889.

Arch himself retired, an old man and disappointed. Many of the early pioneers emigrated. However, the Union had accomplished something: it had won several victories and also proved the value of combination and self-help amongst the labourers.

Until 1916 the fortunes of the agricultural labourer improved, but very slowly. His wage was still less than £1 per week.

GLEANING

The following verses from the Bible are of particular interest in connection with the above title.

And when ye reap the harvest of your land thou shalt not wholly reap the corners of the field, neither shalt thou gather the gleanings of the harvest. And thou shalt not glean thy vineyard, neither shalt thou gather every grape of thy vineyard, thou shalt leave them for the poor and the stranger. Leviticus 19 9 & 10

This injunction was written about 3450 years ago. When Christianity was introduced into this land and the Bible followed, did the farmers accept this and was the custom handed down to the 1900's?

In 1817, from the notice by the farmers at that time, they departed from the original order. The poor of the parish were allowed to glean, but strangers were excluded.

We, the undersigned and occupiers of Farms, Lands and Hereditaments in the Parish of Cubbington in the County of Warwick, do hereby give notice, that from and after the Date hereof, we will not permit any Person or Persons whomsoever, except the Poor of our own Parish, to Glean on any or either of our Lands, in Cubbington aforesaid — and we further give notice that all Persons, except our own poor, who shall be found Gleaning or otherwise Trespassing on any of the lands occupied by us, in Cubbington aforesaid, will be proceeded against with the utmost severity of the Law —

Dated the 12th Day of August, 1817.

John Busby Murcott	Thos. Smith
John Bodington	Joseph Russell
John Smith	James Fell
John Smith the Younger	George Hinde
George Manton	Thomas Knight
Robert Ledbrook	Jos. Ballard

The summer holidays of the school children were known as 'Harvest Holidays' and during this period 'leasing' took place. 'Leasing' seems to have been used as the local dialect word for 'gleaning'.

In the early days the cornfields were cut by a sickle and afterwards by a machine which not only cut but bound the corn into sheaves.

After the sheaves had been 'carried' to the corn ricks the village people were allowed to go into the fields to collect the corn which was left. At one time the Church Bell was rung to herald them in. The Cubbington gleaners all started at the same time and gleaned the same field together. The mothers used to take their children with them to help with this operation. I have joined in with this help for some neighbour.

A large sheet was taken by each parent and on arrival at the field the sheet was spread on the ground at a suitable site. The collection began.

The corn was made into small bunches, held together by twisting some of the straws round each bunch. The bunches were then placed on the sheet with the ears of corn facing the centre. When the leasing was finished the corners of the sheet were tied together and carried home on the head of one of the stronger members of the party. The corn was used to feed the few hens kept by a number of the villagers. It was evident at one period (1817) that people not living in the village had trespassed in the cornfields of some of the Cubbington farmers, in order to lease. Hence the severe admonition issued by the local farming fraternity.

ITINERANT VISITORS

Itinerants were varied but all came for the same purpose — to make money, though in most cases very small amounts.

First, there were the hurdy-gurdy (barrel organ) men. I think that at one period a barrel organ could be hired in Leamington. This instrument was generally accompanied by two men, the pull up from Leamington being very steep. One man was in the shafts while the second helped by tugging at a strap. These instruments played some six or seven very lively tunes. The organ was operated by continuously turning a small handle, and the tune was changed by turning a smaller handle which moved an indicator around a numbered dial so that it would be possible to play a number by request. If the turnout included a monkey, as it very often did, it created an added interest. One man played, the other collected. These visits were frequent.

There were visits from a small number of musicians (generally four) playing on brass instruments. This constituted the German Band, whose members generally wore a kind of uniform hat, and their visits were less frequent than those of the hurdy-gurdy men.

The cheap-jack Crockery Salesmen, I think, came from the Potteries. They came into the village with their well-stocked horse-drawn vehicle and announced their sale on the Village Green, near the school. The wares were spread out on the grass. The naphtha lamps were ready, if necessary, to light the proceedings. People were at liberty to go and bargain privately with the owner during the evening but at a certain time, when a goodly number of people had assembled, he would sell by mock auction. First, asking a price for an article, he would gradually lower the figure until some-one who needed it, afraid that a neighbour might snap it up, shouted out his acceptance of the price reached in its descent. I think most of the villagers agreed that, not only were bargains to be had, but it was also convenient to walk only a short distance to have their requirements supplied.

Salt Sellers sold bricks of salt. The bricks were about 1ft. 6ins. long and about 9 inches square at one end, tapering down to about 6 inches the other end. Since my father kept a general store he used to buy a number of these. They were very cheap. It was my job to saw them into chunks, thinner at the large end, thicker at the small end. I think these sold at about a penny each, so that a chunk of salt, 9 inches square and 1 inch thick, would cost a penny.

Villagers who anticipated killing a pig and salting the sides for bacon would buy one or more large bricks. I have an idea these men came from Staffordshire. Their horse-drawn vehicles were decorated in bright reds and yellows.

The Vocal Soloists were generally men, sometimes accompanied by a sad-looking woman, and when this was so I think they gained a greater amount of sympathy. Normally they came on a Sunday. After Sunday mid-day meals we retired to our sitting room on the first floor. The ground floor of the house consisted of shop, stores, living room and kitchen. The silence of the sitting room, some members of the family sleeping, others reading, was broken by the strains of one or two well known hymns, either 'Lead, Kindly Light' or 'Abide With Me'. Coins were readily available from the family and it gave me great pleasure to open the upstairs window and throw them down to the soloist below.

With a grateful smile and a touch of the cap, he picked them up and continued on his way. The hymns were sung slowly in order to give sympathisers a chance to find their coins. A few coughs and similar gestures to indicate they were cold, added a few pence to the collection.

The Scissors-grinder and Knife-sharpener made periodic visits to the village. The apparatus with which he worked consisted of a grindstone and an emery bob, held together in a frame three or four feet high. Built into this frame was a wheel about three feet in diameter which served a dual purpose. It enabled the whole thing to be moved easily from place to place, and, when the whole apparatus was tipped up on its end, it became free of the ground and able to work the stone or bob, whichever was required, by means of a pulley. The operator sat on a little seat on the framework and pedalled the wheel round, grinding or sharpening away. Customers were plentiful.

Rag-and-Bone Men were very frequent visitors. This is rather surprising, as most of the villagers were very poor. As one lady told the rent collector when he called, 'I haven't any money for the rent, but here we are, rags and bones, you can take us if you want us.' In spite of the poverty, the rag-and-bone men usually went home with a full sack. Rabbit skins were plentiful, rabbits being numerous in the district.

MR. AND MRS. PIG

I mean the variety which has four legs, a curly tail, and grunts.

These animals played a very important part in the economy of the village. The majority of the houses kept pigs, and most had facilities for so doing, the sties nearly always being situated at the end of the large gardens.

The interest in this animal started when a visit was paid to the pig breeder: there were several in the parish. Most of the farmers bred pigs. There might be as many as ten piglets in a farrow, and the buyer would wish to purchase one or two of these. There were certain points of the piglet which indicated that when the end came, the transaction had proved to be a successful investment. One was the length of the animal. It was always assumed that the longer the pig, the heavier it would weigh when its life ended.

There was some bargaining before the decision was made but, this concluded, the piglets were put into sacks and carried to their new home. Soon afterwards the blacksmith came to ring them. This meant piercing the nose and inserting a ring, to prevent the animals routing up the bricks on the floor of the sty. When the ring was there the pig experienced great pain if he tried to do this. From then on they were very carefully tended, bedded down with straw, regularly fed and cleaned out. Critical eyes looked over the pigsty door as they grew. Owners of pigs in neighbouring sties compared growth. A phrase was continually used: 'They're doing well'.

Careful attention to the needs of the animals lasted for a month or two, the length of this period depending on whether the owner wished to sell as pork, or whether he intended to cure the sides of the carcase as bacon. Most of the owners kept their pigs the full length of time to qualify them as 'bacon pigs'. Some of the pig keepers, especially if they were short of money, sold them much earlier to the local butcher; then they were sold as pork.

My father kept pigs, so I have first-hand knowledge of what follows. Its food consisted of all the kitchen waste, placed in the pig bucket, the contents mixed with pig meal — and the animal fed twice daily. Green stuff (cabbage leaves) and occasionally a handful of coal slack was thrown into the sty. Small potatoes, which came to be known as pig potatoes, were boiled and these were mixed with the pig swill. There was little or no waste in the household. The weeks and months passed, the pig growing bigger and fatter, and at last the decision was made, 'The pig must be killed'.

It was a rule that unless there was an 'R' in the month, killing would be unwise. There was an old saying that 'The killing of the pig had to take place during the first two quarters of the moon', for if the pig was killed when the moon was waning, the bacon would shrink in cooking, and it was wanted to plump up. The day was named, the time fixed and the pig killer was informed. There were two pig killers in the village, doing this as part-time work, their normal work being farm labouring. One of the men had the reputation of being a better killer than the other. My father employed the one with the better reputation.

My father had the slaughtering done in the early morning, in winter, as soon as it was light. In writing about this I do so with a shudder, but at that time it was commonplace and no-one took any notice of it. It was often seen by children as it took place outside the pig sties. A rope was put round the animal's nose. It was then led to a low bench. On this it was placed, squealing and struggling, and then its throat was cut. The blood was caught in a jug and carried to the woman who would deal with the inside. The ultimate result would be black puddings.

Mercifully the animal was soon dead. Its body was then placed on the ground and covered with straw; the straw was set alight and all the hairs burned off. The ends of the toes of the dead pig were black. These pig toes, as we called them, were pulled off by the killer and thrown to any boys who were watching, and they were chewed, resulting in a black, slimy patch on each side of the boys' mouths. The various internal organs were removed and the carcase taken to be hung up to cool until next day.

In our case, the 'hanging up spot' was in our kitchen, exactly opposite the front door, so that a visitor was greeted by the view of a dead pig. A large beam ran through this kitchen and my father, in readiness for the arrival, used to put up a prop to support the beam. When the animal was securely hung, a job which required the help of two or three men, the pig killer sat down to breakfast. Our kitchen was thus decorated from the morning of the one day to the early morning of the next. During this period, my uncles and others, on seeing the corpse, would estimate its weight, always in scores of pounds. The length again would be taken into consideration, also the size of the hams. They were quite serious about this and after the weighing they were delighted if their judgement had been near. The discussion was concluded by 'I told you so', and then the remark 'He was a good doer', meaning that the pig had put on weight as it grew, to the satisfaction of its owner.

The following morning the cutting up into joints began. The sides were taken down the cellar to be salted and suitable pieces were cut off to be fried for breakfast after the cutting up. How delicious that breakfast was! I was delighted to watch the pig killer eat the meal. How he enjoyed it, and how he could eat! I have an idea that his drink was ale, but am not quite sure about that. During breakfast the weight of the pig was mentioned again and the phrase, 'Yes, he was good doer' was often repeated.

Breakfast over and the crockery cleared away, work began. My mother had the help of a lady in the village, a real country woman, who used to recall that her son had died of the black todd. I never knew what this ailment was. The smell of the meat attracted all the cats of the neighbourhood, but woe betide any that was seen lurking around. The fatty part of one of the internal organs was cut into small pieces to be melted down into lard. The boiling lard was poured into porcelain pans and put to cool in the cellar. The local baker came to make the pastry for the pork pies and they were baked in the baker's oven. A pie known as a bony pie was made in a large pan. The contents were pieces of meat and bones covered with meat, a lid of pastry was put over all, and this was to be the next Sunday morning's breakfast.

Some of the pig meat was given to neighbours, other joints were sold, but not a tiny bit of pig was wasted. When the ham and sides were salted, they were left for a certain period and then hung up to drain. They eventually found their way into the kitchen, to dry and hang there until used. As most of the country people would say, 'What better picture could you have in a kitchen, than two sides of bacon and two lovely hams?'

FRIENDLY SOCIETIES

In 1601, the first comprehensive Poor Law Act was passed. This made the parish the executive body for all Poor Law administration and as the Church was the unit of government of the parish, the vestry appointed officers known as Overseers of the Poor.

In another part of this book, that dealing with Local Government, you will find their duties given in detail. On reading these, one can understand that it was realised that self-help, by the formation of Friendly Societies, and Sick and Dividend Clubs, was the most satisfactory way of protecting folk against the cost of sickness, old age, unemployment and the dreadful pauper's funeral. In 1843, the Leigh and Knightley Lodge of the Edmonscote District of the Independent Order of Oddfellows Manchester Unity was formed. This branch has done wonderful work during its 127 years of existence. Herewith is a summary of the local balance sheet for 1918:

The Emily Ledbrook Lodge — the Women's Branch of the Oddfellows' Friendly Society

Miss W.M.Payne

NUMBER OF MEMBERS: January, 1st 1918	302
Admitted during the year	7
	309
Died, 9; left by non-payment, 2	11
On the books January 1st, 1919	298

SICK AND FUNERAL FUND

Balance on hand, December 31, 1918	£4005 19 3
Amount paid in sick pay in year	£444 0 4
Number of Members receiving sick pay	107

(The sick pay worked out at about 10/- per week for most members. Twelve of the older members were receiving sick pay for the 52 weeks of the year).

Nine members died: Funeral money	£96 0 0
Two wives and two widows:	£20 0 0

Sick and Dividend Clubs were formed in nearly all the public houses. Members paid weekly subscriptions and the rules enabled the Committee to give financial help to any member falling on hard times. At the end of the year, dividends were given to each member if the calls on the fund had not been too heavy.

Pig Clubs were also formed. In another part of this book you will note what a large part the pig played in the economy of the village. These clubs acted as an insurance by the owner of the animals in case of loss through swine fever or other diseases.

A building was erected in Queen Street and opened on January 24th, 1910 named 'The Cubbington Oddfellows and Working Mens' Club'.

The second rule of the Committee of the Club read as follows:

The objects of this Society are to afford to its members the means of social intercourse, mutual helpfulness, mental and moral improvement and rational recreation.

Rule 19: The Club shall be opened each weekday at 6am. and close at 10pm. On Sundays 12.30pm—2pm. and 6pm—10pm.

At one time there were two lodges in the Village: The Oddfellows of the Leigh and Knightley Lodge, and the Loyal United Sisters Friendly Society.

The lodge known as the Loyal Emily Ledbrook was eventually transferred to the order, but continued as a separate branch until recent years when with the advent of mixed lodges it was transferred to the Leigh and Knightley, to make a mixed lodge in the Village. The District is now known as the 'Edmonscote and Stratford-on-Avon District' and has lodges in Wolston, Marton, Long Itchington, Southam, Bishops Itchington, Tysoe, Shipston on Stour, Kineton, Wellesbourne, Stratford-on-Avon, Knowle, Warwick, Leamington and Kenilworth in addition to the lodge at Cubbington. There are 20 lodges in the District with combined assets of over £285,000. Miss. W.M.Payne, a Cubbington lady, held the position of Provincial Grand Master of the District for a year. She was appointed on 7th January, 1970. She is only the third member of the Leigh and Knightley Lodge ever to have held this high office. There were also in the village, branches of the Foresters' Friendly Society, and the Royal Antediluvian Order of Buffaloes.

OCCUPATIONS

Although agriculture was the chief occupation of the village in the early days, it was never the sole source of employment. The villager needed tools and tackle for his trade, as well as food, clothes, furniture and utensils.

In the early days most of these things were made at home or on the farm. However, specialists were needed and it was the blacksmith who laid the foundation of economic progress. The smith must be regarded as the master craftsman.

By the time of the Norman Conquest the range of rural crafts had increased. In the larger villages were to be found the smith, carpenter, wheelwright, tinker, potter, and miller. Travelling craftsmen performed some of the services.

The craftsman had his place under feudalism like the other orders. He had a cottage, a small enclosure and possibly a few strips in the open fields and rights over the commons.

The total holding would never be large or he would not have time to follow his trade.

He was usually exempt from the labour services incumbent on the villein; instead, he paid rent to the Manor in the form of goods or services relevant to his trade.

But, ultimately, as a result of the economic changes brought about by the Black Death, he was able to discharge all such obligations in cash.

By the end of the Middle Ages, the scope of country crafts had increased. Industrial production had undergone a change. It was no longer confined to isolated craftsmen or the farmer's wife.

In certain parts the village trades were mutually dependent. Smiths, cartwrights, wheelwrights and harness-makers established themselves beside the highways.

In the 13th and 14th centuries, the Urban Craft Guilds flourished. They achieved a high standard of work. In the 15th and 16th centuries, commerce expanded greatly and the Guilds were incapable of adapting themselves to the changed circumstances. They continued for a while, side by side with the capitalist concerns.

At the same time, the decline of the guilds did not mean that the craftsman who owned his own business was immediately superseded by the employer of paid labour. So long as the demands of trade could adequately be met by manual methods of production, the cottager, working for the factor, and the master craftsman continued to work side by side. However, when the demand for goods began to exceed the supply and to exceed all the efforts of the hand worker to meet it, the invention of power-driven machines was stimulated. The development of steam power set the seal on the handicraft industry.

The village was becoming more accessible by the creation of new roads and canals and, after 1840, the railways. All these opened up the countryside at a tremendous pace.

In the 19th century, village commerce (as distinct from manufacture) saw a period of improvement. In the Middle Ages there were only three or four sources of retail trade other than barter: the itinerant merchant, the weekly market held in large villages or small towns, the seasonal Fair, and the village craftsman who bought or grew the raw material and who sold as well as made his particular goods. These conditions continued almost unchanged right up to the Industrial Revolution. With the improvement of communications, especially of the Parish Roads under the reformed Highway Administration of the mid-nineteenth century, the countryside was laid open to outside suppliers.

(Victor Bonham-Carter: The English Village).

Soon, retail shops were set up in villages, stocked by wholesalers from the towns. They were general shops and often the country shopkeeper carried on more than one trade, as my father, who was the village carpenter and kept a general store. At this shop many things were sold, all kinds of food, bread, corn for fowl, oil, hardware, and so on. The village bricklayer was also a chimney sweep. A census taken on May 28th and 29th, 1821, shows that out of 157 families in the village, 107 families were engaged in Agriculture, 44 in Trade, and 6 not employed in trade or agriculture. Cubbington had a brickyard at that time.

In 1884, a Cubbington Sports Programme contained advertisements inserted by the Coal Merchant, Bricklayer and Chimney Sweep, Watch Manufacturer and Repairer, General Draper, Provision Dealer and Carpenter, Saddler and Harness Maker, Photographer, Butcher and Innkeeper, Tailor and Outfitter, Carrier, Land Surveyor, Mineral Water Manufacturer. Trades in the village at this time, but not advertised, included Wheelwright, Well-sinker and Pump Maker, Shoemaker, Blacksmith and Basket maker.

In 1952 a student estimated that 48% of the men-folk worked in Coventry, 10% were farm workers, and a number worked at the Leamington Brewery, Leamington nurseries and Leamington brickyards.

What changes have taken place over the intervening years! In 1970, still a good proportion was working in Coventry, but I should say an equal if not larger number worked in Leamington and Warwick. This estimate includes many housewives. At one time hardly any housewives used to be employed at other than their household duties. We now have in the village itself, however, prosperous firms employing quite a number of men and women.

A closer look at the trades and professions exemplified by their respective establishments in the village is both informative and entertaining. We should, perhaps, start with 'entertainment'.

Outside the 'Queen's Head'; Mr Lambert, the Landlord, with customers. *(See p216)*

THE PUBLIC HOUSE

There were four public houses in the village, more than in most small villages.

Each of these houses brewed its own beer. What a delightful smell there was, especially when the pig-keepers wheeled their barrow loads of 'grains' down the street — hot and steaming corn grains from the vats.

Each public house also had its own skittle alley of nine pins. The sound of the balls hitting the skittles and rebounding from the back boards could be heard in the street. A large room known as the Club Room was available for hire in each pub, where meetings and dances could be held: the music was supplied by two men, one with a fiddle, the other with a banjo.

The pubs were opened very early in the morning. It has been known for men to set out for work, visiting the pub on the way, and to have remained there almost all day. In the evenings, the regulars occupied their own seats. Beer at that time was 2d a pint but wages were low, the attraction during the week was not the amount of beer drunk but a warm fire in the evenings and jolly company. In the summer, long hours of work with the hay and corn harvests meant that visits were mainly on Saturday evenings.

I lived almost next door to a pub, so I heard the activities on these Saturday evenings. Each regular seemed to have his own song, and this he was prepared to sing when invited by his colleagues, so that we knew who was present by the song being sung:

Mr. X — *The Farmyard.*
Mr. Y — *Genevieve*
Mr. Z — *Pretty Polly Perkins*

The soloists sung their respective verses and the whole company joined in the chorus.

A very jolly evening appears to have taken place, occasionally being marred by arguments started inside, culminating in fights outside. These were never of long duration; perhaps the appearance of a wife or the news that the policeman was on his way would end the fray.

The public houses at this time were visited only by men, the ladies came only to fetch beer or stout to drink at home.

On Boxing Day the landlords supplied cold hams or beef, with pickles, to their regulars, to be consumed on the premises.

During the summer months the public houses were calling-places for horse-drawn charabancs returning from tours originating in Coventry. Pairs of horses pulled the loads and I, as a small boy, felt sympathy for the animals which arrived hot and steaming, Cubbington sometimes being the last call of a lengthy tour.

'Glen Roy', 16, High Street, formerly the 'Nag's Head' Public House

The Smithy

The smithy was a hive of activity for about twelve hours a day. The shoeing of horses and the repair of agricultural implements occupied most of the time, and the ringing of the anvil, which could be heard almost continually in most parts of the village, told of busy hours.

On frosty mornings in winter, the horses of the milkmen, baker and other workers, arrived early to be roughed. This meant removing a nail from each shoe and substituting a spike, to prevent the horse slipping. In the evening the ploughboy or the waggoner would bring the coulter to be sharpened and called for the next morning. The coulter is the iron cutter at the front of a ploughshare.

It was normal to work until 7pm. The smithy wall was decorated with horse shoes, made ready, so that with a little adjustment one could quickly be made to fit a horse's hoof. Adjacent to the smithy was a frame, into which were led such horses as, through fear or temper, were difficult to shoe. This fixture consisted of four hefty posts, each about 18s ins. square, with stout iron bars along the sides and front. The horse was generally blindfolded by sacking placed over its head before it was led in. A strong iron bar was then slipped through holes attached to the post behind the horse. A rope was securely fixed to the horse's leg and the rope gently pulled over a wooden roller, thus raising the hoof. The leg was steady until the shoeing was finished. Fractious horses were brought from neighbouring villages to be shod in this way.

The break for difficult horses, behind the smithy

My father, besides being the village carpenter, kept a small grocery business, so I grew up with the problems involved — the long hours, for instance.

The shop opened early in the morning and was open until late at night, 8pm. or 10pm. on Saturdays. After closing time on Saturday, the shutters had to be put up. The windows of all shops were either shuttered or curtained on Sundays — no half day closing.

Most of the groceries arrived in bulk: sugar, in 1cwt. bags, had to be weighed into 1lb. and 2lb. bags. Great care was needed over the weighing if a loss was to be averted. Biscuits came in large tins and the contents had to be re-weighed. Tobacco went through the same process. Cigarettes we did not sell. Vinegar was delivered in barrels and was re-sold in pints or half-pints.

In my early days, late 1890's and early 1900, there was, in the winter, a fair amount of poverty. In severe weather, men were out of work without any pay. Many of these men had large families, and, in our case, knowing the hardship these people were enduring, it was impossible not to be sympathetic, and let them have the essentials, on the promise to pay when their men returned to work. These promises were made in good faith, but the wages were so low that it was impossible to catch up with debts, and efforts were made to pay a little each week, but they never managed to pay off the whole. I know that my father has said to some of these customers, after a period of struggling, 'Now we'll wipe out the debt, and hope that you can now keep straight.' Profits were small and debts could be heavy.

Pennyworths of tea and similar small items could not afford much profit. Some interesting requests were made. There was the chimney sweep from Leamington. He was a tiny man who could have crawled up a chimney, in Dickens' time, quite easily.

I was in the shop. He told my mother that he was suffering from a gumboil, and could she give him a small piece of cheese to cure it? I felt sorry for the sweep. I think that my mother knew why he wanted the cheese, since she gave him a much larger piece than the gumboil needed, and also she knew that he went to the public house next door, not to cure his gumboil, but to accompany a pot of ale with a snack of bread and cheese.

On another occasion, a member of a wealthy family who had an estate in the village called at our shop and asked for some tobacco. Amongst the money offered for this was a French penny. My mother said, that she was sorry, but she could not accept this. He replied, 'If you don't accept that penny, you won't get any more,' thinking that his wealth would overrule opposition. My mother's reply was, 'In that case, neither will you have the tobacco,' so he departed, tobacco-less, from the shop.

Another regular customer was an elderly lady who made an ointment which to us was known as a salve. I don't know the complete recipe, but she used to buy beeswax and a very thin oil, somewhat similar to linseed oil but much thinner. We knew it as sweet oil. The salve was in great demand to heal sores.

We sold only two kinds of tobacco. Two grades of Twist, thick and thin, and another, shag tobacco, which we knew as smoking tobacco, since some of the Twist tobacco was chewed. In each of these cases, ounces and half ounces were weighed from bulk.

Snuff was another commodity we sold, sometimes bought by elderly ladies.

An elderly lady came in fairly often who, when times were bad with unemployment, always had a suggested remedy — a public demonstration. She envisaged a procession, at the head of which would be carried a loaf of bread, dipped in blood, on the end of a pole. She sometimes wore a red shawl.

I sometimes think she should have been born in another country a century earlier!

We had a shoemaker in the village. Boots and shoes were made to individual measurements. At one time, this gentleman made boots for the Leamington Police Force. We also had a shoe repairer.

The tailor was a one-man business. His workroom was adjacent to the footpath alongside the village street. He could be seen, sitting cross-legged on his table, busily stitching away. He was often interrupted by passers-by stopping to gossip with him through the window. He was kept fairly busy making suits.

In the early 1900's there were three busy bakeries in the village. These supplied bread to a number of neighbouring villages. Confectionery was limited to buns, jam puffs, and so on.

The baker provided facilities for cooking cottagers' Sunday joints at a cost of a penny or two apiece. The joint was placed on a stand in a bakery tin, and the Yorkshire pudding in a jug. These were taken to the bakehouse on Sunday morning between 10am and 11am. The Yorkshire pudding was added after the meat had been partly cooked.

It must have been difficult sometimes for the baker to know into which baking tin the particular Yorkshire pudding should be emptied. Baking tins could be exactly alike and occasionally joints almost identical.

On a few occasions, after we had started to eat our Sunday meal, there would be silence. We would look at each other; the silence would be broken by noises with the lips, as if tasting something. A member of the family would then address my mother with the question, "Is this our pudding, Mum?" My mother had been a cook and we were accustomed to a high standard of cooking. As we could decide only by the taste that the pudding could not be our own, we came to the conclusion that the wrong Yorkshire pudding had been put into our tin, and it was eaten rather reluctantly.

One of the bakers whose business was opposite where I lived was successful in gaining the contract to supply bread to the militia at their annual camp in Stoneleigh Park for the duration of three or four weeks. My father was asked if he would allow me to accompany the baker on these trips in order to control the horse while the bread was being distributed. I was highly delighted when I was allowed to go. I was about eleven at the time. We left the village about 7am with a horse-drawn vehicle full of bread. At the entrance to the camp was a steep bank and the baker and I readily gave a helping hand to the horse.

The bugle sounded, announcing time for the distribution, the orderlies arrived, each with a net for the reception of the bread. They assembled in pre-determined ranks under the supervision of a Non-commissioned and a Commissioned Officer. The Commissioned Officer asked the baker to remove a few loaves from the top. Then he would select two or three from below and weigh them in order to check that the loaves were of the standard weight. The Non-commissioned Officer would then take charge. The name of the Company or platoon was called and the private responsible for drawing the ration would step smartly forward. The number of loaves allotted was counted into the net, sometimes including half a loaf according to the number of men in the platoon. A knife was available to provide the half-loaf.

It was at one of these parades that I was introduced to the eloquence and the unique vocabulary used by an irritated N.C.O. An orderly, after his platoon number had been called, stepped forward with a blanket instead of the authorised net. The N.C.O. gasped and, after a few seconds' silence, there followed such a flow of words that the poor orderly who had stepped forward so smartly became utterly crestfallen. The N.C.O. wished to convey that it was unhygienic to collect food in a blanket in which someone had recently slept.

The word 'unhygienic' was not actually used, but after such a torrent of words, there was no doubt that the private knew what was meant. He was sent away without any bread and told to return when the net had been found. It was some years after, in the First World War, when I joined the Royal Warwickshire Regiment that I became further acquainted with the eloquence of N.C.O.'s. I then listened intently with stifled amusement.

In the village was a family of harness makers and repairers. The father and sons were occupied in the trade. They not only made and repaired the harness of the farmers' horses, but also of the Leamington Brewery horses.

On the outside of the premises in High Street, specimens of the work were hung to await a call from the owners or delivery to the clients. This display also served as an advertisement.

In the Sports Programme of 1884 was an advertisement by Mr. E. Duggins, watchmaker and repairer. The illustration of a lady's watch shows a sample of this man's work. Note the engraving on the inside:

'CUBBINGTON 1887
Jane Whitehall'

This watch is supposed to have been given to this particular lady for her 21st birthday. His business was carried on in Queen St. where Mr. Lake's shop is situated.

The well-sinker not only sank the wells but made the pipes. The Cubbington well-sinker was also a wheelwright. He came to Cubbington from Gaydon more than a hundred years ago. The pipes carrying the water from the bottom of the well were made of wood.

These pipes consisted of good straight oak logs about 18 inches wide and from 9 to 16ft. long. These were first sawn into 1 foot square sections. A hole was bored down the length of each pipe. One end was tapered by using an adze and draw knife so that it could be 'married' to another pipe, the end of which had been opened to receive it.

After deciding where the well should be, a circle was marked on the ground and digging commenced. Then a tripod with a pulley and wire rope was set up over the hole. As the well deepened the man descended to the work with one foot in a bucket. The bucket was a small barrel. Water was generally found at an average depth of 15 to 18 feet. Work was shored up with timber before the men started 'quoining' or lining the well with bricks laid dry. The deepest well sunk was 122 feet.

Gas was the worst enemy of the well-sinker, and a grandson of the original Cubbington well-sinker was overcome by gas when digging a well at Ettington and died.

The sawmills have been in the village for about a hundred years but have developed tremendously during the last few, since they have been acquired by Messrs. Bates. My father, as village carpenter and undertaker over 80 years ago, paid frequent visits to the sawmill for elm boards for the coffins. It was English timber that was cut up at that time. I used to accompany him when I was old enough.

The source of power for all the saws was one steam engine. To me, it appeared very large and a little frightening, with steam hissing and the arm of the horizontal saw moving backwards and forwards, cutting the tree trunk into planks.

The transport of the selected timbers was by means of a heavy truck. This is where I came in, to give my father a helping hand, and also to return the truck to the timber yard.

At that time, there was a sawmill where the present mill is on the Rugby Road and a timber yard on the opposite corner where Wise Terrace is now.

Cottage with Draw Well

Messrs Thwaites c.1970

Aerial Photograph of Messrs Thwaites' engineering works, c.1970

Messrs Thwaites' in very early days

Aerial View of Messrs Thwaites, twenty years later

Frank Russell operating a Thwaites dumper truck during the building of the new Office Block in the 1960s

Messrs THWAITES

This go-ahead factory is a great asset to the parish, employing approximately 175.

The chief products are dumpers and small excavators. The latter are capable of digging down to 8ft. quickly and efficiently, doing the work of 8 men.

The dumpers range from 15cwt. to 3 tons carrying-capacity with various attachments to enable the skips to discharge high above the ground, they are hydraulically controlled, and are made in 12 — 14 models.

The number of dumpers dispatched each week is up to 150. Countries to which machines are exported number 65. These include chiefly all the European countries, most African, and some South American, including Chile, and India, Hong Kong and Australia.

The factory is of asbestos and brick construction, almost exclusively portal arch, so there are no stanchions inside the factory, which contains approximately 200,000 square feet of working area for the prefabrication of the component parts. These are manufactured from raw steel drawn from mills chiefly in the Newcastle-upon-Tyne and Cardiff areas, of which substantially over 2,000 tons are used annually in the manufacture of dumpers.

In March 1971 the company received the award of the British National Export Council in recognition of their outstanding export performances. Thwaites' award-winning performance was an 83 per cent rise in export sales from £439,212 in the year ending March 1969 to £718,105 in the following 12 months.

As part of the prize, the foreman of the company's experimental workshop, Mr. Norman Tearne, and his wife, visited the United States and Barbados in April. The company began a major export drive in October 1967, just before the £ was devalued.

At that time, Thwaites had a major share of the U.K. market for dumpers — 29 per cent — and also produced 17 per cent of the dumpers exported from Britain. The company seized the opportunity presented by devaluation and raised its export target. The manufacturing area under cover was more than doubled. The company's share of the export market was raised from 17 per cent to 23.5 per cent.

Weight, space and material cost considerations have stimulated the advance of miniaturisation in many industries.

Messrs STEREOMATIC

A specialist Company which has approached high volume precision manufacture is Stereomatic Limited of New Cubbington. The Company was formed in 1963, appreciating the increased needs of the electronic and allied industries.

Stereomatic readily offers its capacity for large batches of work and also offers the uncommon service of producing small batches on high-precision Automatic Machines for prototype and pre-production development quantities.

The need for cams normally dictates large runs if high precision Automatics are to be used economically but in certain circumstances, as part of their service, Stereomatic have handled quantities as low as only 400. At the other end of the scale they have supplied a single customer with 22 million components over the last 4 years. The emphasis at Stereomatic is on precision. Their machines will hold tolerances of ±0.00025". An instrument component was recently machined at a nominal diameter of 0.016".

Many of the components require second operations, for even the most up-to-date production machines have limitations. Stereomatic score because, besides doing simple machining operations, their production team has often ingeniously modified existing machines to suit more complex components.

Such is the understanding between Stereomatic and their customers that they are frequently able to suggest small design modifications to components that permit worthwhile economies in manufacture.

A special section is also employed on the assembly of Instrument Jewel Bearings in spring and solid type screws or any type of mounting as required by the customer. In addition special components for the metering of fluids and gases are manufactured to very critical tolerances and finishes.

Bechler AS10 in use at Messrs Stereomatic's Works

Components made by Stereomatic Ltd, set in a clear acrylic block

SPARE TIME

VILLAGE RECREATIONS

The Village has always been keen on football, and since the beginning of the century, managed to field strong and successful teams.

Usually, the public house recreations of the time consisted of skittling, darts, cards and so on.

Occasionally, rabbit-coursing took place. The usual procedure was to force rabbits out of their burrows with ferrets and net them. These live rabbits, as I saw them, were housed until the appointed day in an empty pig sty belonging to a public house. They were huddled together, and wire netting was stretched over the top to prevent dogs invading the sty.

On the day of the meeting, these scared rabbits were placed in a sack and taken to a field. The owners of the dogs were there with their animals, usually whippets. I have no doubt that bets were wagered on the result. The dogs, being held by their owners, lined up on the starting mark. A rabbit was taken from the sack, and, being held by its neck, was shewn to each dog by being held a few inches from the dog's mouth. The rabbit was taken to a fixed distance from the dogs and then put on the ground.

I have seen a rabbit so bewildered that it has sat still in fright and has been caught by one of the dogs almost before it has moved.

Another time, the rabbit has been made to move by shouting and making noises. Its movement would be short lived. Before many yards had been covered, the poor creature was caught and killed.

Another sport was Bat fowling which had nothing to do with bats. Imagine a group of men armed with two poles about ten feet long. Attached to these was a net. During the winter months, the men visited ivy-covered buildings or hedgerows, where birds were roosting.

The net would be placed against the building or tree and the ivy or hedgerow poked by another pole, thus disturbing the birds roosting there. As they flew out, they would be caught in the net.

Sparrows were caught this way and killed. I am not sure what was done with the other birds they caught, but the dead sparrows were cooked and eaten.

FOOTBALL

Football in Cubbington has aroused tremendous interest as far as memory goes back, with very successful performances, as the illustration shows. In the season 1931-32, four trophies were won.

In the early 1900's my brother was Secretary, so I had a particular interest. Before each match the task allotted to me was to take the six posts from our house and put them in the appropriate positions in the field, one at each corner and the other two in the centre of the touch line.

The field was frequently grazed by cows, the animals being taken away only a few hours before the match commenced. As a result of this, the players found themselves in some embarrassing situations, much to the amusement of the spectators. After a player had fallen, he often rose in such a state that even his best friend would have preferred to welcome him at a distance. Sliding tackles were obviously out of the question.

The playing pitch had a ditch running only a few yards from the touch line. In dry weather the ditch was sluggish and very smelly. After heavy rainfall it was a fast flowing stream.

When the game was in progress the ball often found its way into this ditch and was recovered with a wire basket on a long pole, as the banks of the ditch were steep. In dry weather the ball emerged in an unpleasant condition. From the 'throw in', sensitive players avoided any heading contact. When the stream was flowing quickly, it was amusing to see the man in charge of the wire basket chasing along the bank to intercept the ball before it went beyond his reach into the next field. Did playing under such conditions contribute to the success of the Cubbington team?

In those days, the Cubbington Albion Club was a member of a Coventry League. The only way of getting to meetings in Coventry, a distance of seven miles away, was by train from Leamington, with an infrequent service, or by cycling. After attending such meetings my brother used to arrive home very late.

Back Row:
Left to right
Herbie Skelsey
Arthur Heath
Chris Cleaver
Les Draper
Harry Kenzett
Jim Timms

Middle Row:
Percy Stone
Harry Goddard
Fred Thompson
Alan Rose
Norman Bass
Bill Hughes
Fred Cleaver
Ernie Hughes

Front Row
Vic Eales
George Chamberlain
Jocky Smith
Frank Hughes
Ernie Thompson
Bill Bruce
Wal Cleaver

Kneelin:
Wal Kenzett
Harry Eales

Cubbington Albion Football Team, 1931-2, with its four trophies

One of the most amusing incidents I witnessed, concerned a spectator and the referee. The match, a vital league match or a cup tie, I do not remember which, was between a visiting team from Coventry and our team. I have an idea that the Coventry League officials anticipated there might be trouble and as a result, the President of the League, who was also a referee, decided to take control of the game. This gentleman was a short man. The match had been in progress some time, when a decision by the referee was challenged by the Cubbington spectators in no uncertain terms, one gentleman in particular being very vocal and slightly abusive. Now this man was very tall. The referee stopped the game, went over to the offender and ordered him to leave the field. After some hesitation and with the advice of the Cubbington officials, who feared the game would be cancelled, he consented. The amusing part was to see this tall man, with the referee who was so short that he did not reach to the man's shoulder, walking side by side to the gate. Heated conversation was taking place between them as they went. The offender ejected, the referee returned and the game re-started.

The changing room for the players was at a nearby public house and there they bathed in tub baths.

THE ANGLING ASSOCIATION

This is a very lively organisation. The meetings for Competitions are very well distributed and take on an air of social occasions as well as serious competition exercises.

In the past they have met at:

Goring-on-Thames.
Dinner at 'Ye Olde Leather Bottle'
River Nene. Dinner at 'The Talbot', Oundle.
River Ouse. Dinner at 'The Bridge', Fladbury.
River Avon. Dinner at 'The Chequers Inn'.
River Severn.
Dinner at 'The White Swan', Upton on Severn.

The list seems to indicate that, however fickle the fish might be at biting, the participants in the Competition were consistently good at it.

The story is told that the members of the Association, on visiting one of the hotels for lunch, found a dining room thickly carpeted. Some of the competitors had anticipated this and had brought clean shoes into which to change, but others had not.

Under these circumstances the only thing to be done was to take off their muddy Wellingtons, leave them lined up in the Hall, and enter the dining room in their stockinged feet!

THE BAND

Some 70 or 80 years ago, the village boasted a Drum and Fife Band.

The Instructor, as he was called, was a member of the Staff of Weston Reformatory School, a residential school where youthful delinquents were sent to be reformed.

So keen were the villagers on their band that youngsters still at school formed their own. Their instruments consisted of tin whistles; their uniforms, lengths of woven tubes of wool, known as cork wool. The latter were woven round tacks driven into a cotton reel. They owned a drum, but unfortunately it had a hole in one side.

On one of their marching tours along the Offchurch Road, a gentleman on horseback became interested. The band, sensing a contribution, halted, formed a circle, and the drummer, unwilling to let the band down, arranged himself so that the battered side of the drum was kept from view of the interested party. A member of that youthful band later became bandmaster of the Village Brass Band.

The Brass Band had its origin in a unique way. During the Boer War in South Africa, several towns including Mafeking and Ladysmith were besieged by the Boers. Great suffering was experienced by the British inside these towns. Late one Saturday, it was announced that Mafeking had been relieved. The news reached Leamington, where a number of our young men were visiting.

On hearing this news, their main concern was to let the village know as soon as possible. They hurried home and on the way decided that, as it was late and most of the villagers would have gone to bed, a trumpet-call was the best method of awakening them.

The father of one of the members of the party had once been in a brass band and at his home was stored a number of brass instruments.

What better way of announcing the news, than to get these instruments (though none of the young men could play) and awaken the inhabitants with sounds, joyful or otherwise? This they did, in the centre of the village. Windows were opened, heads appeared, and the occupants of the houses were ready to tell these noisy intruders what they thought of them, until the news was announced, when the threats turned to cheers. From this incident, a brass band was formed which supplied music in the village and neighbourhood for fêtes and special occasions for many years.

The Original Cubbington Brass Band

Drum and Fife Band

Event 4.—1 MILE HANDICAP, (OPEN,) 4.20 p.m.
1 Prize, £1, Second Prize, 10/-.

1.	J. Hewitt	Scratch.
2.	R. Tandy	10 yards.
3.	J. Smith	30 „
4.	G. Dean	35 „
5.	G. Johnson	40 „
6.	G. Vincent	45 „
7.	C. Dean	55 „
8.	T. Mason	50 „
9.	E. Bastock	80 „

Event 5.—100 YARDS SACK RACE, (OPEN,) 4.35. p.m.
First Prize, [redacted] Second Prize, 2/6.

1. R. Tandy
~~2. G. Heath~~
2. W. Levey
4. G. Gilbert
5. E. Bastock

[redacted]

In this Race the distance will be 50 yards if all competitors wish it.

Event 6.—100 YARDS THREE-LEGGED RACE, (OPEN,) 4.50.
First Prize, 5/-; Second Prize, 2/6.

1. E. H. Godfrey, and T. Hewitt ...
2. G. Vincent, and G. Skelsey ... .
3. G. Gilbert, and M. Levey ... ...
4. G. Johnson, and H. Skelsey ... ...

HURDLE RACE, (FINAL) 5.0. p.m.

All competitors must be clothed to the satisfaction of the Committee.

Any competitor not on the ground at the time for starting will be disqualified.

Handicapper.—Rev H. Allfree. Judge.—Dr. Shapley, Esq.

CUBBINGTON
FLOWER SHOW.
ATHLETIC SPORTS.

Event 1—HURDLE RACE, OVER 8 FLIGHTS. (3.45 p.m.)
First Prize, 10/-; Second Prize, 5/-.
1st—HEAT.

1. G. Vincent
2. A. E. Braidley

2nd.—HE[redacted]

3 E. H. Godfrey
4. J. Smith

Event 2.—220 YARDS HANDICAP, (LOCAL,) 3.50. p.m.
First Prize, 10/-; Second Prize 5/-; No Second Prize if less than Six run.

1.	G. Vincent.	Scratch.
2.	G. Skelsey.	9 yards.
3.	[illegible]	10 „
4.	G. [illegible]	12 „
5.	G. Gilbert	13 „
6.	S. Vincent	20 „

Event 3.—100 YARDS FLAT RACE. (Open only to Youths of the Parish.) First Prize, 5/-; Second Prize, 3/-; Third Prize, 2/-.

1.	G. Heath	Scratch	Age 14.
2.	J. Levey	6 yards.	„ 12.
3.	W. Draper	6 „	„ 12.

Miss Cubbington 1955
(Margaret Middleton)
(Photograph by courtesy of the Leamington Spa Courier)

ALLOTMENT ASSOCIATION

From my uncle's diary, July 29th, 1885:

In the Vicarage Grounds. The 3rd Show of the Cubbington Horticultural Society was held. The attendance not good. Balance in hand after Show, £3. Last year, 1884 £7.

We assume that the first show was in 1883. In 1884, Sports were held in conjunction with the Horticultural Show. It is as well to notice the value of the prizes given for the sports.

First prize for the mile — £1. This is more than an agricultural labourer would earn at that time in one week and so the corresponding prizes in the other events were most generous.

We do not know for how many years the show was run by the Horticultural Society but about the turn of the century shows were held known as 'Marrow Shows'. I was quite young about this time, and my lasting impression is the size of the marrows which were entered in the Class for the Largest Marrow. They seemed colossal to me. One such marrow would easily fill a barrow.

There were classes for other vegetables and flowers, but my memory is of the marrow. At some time about this period, the band arranged those shows. During the Second World War they ceased, but soon afterwards an Allotment Association was formed in 1942. Some two years later, Annual Shows were held. The number of classes increased each year until in 1958 there were 75.

These included not only flowers and vegetables but embroidery, knitting, basketry, cooking, preserves, fruit-bottling, wine-making, children's classes, including painting, collections of wild flowers, and so on. There were twelve trophies awarded. At the present time, not only an annual show is held, but a Sweet Pea Show and a Chrysanthemum and Dahlia Show also.

WOMEN'S INSTITUTE

The Cubbington branch of the Women's Institute was started in 1945. This was a very lively branch. Apart from the Institute's usual activities — demonstrations in cookery, First Aid, Needlework, and so on — the local branch was successful in presenting an annual pantomime. Apart from the excellent performances which were given, a notable feature was the beautiful scenery painted by the husband of one of the members.

They also had a Choir, entered regularly in the Leamington Music Festival.

Their activities were not confined to those of self-interest. The members were always willing to help charitable causes such as the Cancer Campaign or, say, the Lifeboat Association, by the organisation of street collections.

Although activities at the present time are not so varied, very useful work indeed is done by the branch.

MEALS ON WHEELS

When the extensions to the Village Hall were completed, the facilities in the kitchen were ideal for Cubbington to be chosen as the centre for the excellent work the Women's Voluntary Service was doing in respect of their Meals on Wheels for the elderly and incapacitated.

Meals are delivered twice each week. These are cooked in the Village Hall kitchen, and about 60-64 are delivered each week. The area covered includes Leek Wootton, Hunningham, Bubbenhall, Eathorpe, Radford Semele, Whitnash, Baginton, Old Milverton and Cubbington.

The meals are kept warm in heated Hot Locks, 12 meals in each container. There are three drivers and each one has a mate. Each driver and mate cover 15 miles a day, offering a splendid service.

CUBBINGTON OLD AGE PENSIONERS' COMMITTEE

which incorporates Weston under Wetherley and Offchurch, is concerned, as its name implies, with the aged of these villages, and there is no doubt that it does excellent work.

It has been stated that organised sympathy for the old people originated at the Working Men's Club, when the Chairman of that Committee, about 17 years ago, suggested that lonely old people should be invited into the homes of the members of the Club for Christmas Day. It has developed considerably since then.

Outings in the summer and a wonderful dinner at Christmas are the highlights. Those who through any cause are unable to go are given vouchers to cash at the Cubbington Stores. Invalid chairs are provided for use at the outings, and may be borrowed for use at other times. The outing to Longleat which took place recently is typical of the other events.

Women's Institute Pantomime

Women's Institute Choir

Silver Jubilee Celebrations

Nearly a hundred members of the Women's Institute (including several who joined twenty-five years before) and their husbands were at the Silver Jubilee party held in the Village Hall. Seen in the photograph are, from left to right, Mrs W J Robinson (Convenor), Mrs Betty A Underwood (President) Miss Margaret Elkins (Secretary), Mrs W Parfitt and her husband (the Methodist Minister), and the author (Guest of Honour), former Treasurer of the Village Hall. The birthday cake was 'two-in-one'; the real one is on top of the imitation one, decorated with full-size candles, and was the one featured in the Branch's entry in the Village Fête.

Women's Institute Choir

Darby & Joan Choir

Darby & Joan Presentation to Mr & Mrs Peppitt

Darby and Joan Handbell Ringers

About 220 old people left the village at 9.30am. in five coaches. Invalid chairs were packed in the boots of the coaches and a Red Cross attendant rode in each coach. A very pleasant journey ended at Longleat about 1.15pm. In a spacious restaurant, places were laid for 224, where a hot three-course meal was served.

After lunch, the coaches were loaded and driven slowly through the park-like enclosure where the lions were roaming freely amongst the trees and undergrowth, majestic, their coats beautiful and sleek. Zebras and giraffes were free to roam in another large enclosure of the park.

Later, at the restaurant, tea was awaiting them. A pleasant journey home ended a memorable day. Some severe cases of infirmity were taken and the Committee was congratulated on the organisation needed to care for these old people.

The outing will be remembered for a long time, and a re-union anticipated at the Christmas-tide dinner.

All the public houses and clubs help to raise funds for this object.

WORKING MEN'S CLUB

For a number of years, this occupied the Oddfellows' Friendly Society Hall, opened in 1913. A few years ago, they bought the premises and since then have made very useful extensions and are at present building a flat for the Steward. This has proved to be a very successful club.

THE DARBY AND JOAN CLUB

This club for the 'Over 60's' was formed on November 5th, 1954. Meetings are held weekly. In 1955 a Darby and Joan Choir was formed and in that year, and in 1958, 1959, 1960, Certificates of Merit were obtained in the County Competitions.

In 1960, the Club gained a Certificate of Merit for Handicraft.

A Handbell team was also formed from the members. The photograph shows our ringers outside the Pump Rooms at Leamington. Concerts by the members were given in the Village Hall. Drama was introduced and one-act plays formed part of the programme.

THE CUBBINGTON PLAYERS

This enthusiastic amateur dramatic society sets out to present a three-act play in the Village Hall two or three times a year. A high standard of performance is reached and their enthusiasm is shown by their willingness to deprive their homes of needed articles, settees, rugs, and various nick-nackery to provide properties for the plays.

CUBBINGTON VILLAGE HALL TRUST

On the 15th February, 1944, a meeting of a committee comprising representatives of the Combined Services of Cubbington was held. The meeting was called by the Wardens' Association and Mr. J.H.Reeve was in the chair. Present were Mrs. Stickland, Mrs. Church and Miss Payne of First Aid, Messrs. G.F.Peppitt, A.King, and W.Andrews of the National Fire Service, Lt. Beaumont, Colour Sgt. Dawson, and L/Cpl. Grant of the Home Guard, and the Revd. P.T.Broadway, Mr. H.King, Mr. F.Plank and Mr. G.H.Beer (Hon. Sec.) of the Wardens' Association.

After discussion, the following resolution was put to the meeting: 'That after the Parish Council has been informed, it shall be made public that all the profits which may accrue from efforts organised by the Joint Services, shall be invested, primarily for the provision of a Playing Field for Cubbington'.

Proposed by G.F.Peppitt and seconded by W. Andrews. The motion was carried.

During the next seven years, many money-making functions were arranged. In 1950, we prepared plans for the building of a Social Centre, which were submitted to the Local Education Authority and the Ministry of Education. These plans were finally approved.

It was at this point that one of the recurring economic crises arose and we received news by telegram that grants were cancelled for a period. However, we were fortunate in being offered a building for which we paid rent. This Hall was opened on March 3rd, 1951. In 1952, we paid to the Parish Council the sum of £400 for the purchase of a playing field. Up to this time, the fund was known as The Playing Field and Social Centre Fund.

When the playing field was purchased, that part of the original resolution relating to the playing field had been completed, so the name of the Committee was changed to 'The Cubbington Village Hall Trust'. The actions of the Committee are governed by Trust Deeds.

Old Time Dance Members at the Village Hall

Village Hall Interior

Any person over the age of 18 years may attend the Annual General Meeting and may vote. Each organisation in the village is entitled to elect one of its members to serve on the Management Committee of the Trust.

In 1963, we were allowed to purchase the Hall for the sum of £500. Extensions were added in 1964. These consisted of new toilets and cloakrooms, an excellent kitchen and a committee room, and cost £5,000.

The Cubbington Players' Tableau in the Carnival Procession

HIGH DAYS AND HOLIDAYS

CUBBINGTON HIGH DAYS AND HOLIDAYS

Two of these great days in the Village were connected with the local branch of the Oddfellows' Friendly Society.

Whit Monday or Tuesday was the day on which the male members of the Oddfellows had their procession, dinner, and so on. This was known as 'The Club'. The day was greatly looked forward to both by old and young, the excitement of the children commencing weeks before, in recording how much money they had saved for 'The Day'.

The ceremonies began with a procession of members of the Society to the Church where a Service was held. At the head of the procession was a banner, followed by a brass band. The members wore their scarves and aprons of office. It was at such a service, when the collection was being taken that I watched the Verger helping with the collection. He approached a member of the congregation standing a pew in front of me, but there was a hoarse whisper, 'I haven't any change'. As the Verger did not want to be deprived of a small contribution, since the proceeds were for charity, he asked, 'How much do you want to give?' The man told him. A coin — a florin or a half-crown — was put on the plate. The change was duly counted and the Verger continued on his way. One up to the Verger!

While the Service was in progress, the local innkeeper was preparing a sumptuous dinner, to be cooked by the local baker and served in a tent on a nearby field. The Member of Parliament for the Division was generally invited to the dinner. After the Benediction in the Church, the members retraced their steps to the dining tent.

It was the delight of small boys to gather round the tent during the meal. The shape of the large and portly backs of the men sitting round the edge of the tent could plainly be seen. This sight was too much of a temptation to the younger generation outside, and angry shouts and gruff growls were heard as a broad back was slapped, or an unsuspecting youngster was pushed by a companion into a shapely form. The inexperienced boy would venture to poke his head under the bottom flap to see as well as hear what was going on, but this boldness was born of inexperience. A nimble waiter (the same gentleman who was the Church Verger) armed with a springy stick, would quickly but quietly emerge from the tent. Thus armed he would soon impress upon the youngster that quite a large portion of his body was outside the tent. A shriek of pain told of experience dearly bought.

After dinner a second procession visited the large houses of the parish. This procession was also headed by a band and, in addition, a man sitting on a horse wearing a dark cloak and three cornered hat, carrying a large black axe — part of the Oddfellows' regalia. Whenever I saw this man so robed, my mind went back to the executioner of by-gone days.

The horse was owned by the local coal merchant. Whether the animal felt the dignity of his position in leading such a procession, or whether the unfamiliarity of the strains of a brass band upset its nerves I cannot say, but the horse which was docile in performing its every day work of drawing loads of coal, always became restive. Willing hands were there, ready to hold its head, so with gentle coaxing it became sufficiently steady for the man to mount.

The difficulty in mounting, however, must not all be attributed to the horse, for have I not said that the men had just enjoyed a fine repast?

The horseman safely mounted, axe in hand, cloak becomingly arranged, the band struck up and the march to the first house on the itinerary began.

In the same field in which the tent had been erected were side shows, coconut shies, swings and roundabouts, sweet stalls and so on. It was at the sweet stall that a boy realised that an empty hand would go into a sweet bottle, but that a hand full of sweets could not be withdrawn. The stall-holder caught him in this predicament and soundly rapped his knuckles with the toffee hammer.

The evening was jolly with dancing. Such was the Club, when old Cubbingtonians returned from neighbouring villages to enjoy the fun. Married daughters and sons came once more to their native place, and an annual renewal of acquaintance took place.

The celebration in connection with the Women's Branch of the Oddfellows took place on August Bank Holiday, perhaps a little more sedate than the men's affair. Their 'Day' began with Church Parade, followed by High Tea, but no horse led the procession!

QUEEN VICTORIA'S JUBILEE FESTIVITIES

at Cubbington were celebrated right joyously in 1887, on Tuesday, June 21st. Fortunately, we have a contemporary account:

Almost before daybreak, the inhabitants were astir and busily decorating the village which throughout looked quite picturesque. Few houses were left without some sign of loyalty and goodwill.

At 12 o'clock a procession was formed and marched to the Parish Church, which was crowded to excess. The authorised form of prayer was used, and 'Awake, O happy nation' was sung as an anthem. The Vicar delivered a short stirring address on the words 'Rejoice ye with Jerusalem and be glad with her, all ye that love her'. After service the procession again paraded the village.

At 1 o'clock the men, numbering nearly 300, sat down to an excellent dinner. After dinner the Vicar, who presided, proposed 'The Queen!' He alluded to the many reforms of her reign and said that our progress had been real because all classes had shared in it. The toast was most cordially received. The remaining toasts were 'The rest of the Royal Family', 'The Army and Navy' proposed by Mr. Robins and responded to by Colonel Walker and the 'Health of the Secretary' proposed by Mr. Boddington. At 4 o'clock tea was provided and was presided over by 25 ladies of the parish. In the evening there were athletic efforts in Mr. Mann's field, kindly lent for the occasion, and dancing in Mr. Green's field. Mr. Barton of the Ham efficiently acted as judge of the sports.

The aged and infirm who were unable to attend the festivities had a share of the good things sent to them, and the committee must be congratulated on the satisfactory way in which everything was conducted.

On Wednesday the school children were entertained by Mr. Robins at West Hill. Many amusements were provided for them and an enjoyable afternoon was spent.

Prizes were given for races and a medal presented to each child on leaving. Hearty cheers were given to Mr. and Mrs. Robins for their hospitality.

It will be noticed on the copy of the poster advertising the event that people were asked to decorate the streets. Not only were individual houses adorned, but numbers of festoons bright with flowers and foliage crossed the main street.

I have no doubt that after the Cubbington festivities were over, many of the villagers would go to New Cubbington to see the chain of bonfires which were lit in response to a signal from Malvern Hills.

The bonfire on the Campion Hills was quite a massive affair, reaching a height of some 30 feet. This was lit directly after 10pm, on seeing the flickering of a distant fire. Those who were on the hills could see all around, scattered over the vast expanse of country, the glare of 16 or 17 similar fires, some burning brightly and others only as faint flickerings of light against the sky in the far distance.

Fires could be seen at Weston under Wetherley, Shuckburgh, Offchurch, Ufton, Chesterton, Tachbrook Mallory, Burton Dassett, Edge Hills etc.

At midnight the brightness of the local bonfire was rapidly declining, but day was breaking next morning before the last flicker had completely died out.

QUEEN VICTORIA'S DIAMOND JUBILEE of 1897

was celebrated here with much rejoicing. On Sunday, the National Anthem was sung in church at both services and special sermons preached by the Vicar, the Rev. B.M.Bean. The Royal Standard floated from the Tower. On Tuesday, the village was gaily decorated, the inhabitants having almost universally lent a helping hand.
At 11.30am, a procession was formed in Mr. Ferguson's field and, headed by the village band, marched to the Church, where an appropriate sermon was preached from the text 'He that ruleth over men must be just'. After service a dinner was provided for men over 50 years of age.

V. R.

CUBBINGTON JUBILEE FESTIVITIES.

The Committee appointed to carry out the Jubilee Celebration, to be held on June the 21st,

INVITE ALL PEOPLE OF THE PARISH

(excepting the School Children, who will be entertained by J. Y. ROBINS, Esq., on WEDNESDAY JUNE 22nd), to share in the Rejoicings.

There will be provided a

DINNER FOR THE MEN

at ONE O'CLOCK ; and a

MEAT TEA FOR THE WOMEN

at FOUR O'CLOCK.

Each Man to bring his own Plate, Knife and Fork, and Mug for Beer. Each Woman to bring Knife and Fork, Plate, Cup and Saucer, and Spoon for Tea. The Committee will do their best to make the ENTERTAINMENT a success, and hope the Villagers will DECORATE THE STREETS as far as practicable, and make their own homes as attractive as possible.

A FIRST-CLASS BRASS BAND

is engaged, which will Parade the Village, starting from the Schools at Twelve o'clock. The Committee hope that as many Members of the Friendly Societies with their Regalia, and others, will join in the PROCESSION.

During the Afternoon there will be RACES, DANCING, SPORTS, and GAMES, for which Prizes will be given, and for which see Programme at the Post Office.

GOD SAVE THE QUEEN.

PARISH OF CUBBINGTON

Programme

in connection with the celebration of

HIS MAJESTY'S CORONATION

ON

WEDNESDAY, MAY 12th, 1937

AT

CHURCH FARM

(By kind permission of Mr. R. Ellis)

---

1. Open-Air Service at 10-15 a.m. round the Coronation Tree.
2. Lunch at 12-15 p.m. for Mothers with their Children under 14 years of age.
3. Lunch for all Adults over 14 years of age, at 1-15 p.m.
4. **SPORTS** at 2-30 p.m.

GIRLS' and BOYS'	RACE,	6 years and under.	ADULTS'	RACE,	14 to 18.
,,	,,	6 to 8 years.	,,	,,	18 to 30.
,,	,,	8 to 10 years.	,,	,,	30 & upwards
,,	,,	10 to 12 years.			
,,	,,	12 to 14 years.			

GRETNA GREEN RACE. CROSS COUNTRY RACE (Open).

BOWLING, FOR LADIES AND GENTS.

COCOANUT SHIES. DARTS. PILLOW FIGHT, etc.

ALL ENTRIES FREE. Parishioners only will be allowed to compete in any of the above Events.

The Committee reserve the right to refuse any entry, also to handicap at their discretion any candidate or candidates for all events and to alter any race that may be deemed necessary.

The decision of the Judges is final.

5. Tea and Open Buffet from 5 until 7 p.m.
6. Dancing in the Playground from 7-45 p.m.
7. **FIREWORK DISPLAY** at 9-45 p.m.
8. Dancing continued.

GOD SAVE THE KING.

Will all persons please bring their own knives, forks plates glasses, cup & saucer

The Vicar presided, and after dinner proposed the Queen's health, the toast being enthusiastically received. The other toasts were 'The Committee' proposed by the Chairman and 'The health of the Chairman' which was received with musical honours.

The Vicar said how much they regretted the absence of Mr. Yeoman Robins, who had been a generous contributor to the day's enjoyment. In the afternoon the women of the parish were entertained in the schoolroom, and sports were held in the evening in a field belonging to Mr. Amos.

The children had a treat given them in the Vicarage field, where swings, kindly erected by Mr. Flint, races and other amusements were provided. Praise is due to all who helped to carry out the day's arrangements so successfully.

You will notice that dinner was provided for men over fifty years of age. The story is told that one of the villagers whose nick-name was 'Noah' presented himself for the meal. When he was challenged as to his age — the Committee-man thinking he was not old enough — he replied, 'I am Noah, and if you have anyone here older than I am, I would like to see him.'

The Committee-man replied, 'Come in, Noah'.

May Day Procession assembled in the School Playground

MAY DAY

May 12th, or the nearest school day to that date, was the day chosen to celebrate May Day.

For weeks before this date, the May songs were practised and summery dresses prepared. On the morning there were anxious glances at the sky. Would it be a fine day? There was an old gentleman in the village who was a self-appointed weather forecaster. If asked what the weather was likely to be, he would stand still on the roadway, slowly looking round the sky from all points of the compass. After a long pause he would pronounce, 'Well, I think it will be fine, but we might have a shower or two.' A wise, non-committal answer! I cannot ever remember it being wet on this particular celebration day.

It was the custom for girls to carry flowers, and the boys to carry flags. The previous evening the girls had gathered flowers and bunched them, and the boys had made their flags and floral buttonholes. A boy would be proud if his flag was larger than any other. Parents, even those who were very poor, dressed the girls in flowered dresses, or neat, clean white ones.

At the time appointed, the children assembled in the school playground in preparation for a tour of the big houses of the parish. Please note — 'Parish' not 'Village'. The extreme ends of the parish which were visited were 3 or more miles apart!

The Vicarage was the first port of call. The school was noted for its singing, so that the patrons enjoyed our visit and were rewarded thus, for a gift was placed in the collecting box. The other big houses were called upon and then we proceeded to West Hill, the large house on the way to Kenilworth. Here we were made welcome with a glass of milk and a bun for each one.

The next journey, about 2½ miles away, at the other end of the parish, was to Ham Farm, near Offchurch. By this time the flowers were fading, flags more or less furled, feet were weary and everyone, teachers and scholars, were feeling tired. When the visits were completed, we returned home, after a journey of between 5 and 6 miles, anticipating a good tea. For these functions, the children were expected to provide their own mugs. Local shopkeepers prepared a supply of tin mugs, for experience had shown that the harmony of the proceedings was disturbed when small children needed tears to be wiped away and a replacement made of a broken cup or mug.

The tea was enjoyed by all, especially the boys, who would announce how many cups of tea had been drunk and how many cakes had been consumed.

The 'Day' was not yet over, for in the evening the parents had been invited to hear the children sing. A goodly crowd assembled, and at last, parents and children, tired but happy, returned home after another May Day.

When the bills had been paid, any money remaining was divided amongst the children, sometimes amounting to about 2d. each for the older children and less for the younger ones.

The infants assembled on the Vicarage lawn with the Vicar

With a change of Headmasters and the intervention of the 1914-1918 war, the May Day, as described, was discontinued, and after the war the Vicar organised the event in connection with the Church Sunday School. This took a more elaborate form. The children elected a May Queen and attendants. On the day, a crowning ceremony was held, the attendants carrying decorated wands and attended by pages. A May Day concert was given in the evening.

SUNDAY SCHOOL TREATS

In my early days, these took the form of a visit to the Vicarage Field, where sports were held. These consisted of a few races for the various age groups of the scholars. The prizes for the successful competitors were placed on the Vicarage lawn for all to see. The more athletic members of the school viewed them in anticipation, trying to decide which particular prize might be awarded for the race they hoped to win. The field was divided from the lawn by an iron fence, painted white, and we were continually reminded that we must not stand on the fence.

Some years later, Stoneleigh Park became the venue for the treat, and after a few more years, annual visits to the seaside were arranged. On these excursions, the parents and members of the public were allowed to join and so whole families enjoyed a day at the seaside. In fact, a train washired, which could be done if a specified number of seats could be guaranteed. Neighbouring villages added to the gathering — in some cases this meant an early start from home, even as early as 5 or 6am. At the destination, a Church Sunday School room had been hired for the tea; the catering for this meal was done by the teachers, in co-operation with the Church Officials.

The May Day Celebrations organised in conjunction with the Sunday School. The prospective Queen is processing from the Vicarage to the School to be crowned.

CARNIVAL

In more recent times these celebrations have been supplanted by a carnival and procession. The Carnival Queen and her attendants are judged from entrants who must be of school age. The occasion is an evening Social, held a few weeks previously, in the Village Hall, and it is usual to have over 50 entrants.

The procession consists of tableaux, entered by the various organisations of the village, such as The Mothers' Union, Women's Institute, The Cubbington Players (amateur dramatic society), Girl Guides, Boy Scouts, Cubs and Brownies. These are also judged, when they are assembled in the Playing Field. The judging completed, they process through the village, headed by the vehicle bearing the Queen and her attendants, returning to the Playing Field, where a fête is held. In recent years, fêtes have been held in the summer in order to raise funds for the various organisations. As many as three are held in one year. The Village Hall Trust now takes the form of a Carnival and Fête. Earlier annual events were a combination of sports, side shows, and so on.

A correspondent described one of these functions in 1950. After mentioning remarks by the President and Chairman of the Trust and the opener of the event who announced that a temporary hall had been obtained for use by the National Council of Social Service, he continued:

'The programme of sports was curtailed owing to the dearth of entries, but mention must be made of the veterans' race, which included two competitors who, from their appearance, would

Carnival

have made Methuselah look a youngster, but who finished first and second respectively.'

At the earlier fêtes, bowling at nine pins was a popular pastime, and side shows were well patronised.

The prize for the winner in the men's section was a live pig. The animal was brought to the field and placed in an enclosure near the pitch, so that the competitors could see the prize they hoped to win.

On one occasion, the pig was duly placed in the pen in the morning. The helpers were busy erecting stalls and decorations and, at the appropriate time, went home to dinner.

On returning to the field in readiness for the opening, to their dismay the pig had disappeared; somehow he had escaped from the enclosure.

Members of the committee searched the nearby fields and at last found the pig at the farm from which it had been taken.

The final event of the afternoon was the Bull Fight; an extremely fierce bull which had never been defeated, added yet another victory to his laurels.

Having caused the decease of a Bandolero, and having frightened the life out of a Picador, he, however, had to receive first aid from his trainer and the 'vet'.

The famous Matador, scorning the entreaties of his wife, then entered the arena. In fact, it seemed that the bull had met his match, for in a frenzy of wifely devotion, the lady attacked the bull with her umbrella.

However, her nerve failed her and on seeing the bull approach, she ran screaming from the arena. Her spouse, after ineffectual attempts to get to the front end of the animal also fled and the bull would have remained at large but for the blandishments of a waitress carrying two bottles of beer and two glasses.

Crowning the Carnival Queen

Carnival Float

Carnival Fancy Dress Competition for children

2nd of JUNE, 1953

CORONATION DAY PROGRAMME

9-30 a.m.

UNITED OPEN-AIR SERVICE at Village Hall.

10-15 a.m. onwards

TELEVISION in the Village Hall.

12 noon

LUNCH in Church of England School, for Residents aged 60 and over.

2-0 p.m.

CHILDREN'S SPORTS in Field on Rugby Road.

(Kindly lent by Mr. G. R. Parriss)

4-30 p.m.

TEA for CHILDREN age 3 years and over, and those Children attending SCHOOL. Tea will be followed by **Presentation of Souvenirs.** Members of Coronation Committee will deliver Souvenirs to Parents of Children under 3 years of age.

5-30 p.m.

ADULTS SPORTS in Mr. Parriss's Field, Rugby Road.

7-0 p.m.

PARADE will leave Vicarage (accompanied by the **Cubbington Silver Band**) and proceed through the Village to Sports Field, where Maypole and Country Dancing will take place.

9-0 p.m.

DANCE in the Church of England School and Playground. A **Buffet** will be provided.

THE VILLAGE AT WAR

TWO WORLD WARS

Sacred to the Memory
of
Our Brave Lads
who fell fighting for
Their Country's Honour
1914 - 1918

John L Ashfield	Ernest Hancox
John Bastock	Albert Harris
Innes Boreham	George Harwood
Frank Bennett	Percy Harwood
Herbert Bruce	Albert Haynes
Charles Carpenter	Frank Judd
Ernest Carpenter	Thomas Lane
Frank Carpenter	Harold Lee
William Cleaver	John Mitchell
George Cobb	William Mullis
Charles Day	Harold Richardson
John Fell	Harry Tarver
William Fell	Walter Tarver
Edward Green	Frederick C. Taylor
Samuel Green	William R. Watkin

William Walker

I have introduced the efforts of the village in the First World War by a copy of the inscription of the Village War Memorial and the names of the fallen.

Inside the Church is a list of villagers who served in the various armed Services. These number 139. Outside, on the War Memorial are the thirty-one names of those killed.

We must not forget their sacrifice or that of the severely wounded, with loss of limbs, and others seriously incapacitated still amongst us.

I don't think that those of us who were in the Services realise the anxiety and worry suffered by our relatives at home. The waiting for the postman each morning, the relief when the letter delivered told that all was well. The dread that one official letter would be received telling otherwise. Bad news spread quickly and all too frequently they must have learned that John — or Frank — had been killed. In some cases two brothers at the same time. Rationing also added to the worries. No one ever thought that a repetition would take place 21 years later. It was, after all, 'a war to end wars'!

1939 - 1945

Names of those who sacrificed their lives.

Trevor Gallimore	Horace Stephens
Frederick Goodwin	Gordon Wells
Dennis Lissaman	Robert Willoughby
Louis Page	Robert Bradbury
Arnold Page	Dennis Draper

Thank goodness that this list is not as long as in the previous war, but the sacrifice is just as great. It will be noted that the names of two brothers appear in the list. The same anxiety was felt by those at home for their loved ones serving overseas.

There was a difference amongst the general public in that they felt in a small way they were facing similar dangers to those in the Services due to the German bombing. In this parish, as related in the activities of the Fire Service, bombs were dropped near Ford Farm and in Cubbington Woods, and a landmine fell in Lillington, doing quite a lot of damage in New Cubbington. At the height of the raids, the 'Alert' was sounding all too frequently.

Cubbington can be proud of its effort during this period. Besides the personnel in the Army, Navy and Royal Air Force, there were men and women serving in the First Aid, Wardens, Home Guard, Special Constables and Fire Service.

Many hours were spent in a rota system, standing by in case of Call, and stations were manned on the sound of the sirens giving the Alert.

Since I was in charge of the local Fire Service, I can give details of their activities. In February, 1960, the Cubbington Section of the Auxiliary Fire Service was formed as part of the Warwick Rural District Council Brigade. We started with a manual pump. This was operated by two or three men, each side of the pump. There was a piece of wood on each side and the pump was worked by the men on one side pushing their piece of wood up, and the men on the other side pulling it down.

On May 18th, 1940, we had a demonstration at Offchurch Bury, together with Whitnash and Finham, Coventry. Each of these other sections had petrol pumps. Members of the appropriate Committee of the Warwick Rural District Council were present to witness the demonstration.

The difference between the pressure of water coming from the petrol pumps and that from our manual pump was considerable, and the Committee decided to replace our pump with a Beresford Trailer Pump on July 25th, 1940.

Ironically, the first incident we had was at the home of the leading fireman (that was me!). Timbers in the chimney had evidently been smouldering for days, to such an extent that the chimney-breast was hot. I had left home to go to Shirley, Birmingham, when my wife discovered it. She informed two of the firemen who lived quite close, and they extinguished the fire with stirrup-pumps.

Roof timbers smouldering in neighbouring cottages was the next incident on April 3rd, 1940.

From June 24th onwards, Air Raid warnings were frequent. It was the rule that on the sound of the warning, personnel should report to Headquarters. Air Raid warnings were given in this area on June 21st and 25th, August 13th, 18th, 19th, 23rd, 24th, 25th and 26th.

From August 25th, 1940, the Patrol Officer (myself) and one man (on a rota system) slept at Headquarters. Headquarters was at the house I lived in. The front room was given up for this purpose. This rule was in force until April 13th, 1942, when two men and the Patrol Officer slept at Headquarters.

The first call of the section was at 12.45am. on August 25th, 1940, to attend to incendiary bombs. The crew toured from Blackdown to Weston-under-Wetherley. We received a call on October 27th to volunteer to go to Finham (Green Lane, Coventry) to man a post while they were engaged in part of Coventry, from 9pm. to 1.30am.

On October 29th, incendiary bombs fell at Blackdown. The Call was received at 11.45pm. The Officer and three men turned out.

Mr H.J.Lloyd

Chief Officer of Mechanisation and Aero Ltd Works' Fire Brigade
(part of Morris Motors Ltd of Coventry).
He was awarded the British Empire Medal for the work he and his crew did
on the night of the big raid on Coventry, the 14th of November, 1940

Top Row, L to R:
Frank Knight
Eric Houghton
Edgar Davis
Bill Cox
Albert Whitehead
Will Smith (Smiggy)

Middle Row:
Bert Clements
Bill Goddard
Alan Rose
Alf Morris
Alf Belcher
Harry Arnott
Ken Ellis

Front Row:
Claude Dawson
Tom Andrews
Gus Peppitt
Ken Plank
Bob Lambert (Foggy)
Bill Heath
Ernest Merriman

Auxiliary Fire Service Members, 1939 - 1945

Home Guard, 1939-45

Wardens, 1939 - 1945

Incendiary bombs were found at Quarry Bank, emitting a strong smell of carbide. We returned at 1.20am.

On November 12th the District Warden (Vicar of Cubbington) reported incendiary bombs down Coventry Road, but they had burned out.

We had another call to go to Green Lane, Coventry, on November 14th, about 8pm. When nearing Green Lane, hundreds of incendiary bombs were falling. Luckily we were not hit. Later we were again fortunate. I was driving the car without lights, as it was a beautiful moonlight night. Suddenly a car came from Coventry, evidently to escape the air raid, at a terrific speed down the hill before the turn to Green Lane. I was driving in the middle of the road and a collision seemed inevitable when the oncoming vehicle passed our car safely on the wrong side. We reached the Green Lane station when the bombs were falling fairly close, the blast shattering shop windows. We were told to go to the nearby sewage-farm, where incendiaries had set fire to a straw rick. It was realised that the following bombers would be guided by the flames and encouraged to bomb the sewage-farm.

After the fire was extinguished I brought the crew home at 3.30am. as they were wet, and then returned to Coventry with another crew who had been standing by at home.

The All-Clear went about 6.45am. and we all returned to Cubbington. This was the night of the great raid on Coventry.

On November 19th, the Head Warden reported incendiary bombs at Eathorpe, which were dealt with by the crew. At 1.45 in the morning of April 10th, 1941, a message was received from the Warden's Post that incendiary bombs had fallen at Cubbington. Burning bombs were found by the Patrol Officer and crew down Leicester Lane, and buried.

Activity in the district occurred on April 7th, 15th and 22nd, May 2nd, 4th, 10th and 16th, June 4th, July 4th and 8th, and November 1st and additional men reported on the sound of the sirens.

The station was manned every night. Local enemy air activities became fewer during the following years.

The bombs dropped near Ford Farm, Offchurch and in the Cubbington woods were obviously mistakes. These bombers were evidently trying to drop their missiles on Coventry. I am not sure how enemy aircraft were guided to their targets, but the idea was prevalent at the time that our scientists had succeeded with an invention which misled them slightly. After the November 14th, 1940, raid on Coventry, a decoy station was set up at Weston Mill, about half a mile from where the bomb had dropped at Weston-under-Wetherley.

This consisted of containers filled with inflammable material, set up on standards about 8ft. high. The containers were about 6ft. long and 3ft. square at the ends. Each one (and there were some dozen set about twenty yards apart) was connected electrically to an operational dug-out, about a quarter of a mile away. The idea was that if the authorities thought that a large-scale bombing raid was taking place on Coventry, the containers could be set alight electrically, from the dug-out. This process, together with the previously mentioned though unspecified invention, would entice the aircraft to drop their bombs in the Weston Mill area, which is about seven miles from Coventry. The decoy was never used for the purpose for which it was erected.

The local station during the ensuing years dealt with several farm fires at Princethorpe, Southam and Cubbington.

On February 25th, 1944, the crew was assembled to go to Leamington for duty at 7.50pm. when a villager informed us that he had heard an aeroplane making strange noises between Cubbington and Offchurch. The sounds had suddenly stopped, and he feared there had been a crash. We went to investigate and found that what he feared was correct. The plane had crashed on the hill, opposite Ford Farm. The pilot was dead.

The farmer from Ford Farm and his wife came up and we asked them to telephone the Police and Ambulance. We searched the neighbouring fields to see if there had been a second occupant of the plane, but we learned afterwards that the dead pilot was the sole occupant.

Besides manning the station every night on a rota system, drills and exercises took place at weekends.

About August, 1941, the National Fire Service assumed control from the Warwick Rural District Council. In 1943, the station was transferred from the home of my wife and myself, to a wooden building erected by the National Fire Service.

To keep the local firemen on their mettle, competitions were arranged which were entered into by the local brigades with the greatest zest, and we at Cubbington had excellent results.

The first competition was under the direction of the Warwick Rural District Council and was held on June 8th, 1941, at Lapworth.

The brigades taking part were those of Cubbington, Whitnash, Finham (Green Lane, Coventry) and Lapworth.

This competition will always be remembered by those taking part.

Some months before, we had received details of what was required in the competition. As far as we were concerned, the vital rule read as follows — 'The mackintosh coats shall be folded up, placed on the ground, and each member of the crew shall be flat on the ground with his head resting on the coat. At the given signal, the crew shall get up, don their coats, and at the end of the competition, a definite number of buttons must be fastened.' (I think it was four). Then followed the rules with respect to running out the hose, branch pipes, and so on.

We had sufficient men to enter two crews.

Carefully studying the rule with respect to the coats and the number of buttons which must be fastened at the end of the Competition, we realised that nowhere had it said that the buttons had to be fastened during the competition. So long as they were secure at the end was all that mattered. By fitting out one of our crews with the largest size coats we had, we found that, by buttoning the coats up before the competition started, folding them and putting them on the ground, on the given signal, the buttoned coats could be put on quite easily and quickly by putting them over the head like a shirt.

Therefore, it was decided that one crew should deal with the coats as described, while the other crew should start with their coats unbuttoned, as we expected that the crews of the opposing brigades would do. The latter, the unbuttoned coat crew, we decided to put in the first of our two crews. Everything was going smoothly, with times recorded. Some of the brigades realised that they were not quick enough, and the fastest crew up to that time was expecting that they would have the honour of winning the Shield which was to be presented to the winners.

The time arrived for our second crew to take part. I will call them the 'Buttoned-up-coat crew'. In practice we found that these members were very quick. We also found that one man could carry two pieces of apparatus instead of carrying one and then running back to the pump for the other part. There was no rule against this, since it was left to the initiative of the crew to find out.

All was ready, buttoned coats duly folded. None of the officials inspected the coats. The men lay down and the signal was given. The coats were donned, as practised, shirtwise. Then the uproar broke out, shouted protests from the watching crews. Each group operated singly and was timed by a stop-watch.

The Cubbington men ignored the uproar but continued with the competition, recording the fastest time.

However, all was not over. Official protests were made and we were penalised for every button previously fastened, a total of 29 seconds added to our time.

Even with this heavy penalty *WE WON* and the Shield was proudly brought to Cubbington.

This was only the start of our successes in following competitions, *EVEN WITHOUT BUTTONED COATS!*

The next competition was held for part-time crews, under the auspices of The National Fire Service.

This division comprised Leamington, Stratford, Rugby and Solihull and their respective Districts. The result was Cubbington First and Second, and Kenilworth Third. Consequently, Cubbington competed for the Area Cup. This comprised the area from Worcester to Rugby, but did not include the Cities of Birmingham, Worcester or Coventry. Cubbington won the Area Cup too!

THE AREA TRAILER PUMP COMPETITION

The following are the results of the Area Trailer Pump Competition Finals held at Pitchcroft, Worcester on Saturday, August 23rd, 1942. The winning team will hold the Senior Officers' Cup for six months.

Placings	Actual Time of Drill(mins)	Penalties	Total Time
1 B.1.X Cubbington A	1.48.2/5	2secs	1.50.2/5
2 A.3.Z Peterchurch A	1.51.1/5	Nil	1.51.1/5
3 B.1.V Kenilworth D	1.58.3/5	Nil	1.58.3/5
4 B.1.Z Whitnash A	1.58.4/5	2secs	2.0.4/5
5 A.3.Y Hereford A	2.04.3/5	Nil	2.04.3/5
6 A.3.Z EwyasHarold A	2.11.1/5	Nil	2.11.1 /5
7 B.2.W Studley A	2.18	Nil	2.18
8 A.3.Z Peterchurch B	2.28.3/5	Nil	2.28.3/5
9 B.1.V Kenilworth A	2.44	Nil	2.44
10 A.3.Z Ewyas Harold B	2.46.4/5	10secs	2.56.4/5
11 A.3.Y Hereford B	3.11	Nil	3.11
12 B.2.W Bidford	Drill not completed		

A.J. Bridle,
Fire Force Commander No 23 (Worcester Area)

The next competition was for the whole Division: 10 teams from Leamington, 11 from Stratford, 26 from Rugby and three teams from Solihull and their respective associated districts entered — a total of fifty teams. Cubbington entered three teams, and the result on this occasion was Cubbington First, Cubbington Second, and Cubbington Third, and Kenilworth fourth!

I have related some activities of the Fire Service because I was actively engaged, but the Home Guard, Wardens, First Aid and Special Constables were equally enthusiastic and conscientious about their duties and deserve the highest praise.

The First Aid Post was in the schoolroom of the Methodist Chapel. It was manned on a rota basis and equipped to deal with any emergency.

Looking down Queen Street towards the Methodist Church

PEOPLE IN PARTICULAR

THE COLONEL'S DAUGHTER

This lady was the daughter of an Army Colonel who lived in a Manor House type of dwelling known as The Cottage. I only knew her after her father and mother had died. She employed maids and a manservant who was both gardener and coachman. The trap was drawn by a smart pony.

This lady was determined to impress upon the youngsters of the village that she was the daughter of an Army Colonel. She expected the boys whom she met in the street to salute her by touching their caps or forelocks and the girls by making a curtsey, in return for which she would give a gracious smile.

My sister tells the story that she was playing with a friend in the street when 'the lady' came by. My sister dutifully curtsied; the other girl, whether intentionally or by accident, did not. The lady stopped and, addressing both girls, said, "One polite little girl and one impolite little girl".

I remember at school one day her manservant arrived with an attractive looking box. Since the box was attractive our expectations ran high. These were quickly dashed when the headmaster, after calling the school to order, opened the box only to disclose a large number of pebbles which had been found on the lady's lawn. These had evidently been thrown over the 6 feet high wall which bordered the garden. After the children responsible had been admonished and the others warned, normal work resumed.

CLOVER HEAD GATHERING MACHINE.

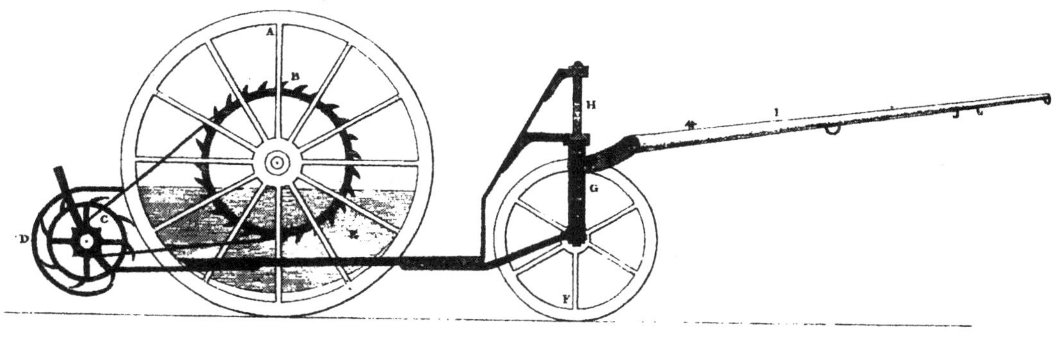

A. One of the wheels that carries the box.
B. Chain wheel.
C. Cylinder with the cutter.
D. Cone with a comb under the cylinder.
E. Box to receive the clover heads from the cylinder.
F. Centre wheel to carry front part.
G. Iron carriage for the centre wheel to work in.
H. Upper part of the centre wheel carriage made round so that it may turn freely at lands end.
I. Shaft attached to the carriage. G. H

JOSEPH RUSSELL,

Agriculturist and Author

The poor people of Cubbington, nearly two hundred years ago, were greatly indebted to Joseph Russell, who farmed at Ham Farm and at Cubbington Heath in 1780.

He had a man in the village taught to slaughter cattle. He sold the meat at cut price to the poor families, and also bought cheap joints of meat at Coventry for their benefit.

He grew large quantities of flax. This was dressed and spun on his farm, afterwards being made into linen by private hands in the neighbouring villages.

A row of cottages which stood at the back of the present Post Office was known as 'Weavers' Yard'. No doubt the people living there were engaged in the making of linen. The bleaching mills were extensive and he is said to have employed more than 100 men.

He planted a few acres with asparagus to supply the Coventry market and the rising town of Leamington.

As a practical farmer he was outstanding, always willing to experiment and to try out new crops, as explained previously. The seed of new varieties of potatoes were used, some costing as much as £2 a bushel. He also introduced the breed of Leicester sheep into Warwickshire.

The threshing machine was introduced into this area by him, and was hired out into the surrounding country. The 'G.O.', or sub-soil plough was first seen on his farm and he invented the Clover-Head Gathering machine.

In another venture he went to London and engaged in business, but this failed, and he returned to Kenilworth in 1827.

In 1830, at the age of 70, he published his first work, entitled 'A Treatise on Practical and Chemical Agriculture', followed in 1832 by a tract, entitled 'Observations on the Growth of British Corn'. Another work was published in 1840 on a new system of tillage. He advocated the system of alternate cattle and corn crops, without the aid of fallows.

Joseph Russell was a keen churchman. One of his daughters went as a governess to a family living in Birmingham. On hearing that the family were Unitarians, he journeyed to Birmingham with the intention of removing his daughter, but, on the assurance that no one would influence or interfere with her belief or attendance at church, he allowed her to remain.

He died suddenly at his daughter's home on Abbey Hill, Kenilworth, in 1847 and was buried with other members of his family in the south side of Ashow Church. The tombstone reports:

In Memory of Joseph Russell, who departed this life, March 7th, 1847 Aged 87, also Frances his wife, who died 3rd, January, 1848 aged 80.

THE VILLAGE BRICKLAYER

The village bricklayer and chimney sweep as I knew him was an extremely good tradesman. Since my father was the village carpenter the two worked together frequently on repairs and new buildings. When working on alterations he was most careful in salvaging any items of bolts, hinges and the like. These were carefully stored in such a way that if any article was required he could go to his store room and instantly find it.

He was also the owner of funfair equipment, swinging boats, round-a-bouts and coconut shies. He was in great demand during the summer, visiting neighbouring villages for their annual functions, flower shows, fêtes and general festivities.

Now this man was a most respectable business man, with not the slightest sign of excessive drinking. However, almost regularly at the end of the summer season, when the fêtes were finished, he celebrated by having a week from his regular work. During this particular week frequent visits to the public house were made. The effect of these visits was seen in this gentleman's behaviour, by nature an exceedingly jolly, generous man. At this time when the children came out of school at mid-day he would stand at the public house door and await their arrival. He would be armed with a pocketfull of pennies. These he would throw into the road at intervals for the children to scramble for them. He would stand there and shake with laughter as the pushing and shoving went on to get as many pennies as possible. He never became incapable, but was out for fun. When the week was over he would resume normal work. One alternative to a week at the seaside!

MISS EMILY LEDBROOK

The Village has been greatly indebted to the Ledbrook family, especially to one member, Miss Emily Ledbrook. This lady lived at Ford Farm, Offchurch Road, with her parents and sister. She regularly attended Sunday School as a Teacher, walking that distance of more than a mile each way.

About 1890 she started a Lending Library in a large room attached to a house they owned. The room was known as the Reading Room. In the evenings it was used as a Men's Club where bagatelle, dominoes, cards, darts, and so on were played.

The Library was opened on alternate Saturdays between 2 and 4 o'clock. The subscription was 1d. a month to be paid in advance, with payments of half the cost if the book were lost, a quarter if damaged.

Fairground

The library was run by two ladies. Books were covered very carefully in brown paper, making them very much less attractive to look at than the very attractive dust jackets of today's novels.

The work of covering the books was done by Miss Ledbrook herself, as also was the purchase of new books. I remember when I was quite young a book known as the 'Chatterbox' was eagerly read. This was an annual publication.

I have in my possession now a library book of this period:

'The Prince and the Page'
by Charlotte M. Yonge
An historical novel.

On the fly leaf of this book is a printed sheet giving the rules of the Cubbington Lending Library and spaces in which the dates of issue to the members are shown.

The first date is 5.3.92, the last 9.12.22. This book was in circulation for 30 years. It is still in excellent condition. The number of books in the Cubbington Library list is 483.

Sunday School Procession headed by the Cubbington Band and the banner painted by Miss Ledbrook

This lady also used to collect subscriptions from her friends in order to purchase coal. This was delivered to very deserving cases in the Village during the winter. She also bought packets of tea which she delivered to poor widows.

Her hobby was that of an artist of no mean merit. She was responsible for painting the Sunday School banner. This is a design painted on silk of an open bible on which was inscribed 'The Secret of England's Greatness', bordered on each side with a design of oak sprays.

When the Old Wesleyan Chapel was up for sale she purchased it and gave it to the parish to be used as a Social Centre. The room was eventually equipped with an indoor air-gun rifle-range, billiard table, and the like. When Miss Ledbrook became older she gave the premises to the Vicar and Wardens of the Parish Church.

At this time she was living in Leamington. She did this social service work quietly and without fuss. I never saw her on any public platform or at any public function. She did indeed realise the value of 'Social Service'.

A road in the Village is named after her, as is the ladies' branch of the Oddfellows' Friendly Society — the Emily Ledbrook Lodge.

On October 27th, 1969, Mrs. Mary Bastock reached the ripe old age of 100 years. She was born near Banbury, and came to Cubbington and lived with her aunt when she was ten years old.

For a number of years she taught in the village school.

After leaving the profession, and on becoming a widow she became a newsagent. Travelling on a tricycle, she journeyed to Leamington at an early hour to fetch the morning papers, which she eventually delivered to the individual customers' homes.

On her 99th birthday, accompanied by her daughter, she went to Banbury, not on a tricycle but by taxi.

She declared that her long and healthy life was due to the exercise from tricycling and walking, with an occasional glass of ale.

Opposite, above: Miss Mary Bastock at 100
below: Delivering newspapers.

MR. T. WHITMORE,

(born 1847)

His father kept a shop and bakehouse in High Street. His son (my uncle) inherited the business. The advertisements in a Sports Programme show the variety of business interests he had:

T. Whitmore, Jun., General Draper.
Messrs. Whitmore and Bass, Land Surveyors.
Messrs. Bass, Whitmore & Co.
The Midland Steam Mineral Water Works.

This was about 1884. He afterwards took over the bakery business of his father. He became Registrar of Births and Deaths, Clerk of the Parish Council, Rate Collector, Sidesman of the Church, Secretary of the Local Committee dealing with Evening Classes, and an official of the Horticultural Society.

He was a man of deep religious convictions and of a high degree of intelligence. An extract from his diary describes an attempt to make gas out of petroleum, which, he says, was fairly successful.

He used to give me a small amount of money to deliver rate-demand notes. Some of these were to farmers who lived a distance of 1½ to 2 miles from the village. I remember very vividly going to one of these farms with such a note. The house was a great distance from the road, with a long drive. I entered the gate and had gone a short distance up the drive, when I could see some distance away, a great mastiff, a dog of extreme size. I quickly reversed and came out of the drive, walked back home with the undelivered note. I went to the Post Office and bought a postage stamp and posted the letter. This was my procedure afterwards with all those long distance, isolated houses. In fact, I spent all the money given to me on postage. Only the really local notes did I deliver free of charge.

MISCELLANY

GUNPOWDER PLOTTERS

One can imagine the excitement in the village on the morning in early November, 1605, if any of the villagers — as quite likely — heard the sound of galloping horses in the middle of the night. They would be ignorant of the happenings in London and even of those at Dunchurch. News would travel slowly but eventually the true facts would trickle through. Until then, surmises would be numerous. The following is a summary of the facts concerning the plotters' dash along the Rugby Road to Warwick and ultimately to capture, at Holbeach House near Dudley.

On November 5th, 1605, after Guy Fawkes was discovered and seized, Robert Catesby and some of his fellow conspirators set off along the Holyhead Road to meet their confederates at Dunchurch. Arrived there, the group of Midland Roman Catholics hastily dispersed. Catesby and his close followers made a wild dash by night for Wales, tearing through Princethorpe, Weston, Cubbington and Lillington until they reached Warwick, where, being in need of re-mounts, they stole horses from the Castle and from the stables of a horse-trainer named Benock.

Their story ends at Holbeach House near Dudley, where they were caught by the Sheriff's party, and Catesby and all were shot dead, except Thomas Winter who escaped with wounds, and later wrote his narrative.

CIVIL WAR

During the Civil War, the inhabitants of Cubbington petitioned that no more troops might be quartered on them, owing to the scarcity of provisions. The following description shows how the raising of the troops in the opposing forces and their subsequent movements during the month of October, 1642, must have aroused considerable interest in the conflict, especially as on the 21st October, 1642, King Charles led his troops from Kenilworth to Southam along the Offchurch Road, Cubbington.

Troops had been raised on all sides. Lord Brooke's purple-coated Warwickshire Regiment was early in the field, Hampden's green coats were not far behind. Holles' redcoats followed so that in the course of a month the Earl of Essex, as Commander-in-Chief for the Parliament, found himself with a formidable army. He crossed Warwickshire in the month of September on his march to Worcester, where he rested to watch the movements of the King who was raising troops at Shrewsbury and Chester. Charles I evidently felt the importance of marching on London and striking a blow at the headquarters of Parliament before the Earl of Essex could intercept him.

He left Shrewsbury on the 12th October, 1642, and proceeded to Bridgnorth, whence on the 15th of that month he went to Wolverhampton, thence on the 17th to Bremichem (Birmingham) to the mansion of Sir Thomas Holt, Aston Hall; on the 18th he went to Packington, the house of Sir Robert Fisher; on the 19th to Killingworth (Kenilworth). Whether the Castle was then garrisoned by the forces of Parliament, or abandoned by them, whether for the night he stayed in the Castle or elsewhere, the writer does not inform us. Lord Clarendon, however, states that it was 'a house of the King's and a very noble seat'. He was now between the two hostile garrisons of Coventry and Warwick Castle. On the 21st of October he journeyed with his army to Southam, probably by way of Chesford Bridge, Cubbington and Offchurch. At Southam, the house in which he slept may still be seen. On the 22nd October he proceeded to Edgcote, Prince Rupert taking up his quarters the same night at Wormleighton at a fine Tudor mansion belonging to the Spencer family. An anecdote is related by Dr. Thomas, of Mr. Richard Shuckburgh, of an ancient family in Warwickshire, the possessor of the Shuckburgh estates in the County at the time of the Civil War, in no way inferior to his ancestors.

He continues:

As Charles 1st marched to Edgcote, near Banbury, on the 22nd October, 1642, he saw him hunting in the field, not far from Shuckburgh, with a very good pack of hounds, upon which it is reported that he fetched a deep sigh and asked who that gentleman was who hunted so merrily that morning, when he was going to fight for his crown and liberty, and being told that he was this Richard Shuckburgh, he was ordered to be called to him, and was by him graciously received, upon which he went immediately home, armed all his tenants and the next day attended him in the field where he was knighted and was present at the Battle of Edgehill. After the taking of Banbury Castle and

His Majesty's retreat from those parts, he went to his own seat and fortified himself on the top of Shuckburgh Hill, where, being attacked by some of the Parliamentary forces, he defended himself till he fell with most of his tenants about him, but being taken up and life perceived in him, he was carried away prisoner to Kenilworth Castle, where he lay for a considerable time and was forced to purchase his liberty at a dear rate.

There is, in the Church of Upper Shuckburgh, a bust of this Warwickshire worthy and staunch Royalist.

The Battle of Edgehill took place on Sunday, October 23rd, 1642, the first battle of the Civil War. Although neither side could claim the victory, advantage rested with the Royalists who were able to capture Banbury and so march to Oxford without resistance.

CUBBINGTON MEN'S INVOLVEMENT in the WARWICK BOROUGH ELECTIONS

The following is taken from The Warwick Advertiser of December 15th, 1832.

Warwick during the whole of last week, was a scene of considerable disturbance, the partizans of the various candidates exhibiting the greatest rancour towards each other, whenever, in their canvassing progress through the town, they came into collision. Scarcely a day passed but what someone, or more, individuals were seriously, if not dangerously wounded, the houses of many of the inhabitants were attacked, and the front windows of some, demolished. On Friday an affray took place which at one time threatened the most serious consequences; the Blue party, rushing out of one of the Committee Rooms, attacked the Orange Men with iron bars and sticks loaded with lead: a considerable number of whose wounds were deep and dangerous.

A meeting was then held at the Mayor's house, and the wounded men were taken there, that he might himself see their actual state.

After a deliberation of some time, and a consultation held, it was decided that the Military should be called in and a troop of the Scots Greys arrived about 11 o'clock. At that period, however, all was quiet, and after parading the streets the troops retired to their quarters.

The Military having disappeared, however, the rioters took fresh Courage, and in the course of the night attacked the Gas Works, broke the large entrance door, and pulled down the iron palisades. A Constabulary force making their speedy appearance, the mob dispersed and the town was tranquil during the remainder of the night.

Many serious battles took place on Monday and the Orange boys, flushed with conscious triumph – for they had overpowering numbers during the whole of the day – became altogether ungovernable, under the management of two hundred special constables appointed by the Magistrates. The Worshipful the Mayor and several other Magistrates were closely engaged during the whole of the morning in hearing cases brought before them, not only as to the dreadful depredations of Friday night, but the various personal attacks made at that period.

Men were taken on both sides, with bludgeons on their persons, which were of course, deposited with the Magistrates and the men on either side were then set at liberty. The spirit of mischief was abroad, the hot blood of revenge was flowing in the veins of a misguided multitude. The fights became every hour more formidable. The Constables were set at defiance. After a desperate engagement in the Market Place, about noon, we saw several poor fellows severely beaten, and one carried off by the Pinks and Blues, perfectly senseless, with his face so horribly disfigured that it bore no resemblance to human features, and was but a frightful mass of contusion. He was removed to a public house and a surgeon was called in. He seemed beyond the possibility of recovery, and more than once it has been reported that he was dead.

We understand, however, that he has at length returned to feeling though unhappily not to sense. We are informed that yesterday he was in a state of distressing delirium. Should he continue to live, which it is yet considered very doubtful, it is feared he may never recover from the effect of the dreadful wounds he received.

Another unfortunate man, who was wounded on Friday evening, during the dreadful battles between the parties in the Saltisford, and who was thrown over a wall and left for dead, is, we are informed, so dangerously injured, that it is certain he can never again be fit for employment. It is very doubtful whether he will recover.

How lamentable are these facts. They reflect the deepest disgrace upon our character as an enlightened people.

Immediately after the alarming affray in the Market place, to which we have alluded, the Magistrates very properly resolved to call in a troop of the Scots Greys. They came in the evening of that day, and soon after their appearance in the town, it was restored to some degree of order. In the meantime,

Monday being the day appointed for the nomination of the Candidates, the Committees were much engaged in consultation with the worthy Mayor and his colleagues, upon the subject of the arrangements to be made at the County Hall.

The friends of Mr. Tomes and Mr. King had received a secret communication, to which we do not consider it advisable at this period to allude more particularly than to say it was the cause of the ulterior arrangements as to the nomination of Candidates. That communication was of such a nature that the Committees applied to the Mayor, and suggested that the three Candidates should be advised not to appear before the excited people at the time of the nomination.

To this arrangement the Candidates all gave their consent in writing, and the gentlemen who were appointed to propose and second the respective nominations, having agreed that no speeches should be delivered, the Mayor and his colleagues, accompanied by the Committees and friends of the Candidates and a large concourse of the people, proceeded from the Court House to the County Hall about half past one.

After the usual ceremonies, the readers of the Writ – the Act against bribery, etc. – the Worshipful the Mayor (Thomas Collins Esq.) announced the arrangement made, and stated that it had been thought advisable, in the excited state of the people, to nominate in the absence of the Candidates and that further to prevent excitement, the gentlemen who would propose and second the nominations, had recently consented to forbear making any observations.

John Edwards Esq. then proposed
John Tomes Esq.
and was seconded by Richard Saunders Esq.

Edward Bolton King Esq.
was proposed by Mr. Alderman Burbury
and seconded by Charles Lamb Esq.

The Hon. Sir Charles Greville KCB
was proposed by W. Staunton Esq.
and seconded by Henry Wise Esq.

A Poll was then demanded by Mr. Haynes, the solicitor on behalf of Mr. Tomes – by Mr. Heath, the solicitor for Mr. King – and General Mansters for Sir Charles Greville. The Court was nearly filled by the Orange party and we need not add that, when the gallant leader's name was announced, it was received with loud shouts of applause.

The crowd then dispersed without any excesses of a riotous character, the gentlemen being conducted by a numerous constabulary force back to the Court House.

The town was now a scene of anxious solicitude for the opening of the poll – nine o'clock the next morning being the hour appointed.

On Tuesday morning at a very early hour – long before day light – the people were preparing to assemble and large bodies on both sides in the approaching contest collected together.

The Orange men, elated with their exploits of the previous day, rose in high spirits and evidently anticipated the glory of carrying everything before them. The Pinks and Blues, however, had contrived to be prepared with their stronger band.

Before daybreak they had safely introduced into the town their heroes from Coventry and Birmingham to match the worthy lads of the Orange from Cubbington, Rugby and divers other places, according to the busy tongue of rumour.

The matter stood, according to the information given to us. The hour of action now arrived. Crowds of Orange men collected at the Polling places, full of anticipated success in their plans. The Pinks and Blues appeared in formidable numbers at the bottom of the Butts, a few stragglers of their party were just surrounded and driven into a corner by the Orange lads, and they were about to be assailed with violence, when the body of Pinks and Blues came to their fortunate rescue.

We cannot help stating, whether it may be deemed 'partial' or not, we neither know nor care, for the fact deserves to be mentioned that, when the Pinks and Blues gave battle to the Orange, they took from the latter several bludgeons and instantly threw them over a wall, telling them they wanted no weapons.

Sir Charles Greville and Mr. King were, at about 4 o'clock on Wednesday, declared fully elected, the number of votes being

Sir Charles Greville 701
Mr. King 553
Mr. Tomes 463

Mr. King, in his address after the election, referred to the ballot system. He said he had formerly held opinions against the adoption of that system, but he was now convinced that it had become necessary for the protection of the poor voters who were in a state of bondage, and brought to the polls under the in-

fluence of bribery or intimidation, he should therefore most readily vote in favour of the ballot.
He should also vote for the reform of the Church.
The Hon. gentleman very feelingly alluded to an attack which had been made upon Mr. Tomes and himself by the infuriated mob, observing that had it not providentially happened that 'the Venerable and Respected gentleman with whom he had the honour of sitting in Parliament' and himself made their escape into the house (the attack being made at Mr. Tomes' door) before the ruffians could rush in a body up the steps, although a desperate blow with a bludgeon was aimed at the head of Mr. Tomes, and he himself was knocked down, he should not now have been a living man to return his grateful thanks to those who had exerted themselves in his cause.
He concluded amid loud and enthusiastic cheers.

The writer of this next report evidently took great exception to the phrase in the paragraph at the beginning of the previous report, viz.
"the Blue party rushing out of one of the Committee rooms, attacked the Orange men with iron bars and sticks loaded with lead".

With respect to this paragraph we feel it our duty to state that a more scandalous misrepresentation of facts never issued from the public press. With this brief declaration, which we will readily repeat to the face of the Writer, whoever or whatever he may be if he be not ashamed to acknowledge his distorted bantling with this declaration we leave our readers to contemplate the enormous evils attendant on that lamentable party spirit by which this town has been so long disgraced.
It is not by any means our desire now the Election has been closed, to re-open the wounds that are, we most anxiously hope, already, at least in some degree, healed, but we could not read the paragraph without expressing our disgust at its infamous falsehood. What! Could we suffer it to go forth to the World as an uncontradicted fact that the Committee for conducting the Election of Mr. Bolton King (now one of our worthy members) was composed of blood-thirsty ruffians. Had we been silent on this occasion, we know that we should have incurred the deserved censure of every honourable man in Warwick.
We solemnly declare before the face of heaven that had the same malicious statement been made against Sir Charles Greville's Committee, we should have felt equally earnest and sincere in the expression of our abhorrence at the infamous falsehood of the charge and we are convinced that should Sir Charles read the atrocious paragraph he will readily see that it is calculated to reflect the deepest disgrace on his native town, and we feel disgusted at the imputation cast upon the Committee of his late opponent and present colleague.

DEMOCRACY AT WORK - 1946

Two rival claims of fish vendors to open shops at New Cubbington form the subject of a public enquiry at the offices of the Warwick Rural District Council.

This enquiry was a sequel to the action of a Mrs. C who, when refused permission to establish a fried fish shop in Rugby Road, wrote to the King and to the Home Secretary. At the same time, she appealed against the County Council's action in imposing restrictions under the Ribbon Development Act.

A Mr. H was already the owner of a fish shop next door to where Mrs. C wished to trade.

A former member of the Warwick Rural District Council said that when the rival plans were considered, he gained the impression that someone was pushing Mr. H's plans in preference to those of Mrs. C.

This Councillor was rebuked by the Clerk of the Council for making public matters which were discussed in Committee.

The Inspector, at the end of the evidence, said he would submit his findings at a later date.

The result — two fish shops (one wet fish, the other fried fish) were established in Rugby Road, Cubbington, very close to each other.

A letter from a humble villager to the King, and to the Home Secretary, started an enquiry which, in my opinion, had remedied an injustice.

A triumph for Democracy!

EXTRACTS FROM
A CUBBINGTON DIARY

July 9th, 1886. Election.

This was also the day of Election for the Rugby Division of the County of Warwick. The Candidates, busy for the union, M. C. Buzard – for the disunion, the ardent followers of the insane 'Grand Old Man' viz. H. Cobb.

Polling during the day was very slow, the last 2 hours being the most busy.

During the time of polling, both candidates drove through the village. The Unionist (Buzard) having carriage and four with postilions dressed in the colours, red, white and blue. On his progress through the streets he was presented by Mr. T. with a basket of fruit and flowers.

The Gladstonian Cobb carried in his conveyance a representation of his deity, whom he servilely worships.

On the whole, things passed off very quietly.

July 10. Result of above, Cobb returned, Majority 478.
July 14th, 1884. Hospital Saturday Collection started.
March 22nd, 1893. Technical Education

A meeting of the Divisional Committee was held on Thursday last week at Cubbington for the purpose of electing officers for the district. Representatives attended from Leek Wootton and Bubbenhall. The Rev. B. M. Bean was elected Chairman, Mr. Donne (Leek Wootton) Treasurer and Mr. W. Rowbottom, Secretary. Large ambulance, mensuration and dressmaking classes have already been started and it is proposed later on to add 'Continuation' Schools and sick nursing to the curriculum. The movement promises to be very popular.

.............1896

Meeting to elect committee of Cubbington Vegetable Marrow and Late Root Growers Association.

May 3rd, 1905.

Meeting to consider a presentation to the Vicar of an Illuminated Address and Present, on the completion of a quarter of a century's residence and work amongst us as Vicar and also to mark the celebration of the 25th Anniversary of his Wedding Day.

May 4th.

Order given for Illuminated Address. Presentation present. Silver Inkstand and two candlesticks.

LETTER FROM A CUBBINGTON MAN WHO HAD EMIGRATED TO CANADA IN 1897.

My dear Friend. Feb. 7th, 1897

I write these few lines to you hoping to find you quite well as it leaves me at present very sick, dear friend. I have not heard from anyone since I left dear old England. Dear friend, write to me and let me know all the news for I feel lonesome out here. Dear Ted how is all the children and your wife are they all well. Tell me all the news you can think of dear Ted. This is the country for a single man and a married man you earn more money out here than in England but it is a new country and it is not opened up yet. It is all woods, all but just the cities but it was a very hard country when I first landed in it was very hot. This is the country for work and more than work. This is a very hard country on a man the summer is too hot and the winters are too cold I am working in the wood this winter a good Chopper gets about five pounds a month and all he can eat and wash his clothes. I get this winter about four pounds a month and all I can eat. We have about five feet of snow. It is hard work when you get down in the snow I think I will be home when the hundreds come in don't forget to tell me all the news about dear old Cubbington is the many of the people been summoned since I was there I have just began to feel my feet I have just began to do good for myself if I was some of them at Cubbington I would have a heart in me not stay there and be poor when they get old and go to the poor house. My mother as old as she is gets two pounds ten shillings a month at a house where she is living and she can earn that as long as she will stay there. Young girls have a good chance to do some good for themselves. This is the country I will just tell you a little about it. Every man for himself and the devil for us all. You can buy a good farm for about forty pounds, but I think I will not buy a farm I will save my money and I think I will come and see if I can find a wife somewhere.

from your friend

....

Lenoxville, Canada.

EFFIGY BURNING

I was quite young when the last effigy burning took place in the village.

Two people in the village were accused of loose living and the event which took place was the method used to show, publicly, the disapproval of the Community.

Before the appointed day, effigies of the people concerned and torches were made.

I lived next door to one of the organisers and was aware of a certain amount of the activity which took place in the communal washhouse. In this building was a copper to hold the water, which was heated by the fire in the grate underneath, the fuel used being slack. It was in this building that the sound of men's voices was heard for a few evenings before the appointed date. When the time arrived a procession was formed and at the head were carried the effigies on long poles. The torch-bearers followed behind, adults and children trailing at the end. The procession deliberately passed the houses of the people concerned, to the accompaniment of cat-calls, hoots, jeers and songs.

I followed in the rear until the procession reached the bottom of Windmill Hill, then, being young and a little nervous, I returned home. By this time the participants were lustily singing,

> The brave old Duke of York,
> He had ten thousand men,
> He marched them up to the top of the hill
> And marched them down again.

The site of the burning was in a field along the Rugby Road, opposite Mr. Compton's Garage.

The effigies were placed in a heap and the bonfire ceremoniously lit, to the cheers of the surrounding crowd. When the fires were out the men returned to their pubs, with the satisfaction that justice had been done.

There was a sequel to all this. The ringleaders were summonsed by the man concerned. These had to appear before the Magistrates, and a Leamington solicitor was to defend them.

After the man had given evidence the Defence solicitor asked him if the effigy they carried was anything like him. He replied that it certainly was not. The next was 'How do you know that it was your effigy they were burning?' This he could not answer satisfactorily and so the case was dismissed.

John Nutt with pupils of the Church of England School on their way to dance round the Maypole as part of the school's bi-centenary celebrations (see p 203)

(Photograph by courtesy of the Coventry Evening Telegraph)

MOVING ON

The content of this chapter is arranged in the same order as the original book. A little of the material relates to the period before the first edition was published, but most covers just the last quarter of the twentieth century.

THE CHURCH

In the twenty-eight years since the original publication of Mr Peppitt's book, various changes have been made to Saint Mary's Church to accommodate the continuous unfolding of the life of the Church.

Following the retirement of the Reverend Glyn Lewis, the Reverend Kenneth Lindop was appointed to the Parish in 1980. Under his care and guidance the Church has continued to be one of the focal points and strengths of the village. Members of the congregation are actively involved in many different aspects of life in the local community and the Church has received much support and encouragement from the parishioners.

In the early 1980s, a major programme of restoration work to the fabric of the Church began. This included a complete overhaul of the roof, clerestory windows and parapets, as well as the re-wiring of the Church's electricity supply. Floodlighting was also installed around the outside of the Church. A Charitable Trust was created to oversee the programme and it is important to note that the Trustees were members of the wider community, which helps to reflect the high level of involvement from the village. Phase 1 was completed in 1987 thanks to the enthusiastic support of many friends and a generous grant from English Heritage. The tower had been completely restored at a cost of £65,000 and new drainage completed on the North wall.

Phase 2 included repairs to the Nave, Chancel and porch, to the stone tracery around the windows, and to the timber floor. The programme of work was completed in February 1992 and in total had cost nearly £230,000 — raising such a huge amount of money from activities, donations, gifts and grants was a remarkable achievement and a reflection of the commitment and dedication of many people.

The land around the Old Vicarage was developed in the early 1980's, together with the land from the Cubbington Sawmills, to form the Pinehurst Estate and the Westminster House Nursing Home. The Old Vicarage was vacated and a new Vicarage built on the estate and conveyed in May 1983.

There have been many notable events in recent years. One of the most memorable was the celebration of the 50th anniversary of VE Day in May 1995. A display of memorabilia was mounted in the Village Hall. This was a moving opportunity for people to bring treasured items from the war years and put them on view. The Reverend Kenneth Lindop and a team of people co-ordinated the collection and display of items on loan, which included ration books, medals, photographs, uniforms and the like; the day gave many of our younger generation a brief insight into day-to-day life during the war years.

There is a dedicated group of Churchyard workers, led by John and Audrey Thornley, who maintain the churchyard to a high standard. In the Best Kept Churchyard competition, having been placed in the top three in the Warwick District many times, S Mary's went on to win first prize in the Coventry Diocese in 1989, 1997 and 1999. S Mary's was placed second in the Coventry Diocese in 1992 and third in 1994.

Cubbington also won first place for Churchyards in the 1997 'Warwickshire Best Kept Village' competition.

S Mary's Church Choir with the Organist and the Vicar

The Rt. Revd. Anthony Priddis, Bishop of Warwick (left), with the Award-winning S Mary's Churchyard Team in 1997

The 2nd Cubbington S Mary's Rainbows, Brownies, Guides and Rangers continue to flourish. The original group was founded by Joyce Beckett in 1962 and has grown considerably over the years. A Rainbow group for the 5-7 year-olds has been established and Joyce's two daughters, Joy Lingard and Cathy Thorpe, continue to play an active part in leading the young people.

THE MOTHERS' UNION

The Cubbington S Mary's branch has fifty members, one of whom, Mrs Hilda Joyner, who passed away in April 1999, cherished her card celebrating more than sixty years of membership. Two others, Mrs Nesta Davies and Mrs Carrie Timms, hold cards recording their half-century. Members are involved in every aspect of Church life: preparation for baptism, supporting new church members at Confirmation, running the library and singing in the choir. They also promote and support projects which help needy people at home and abroad, and happy afternoons are spent entertaining under-privileged children. The Cubbington branch is dedicated to supporting all initiatives which make life better for others.

Members of S Mary's Mothers' Union working on a project

THE METHODIST CHURCH

In 1988 the Methodist Church in Cubbington celebrated the centenary of the present building in Queen Street. A detailed centenary booklet was produced and the following are extracts from this booklet. The Methodist Church referred to briefly in Mr Peppitt's original book has been an important social feature throughout the past 150 years in the village. After early beginnings in the cottages in Chapel Yard, now North Close, the first real development was the opening of a new church in 1844 in Regent St., later Ledbrook Road, with seats for 110 people and built at a cost of £210. Underneath was a School room, and a Wesleyan Day school functioned from 1863 until about 1870 when the 1870 Education Act effectively caused it and many similar small non-authority schools to close. An early preaching plan of 1867 shows that Joseph Arch the agricultural workers' champion and local Preacher once took services here.

Few Chapel records have survived before 1888 but in 1886 a decision was made to construct a new church in Queen Street on land owned by Lord Leigh which he generously gave for a peppercorn rent. For a while the old chapel was used as a Sunday school until, in 1891, the extra rooms were built behind the Chapel. The old building was sold eventually to the Ledbrook family, hence its familiar name.

The new church opened in 1888, costing £750, with seating for over 200 people. Ever since 1837, the Cubbington Church has been part of the Leamington Methodist Circuit, though, interestingly, before that it was part of the Coventry Circuit. The new chapel must have looked and felt really grand with its gallery and adequate coke boiler. Mention should be made of Imri Flint, a member who lived near the Cubbington Sawmills, being the manager there. He personally paid for the wood for the construction, and provided extra funds where necessary. Other stalwart members of the day included Mr H.Bass who played the organ, and Mr George Carr who filled many rôles in the church.

By the 1930s the church was having a hard time and might have closed had it not been for Mr William Rogers, a Cubbington farmer whose wife ran one of the many Cubbington shops. He undertook many duties and provided fuel for the boiler; the church for a while was fondly known as "Mr Rogers' Church". However in the 1950s came a boom in house building which introduced many new families to the area and to the church.

Some of them are still with us, but particular reference should be made to the work undertaken by Mr and Mrs Harold Law who encouraged many of the improvements in those days. A new Church trust was formed and leaders encouraged to start a Brownie Pack and a Guide Troop. Scouting was also begun at that time, along with a junior Cub Pack.

Perhaps the greatest consideration was the decision to appoint its own minister. Until then the church had been cared for by the Minister of Dale Street Methodist Church in Leamington. The Revd. Walters Ensor, a recently retired minister, agreed to take charge of Cubbington in 1959. During his time of office the church flourished and grew.

The opportunity arose to purchase allotment land at the rear which was being developed, and a lovely new hall was built in 1965 at a cost of about £12,000 with facilities for stage events. Many people are unaware of the range of buildings behind the church. New lavatories were built to replace the old earth closets outside. Mr Ensor finally retired in 1966 and the Leamington circuit increased the number of its ministers to four. This meant that Cubbington could share a minister with the Kenilworth church. In the September of that year the Revd. Wharton Parfitt came and since then the ministers have been the Revd. Rob Lewis in 1971 and the Revd. Ian Duncan in 1977. In 1986 the Revd. Bob Sneddon was appointed, and, finally, in 1991 the Revd. John Clarke took the helm as a part-time Minister, combining his duties with his on-going Directorship of the Arthur Rank Centre at Stoneleigh. He and his wife Hazel retired in August 1999

The most recent capital development in 1997 has been the construction of a better foyer at the rear, new toilets including ones for the disabled, and wheelchair ramps.

The church is certainly important in the village provision of care. The playgroup, begun in 1967, continues to flourish, and a Mother and Toddlers' Group meets weekly. The Cub and Brownie Packs are continuing in strength and a very recent formation of a Beaver Colony has taken place.

Unfortunately there are no longer Scout and Guide groups. Provision for the development of young people has always been a priority, over the years. Some twenty years ago the Jubilee Room was built as a centre for the youth club to meet. The church is a polling station at elections and the Village Policeman has recently installed himself in a room on the premises. Other organisations use the premises and at present there are ballet dancing and line dancing classes, and the Cubbington Silver Band rehearses in the hall.

THE ROMAN CATHOLIC CHURCH

The future of the temporary church used by the Roman Catholics in Cubbington began to be in doubt when, on September the 23rd, 1963, a splendid new church was opened in Lillington. Use of the old church continued for a time, but, when finally in 1969 it had become redundant, the land it stood on was sold and houses built there instead.

Cottages on the site of Brookfield Road and Ladycroft
The occupants were Mr & Mrs Betts, and Mr & Mrs Harry Eales

New Street suffered serious flooding on Good Friday, 1998

Queen Street in March, 1999. Doug Dennis stands outside his DIY shop
This was formerly the Post Office

THE MANOR, CHURCH LANE

Since publication of Gus Peppitt's first edition there have been many changes at The Manor. The present owners, the Coad family, bought the house in 1995 to find that the dovecote had sadly been demolished several years earlier. However, many of the original features, both internally and externally, of this centrally positioned Grade 2 listed Georgian house still remain. One feature in particular is the illustrated stained glass window.

Other features such as the chimneys, stonework, attic rooms and roof needed considerable attention. Subsequently, the owners embarked upon a course of both renovation and preservation which included builders living with them for six weeks.

During the renovation of the attic rooms, items were found from several generations of previous occupants including a maid's glove, sewing and knitting implements, and numerous coins, buttons and beads. It was therefore an exciting moment at the end of this time that the new roof and main chimney was inaugurated by the current publican of the King's Head, Marcus Easterlow, who ventured up the scaffolding to place the final stone.

The house is an integral part of the village conservation area and the renovation process is still being continued by the Coad family. Undoubtedly, much work still remains to be undertaken to ensure that the house and its surroundings continue to be preserved for future generations.

THE FREEHOLDERS

The land owned by the freeholders is still, nearly thirty years later, leased to Warwickshire County Council. It is used as a highways depôt for the storage of road-making materials and equipment.

The revenue from the lease continues to provide a useful source of funds for the Parish. In these days of comprehensive local authority services, the trustees place the greatest emphasis on supporting community-based organisations — the Village Hall Trust, the Methodist and Anglican Churches, the two schools in the Parish, the OAP Association, among other organisations, and the Parish Council.

The Freeholders have recently provided substantial funds for the extension to the Village Hall, computer equipment for both the schools, complete refurbishment of the Village War

Memorial, the provision of floral poles in the centre of the village, roadside seats, and playground equipment. Last, but not least, the re-established Cubbington Silver Band was assisted with its start-up costs.

These benefits are of recent years. It seems quite remarkable, however, that the fund has been in existence for over two hundred and thirty years, vested in the Freeholders of the Parish, and administered by their Trustees for the whole of this time. Long may it continue!

In similar vein, one might applaud the continued flourishing existence of Sotherne's Charity, still benefiting the community three hundred and seventy-five years since its inception!

POPULATION STATISTICS

The estimated population of the village quoted for 1971 in the First Edition was 4,400, and the number of houses 1,470. Peppitt noted that in 1969 there were 216 Council houses; this number had reduced to 157 by 1991, but there were 8 properties rented from housing associations, marking the new freedom of council house tenants to purchase their dwellings, and a corresponding need for a flexible housing pool. The population in 1981 was 4,260, and by 1991 had fallen further to 4,077. An estimate suggests that the figure for 1999 is little different. The balance between the sexes is almost exactly half and half. But the marked difference between these latter figures and those for the early nineteenth century lies in the grouping of ages. In 1821, the largest age group in the village was the 20-30-year-olds, which represented 16%: at the last census, that group represented only 11·7%. On the other hand, the 30-to-Retirement group in 1821 was approximately 29%, whereas in 1991 it was no less than 70·8%. And those in 1821 who survived beyond their 60/65 span amounted to a mere 8% — in 1991 that group amounted to 20·1%.

It is not possible to compare unemployment figures, because the Poor Laws in operation in the early days of Census-taking meant that, technically, there were no unemployed. At the 1991 Census, 5·2% of the employable population were not in work.

The housing stock movement is interesting. Hearth Tax returns for 1663 show 55 houses. By 1811 this figure had risen to 113, an almost exact doubling in c.150 years. 1969 is another c.150 years later. The housing stock then was 1,470 — a thirteen-fold increase. In 1991, there were 1,601 occupied houses, and in 1999, 1,650.

The average number of people occupying a house in 1821 was 4·65: in 1991, it was 2·55 — little more than half as many.

We are all aware of inflation these days, but it is not possible to compare realistically rates for the early 19th century with today. However, in 1967, the rateable value of Cubbington was £139,704, and, in 1999, £2,376,656. Considering that the housing stock had risen by only 12%, the massive increase of 1600% in the rateable value speaks volumes for the ravages of inflation over the last thirty years.

The growth of the area of the village is difficult to assess, as the 'hideage' of Domesday Book is not wholly reliable. In 1086, the figure was approximately 1,200 acres, but is now 2,100. Quite clearly, a vast proportion of the 11th century village was field and woodland. Thankfully, there is still a good proportion of open land, farmed or fallow, but a 46-fold increase in population in nine hundred years from eighty-eight to over four thousand means there is rather less land to farm. As the majority of the Domesday population would have been employed in agriculture, it is ironic in the extreme that there had been a four-fold *decrease* in the number of people involved in agriculture to the year 1991 — a mere 20, the same number as in 1968! It is extremely unlikely that an individual agricultural worker in 1086 owned a horse: in 1991, the households owning at least one car amounted to 96·4%.

The few shops remaining in 1971 have been augmented since then and there are now some 17 or 18.

Of the estates existing before 1971, the 'Scottish' estate north of the Rugby Road was built on land belonging to the McGregor family, and of the stipulations on the sale of that land one was that there should be no public houses, and the other was that the streets should be named for towns in Scotland.

The 18-year-old estate of Austen Court built on the Church Farm site was named for James Austen, Jane Austen's brother, vicar of the parish in 1792.

Pinehurst Estate, referred to above (p.193), is a beautiful estate of 18 houses built around the renovated centre-piece of the Old Vicarage and occupying its former grounds.

The streets of the new estate built by Coventry Road are derived from an old map of the Stoneleigh Estate which, with all the Stoneleigh Estate Papers, is held by the Shakespeare Birthplace Trust. They are the names of fields in the vicinity: Cotton Mill Spinney; Thorn Stile Close; Three Cornered Close; Willow Sheets Meadow. The names are at once descriptive and enigmatic and are in marked contrast to street names derived from, say, local noteworthies.

LOCAL GOVERNMENT

A major change to the arrangements for the people in England to be represented at local level took place on the first of April, 1974. On that day the former county, county borough and county district councils were abolished. In their place a two-tier system was established, namely the County Councils and the District Councils.

Two Councillors represent the village on the District Council, and one on the County Council. However, the Parish Council exists as before with 12 members elected every four years; this looks after the interests of the village, but has no involvement in finance or administration, and is restricted to making representations over roads, road-signing and planning applications.

Council involvement in the village since 1971 is visible in the traffic calming scheme installed at the top of Windmill Hill — where previously there had been a spate of accidents — speed restrictions on the principal roads, and the provision of school crossing patrols.

Until 1983 the two District Councillors represented Cubbington only. Since that date they have represented Old Milverton, Blackdown, Bubbenhall, Weston-under-Wetherley, Eathorpe & Wappenbury as well.

The County Councillor has been responsible since then for all those villages and for Hunningham, Offchurch & Radford Semele as well.

Population of Warwick District Council was 118,300 in 1990/1 and 123,100 in 1997.

CHURCH OF ENGLAND PRIMARY SCHOOL

In September, 1996, Warwickshire County Council reorganised all its schools, and Cubbington C of E Combined School became Cubbington C of E Primary School, with provision for 4-11-year-olds. At present there are 211 pupils. A Parent and Toddler Group is held in the temporary class room on two afternoons each week.

The school currently has seven classrooms, a computer room and library. There is an indoor swimming pool, built by the parents, and later covered over and tiled. It is used by several schools and community groups. The PTA remains a strength of the school, and has recently designed and built an adventure playground for the children's use. Their most recent effort has been to renovate "Annie's Room" — the Old School House — as a place for group activities.

OUR LADY AND S.TERESA'S ROMAN CATHOLIC SCHOOL

This has now become a primary school, and at present has 180 pupils. A Montessori nursery occupies part of the site.

The original building has undergone a refurbishment programme over the last two years, with new doors, windows and internal developments. A new entrance area has been built, and the provision of a prayer room enhances the building.

Before- and After-School Clubs have been formed for the benefit of pupils and parents.

THWAITES

In recent years, the company has come under new ownership, following the death of its chairman, Basil Thwaites, on June 16th, 1989.

In the ten years since then the company has continued to develop, test and manufacture new dumpers ranging in load size from one ton to sixteen tons, to meet the requirements of the construction industry. The photographs of the site between pages 137 and 141 show the expansion that has taken place.

The present chairman is Lord Dulverton.

THE WARWICKSHIRE BEER COMPANY

Gus Peppitt records that, in years gone by, the pubs in Cubbington brewed their own beer. That practice ceased long ago, but a new venture in the village, started up last year, has gone some way to reversing the trend of buying from breweries far away. The new Brewery is located in Queen Street and offers a range of eight beers to free houses in Warwickshire and beyond. The brand on pump at the King's Head beside Cubbington Church is known as 'Earbiter', not because of any physical property it might possess that endangers drinkers' auditory organs, but in recognition of the Albion Football Team that acquired the name after an incident during a match many years ago — an incident which has never been allowed to sink into oblivion.

Church of England Primary School Reception Class prepares for Christmas, 1998
(Photograph by courtesy of the Coventry Evening Telegraph)

There were 25 pupils in the Reception Class at Our Lady & S Teresa's School in 1998
The twenty-two in this picture seem, on the whole, very happy about their new surroundings!
(Photograph by courtesy of the Coventry Evening Telegraph)

Children from the Church of England School dance round the Maypole — part of the Celebrations in 1980 to mark the 200th anniversary of the founding of the school

June 1986: The 25th anniversary celebration of the Pre-School Playgroup Association (now the Pre-School Learning Alliance) with children of the Methodist Church Playgroup (Photograph by courtesy of Christine Daly)

Ted Fairbrother — The 'King of the Bottle Tops'

William Franks bought his milk business on the 6th of November, 1934, from Charles Pickering of 'Stonehouse', Cubbington'. Franks died in 1949 and his son-in-law, Edward (Ted) Fairbrother took over until his retirement in 1990
(Photo courtesy Christine Daly)

Another Cubbington Dairyman, Sam Cleaver, who delivered his milk from 1919 to 1957, perhaps not always by the means depicted.
(Photo courtesy Phil Carpenter)

1920s photograph of Jack Harwood, — with the horse — the owner of the coal round, & Jack Coye. Photo taken outside 'The Manor', Church Lane

Potato-picking on Old Ridge with Norman Cowley (farmer, left), Florence Lee, Joan Kirby (and child, Kathleen Kirby), Nellie Eales, Mary Richardson. Others unknown

CUBBINGTON ALBION FOOTBALL CLUB

In the early 1950s, the Albion joined the newly formed Warwickshire Combination, a semi-professional league which covered an area from South Gloucestershire to Staffordshire, including Leicestershire and Oxfordshire. This League ceased to exist in late 1960s. Since then, the local Club has played in the Leamington and District, the Rugby and District, the Coventry Alliance, and Stratford and District Leagues.

In the late 1970s, a boys' section was formed, playing in the Mid-Warwickshire Boys' League, and at times in the Coventry Minor League. Boys' teams from under-10s up to under-17s have participated in Club activities.

Currently, the men play in the Saturday Stratford League and the Sunday Leamington and District League; the under-16s in the Mid-Warwickshire Boys' League; and the under-12s in the Coventry Minor League.

A highlight of recent years has been the matches against Aston Villa Old Stars. 1997 was the Club's Centenary, and part of the celebration was a 'Villa' game; the opportunity was then taken to make this an annual fixture. Money raised from the event goes to local charitable organisations.

CUBBINGTON SILVER BAND

Mr Don Robb, formerly Musical Director of Coundon Wedge Band in Coventry, together with the Reverend Ken Lindop of S Mary's Church, Cubbington had conceived the idea of re-forming a brass band in Cubbington. A request for local people interested in helping to form such a band was printed in the S Mary's parish magazine "Contact". On a sunny Sunday afternoon in 1995, six Cubbington residents came to S Mary's Church to meet Don. Later that month at an Inaugural meeting, Cubbington Silver Band was formed with twelve local people whose ages ranged from 11 to over 60 and many of them had never played a musical instrument. It was suggested that the Band aim to purchase silver instruments (considered to be better quality than brass), hence the name Cubbington Silver Band.

Mr. Don Robb was appointed Musical Director, Councillor Hughie Griffiths Treasurer and Mrs. Sue Kendall Secretary.

Back Row
Left to right
Gavin Smith
Stuart Lawson
Darren Pettifer
Rob Reading
Paul Cronin
Rick Hollingsworth
Ian Crofts
Sati Mann
Tim O'Mahoney
Dave Shilton
Chris Ovington

Front Row:
Tom Donovan
Tony Lambert
John Sullivan
Phil Hollingsworth
— (Captain)
Michael Fitzpatrick
Warren Shepherd
Macki Haer
Nav Brahma

Cubbington Albion Football Team, 1999

The Silver Band in their Practice Room — the Methodist Church Hall

Band rehearsal night is Friday. Rehearsals were originally held at S Mary's Church, moving early in 1996 to Cubbington Methodist Church Hall to accommodate the growing number of players and provide more facilities. In February 1996 a Management Committee was formed and the Reverend Ken Lindop was invited to become the Band's Chairman.

A generous start-up loan from Councillor Hughie Griffiths, followed by grants from Cubbington Freeholders, Cubbington Parish Council and Warwick District Council (among others) helped to purchase instruments.

In April 1996 the Band played in public for the first time at a Coffee Morning at Cubbington Village Hall.

On Sunday 12th May 1996 a Service of Thanksgiving for the re-formation of Cubbington Silver Band was held at S Mary's Church. In the August of that year the Band played in Jephson Gardens for the Gardens' 150th Birthday. By the end of the Band's first year it had 26 members aged 7 to 60+ and had played at 12 engagements.

During the Band's second year it travelled farther afield and played at 21 engagements. It also played at the 150th Birthday celebration of the Queen's Head public house in Queen Street, Cubbington and at fêtes at both Cubbington schools. In September 1997 the Band played in the Pump Room Gardens Bandstand.

In October 1997 the Band received a Highly Commended certificate at Warwickshire Village Venture Awards for "active involvement in the enhancement of community life in Warwickshire". By the end of the Band's second year it had 25 members, 23 of whom were players, with ages ranging from 9 to 60+.

During the Band's third year it played at 31 engagements. In January 1998 the Band was registered as a Charity. In October of that year the Anniversary Concert held at Cubbington Methodist Church Hall was a sell-out! By the end of the Band's third year membership was 31, 29 of whom were players.

In February 1999 the Band received its largest grant to date, almost £6,000, from the Telephone Engineers' Social Club after the winding-up of that Club's affairs.

One of the current members, Mr. Dick Heath, was a member of the former Cubbington Brass Band, joining them in 1937 at the age of 6. He left when he was 30 in the 1950's. His father Bill and his uncles Arthur and Philip were also in the original Band.

THE WOMEN'S INSTITUTE

With an active membership of 55, the WI continues to thrive,meeting each month in the Village Hall to listen to visiting speakers, and enjoying a programme of outings. Members are seen here in 1989 with woollen clothes for premature babies at the Warneford Hospital (now closed).
Left to right: WI Chairman Florence Lindon; midwife Eileen Critchley; WI Member Kathleen Dealtry; Sister Christine Sidgwick & baby Caroline; Yvonne, Caroline's mother, daughter-in-law of Mrs Dealtry
(Photo courtesy of The Leamington Spa Courier)

CUBBINGTON AND DISTRICT OLD AGE PENSIONERS ASSOCIATION

In 1999 the Association celebrated its 40th anniversary. It is rather significant that the adopted emblem is an acorn, because although it is not a static 'big oak' it has certainly grown into a large, lively sapling. Cubbington is the place to live when it is time to become an Old Age Pensioner. During these 40 years, a first-class Association, organising social functions, outings and help for the sick, has kept to the principles of its founders — that it should be free of charge.

The present Association, founded by Norman Bass in 1959, organised a darts competition between local pubs and the Working Men's Club. They formed a committee consisting of Norman Bass, the Chairman, R. Patstone, the Secretary and E. Davies, the Treasurer. The money raised provided a Christmas Dinner for the pensioners and as the Association expanded, outings were organised, based on £2 for a meal. Membership in those days was around 200. When Norman Bass died in 1964, C. Lovell became Chairman.

As expansion continued the outlying villages were invited to join and in 1985 the Association applied for, and was granted, Charity Status, with the Constitution stating: "The object of the Organisation shall be to promote the welfare of the aged, in any manner which now is or hereafter may be deemed by law to be charitable, within the villages of Cubbington, Offchurch, Weston-under-Wetherley, Eathorpe, Hunningham and Wappenbury, in the County of Warwickshire." As the membership increased, Darts, Dominoes and Crib continued to be the main source of the income. At its peak the then Darts Secretary, Michael Serhyniuk, (now Chairman and Treasurer of the Association), had 74 teams, consisting of 5 Divisions (of 10 teams) for men and 2 divisions (of 12 teams) for ladies.

All the fun of the fair!
Mr Eales &
Keggie Chamberlain
battle it out
in the Pillow Fight:
about 1914
at the Annual
Flower Show
of the Allotment Assn.
(Photo courtesy
Marion Avern)

Sadly, this source of income dried up in March 1995, because of the lack of volunteers to run it. But, in 1997, Terry Morgan, approached the Association with a proposal to try to reform the Summer League. To date, he has had two successful seasons.

Of course the darts and similar games were not the only source of income: there evolved, with the Working Men's Club, an annual Plant Sale which is now held at the Village Hall, a Field Day, and, more recently, an annual Garden Party organised by Secretary Marion Lee. One of the newer annual events has been a collecting day with a theme, when the Committee, wearing fancy dress, walk round the village with buckets for the money and distributing sweets for the children. 'The Circus', 'Wild West', and 'Father Christmas' are some of the themes used. Two Auctions are held each year in the Village Hall, with the Association taking commission on the sale, which is run entirely by the Committee.

Nowadays, with 700 members, money raising is continuous but is supplemented by donations. There have been several occasions when funeral donations have been received. With more money coming in, more can be spent for the benefit of the pensioners.

In 1997 two modern wheelchairs were purchased to augment the ageing fleet. These are lent to any member in temporary difficulty. Vouchers worth £10 are given to members who have been in hospital or had a serious illness. The social events have increased: Bingo started in 1987, and is very popular. The difference with recent outings is the availability of many more venues for members to visit.

In 1998, there were three long-distance outings, and one short distance one to a concert. On all these occasions, members were taken door-to-door. In addition there was a dance organised with live music at the Social Club.

To keep everyone informed of events the Association produces a 20-page monthly magazine called the 'Acorn', with advertisements offsetting the costs.

What of the future? The first priority will be to try to do more for the housebound, by making special provision for their needs.

Provision will also be made for the active: if the younger members take an interest, this will surely succeed. The Association is financially sound, the cause good, and who better to be pampered in their twilight years than the Old Age Pensioners?

FURTHER PROVISION FOR THE ELDERLY

A newcomer to Cubbington is 'Westminster House', a residential nursing home built on land belonging to the Old Vicarage and the sawmills by Westminster Health Care. It is an extensive, modern, characterful building, opened at Whitsun, 1992, and designed to make the latter years of the elderly dignified and comfortable. The emphasis in the internal decor is 'local': the many Cubbington people who have chosen to live there have been made to feel still 'at home'. Fewer local people now have to leave the village when they decide they are unable to look after themselves in their own homes.

The OAP Association Garden Fête
held in Secretary Marion Lee's garden, 1990

The OAPs gather for their Summer Outing, 1980
(Photo by courtesy of the Leamington Spa Courier.)

Old Age Pensioners Association outing to Matlock, gathering at Windmill Hill, June 1994
(Photograph by courtesy of the Leamington Spa Courier.)

1996: Members of the Old Age Pensioners Association set off for a 5-hour tour of the village collecting money
Left to right: Keith Timms, Maggie Guest, Norman Guest, Marge Longden, Doreen Hodkinson, Olive Insull, Fred Gurney, Ron Insull, Michael Serhyniuk, Marion Lee, Joan Thornicroft and Brian Mullis as the Tiger.

Cubbington Brewery

Cubbington's answer to 'Last of the Summer Wine':
Derek Newman, George Lee, Dennis Taylor, Bernie Collins & Neville Walden
(& dogs) set off for one of their regular forays into the hinterland.

Westminster House Retirement Home site when occupied by the Sawmills
(Photo courtesy of John Lambert)

Westminster House Retirement Home

THE VILLAGE HALL

The Hall has been much used through the years, home to many organisations and groups — the Brownies, the Guides and the Rangers hold their weekly meetings in it — and martial arts groups meet there too. It is also a popular venue for weddings, christenings and children's parties. S Mary's Church holds a monthly whist drive there, and its Christmas and Summer Fairs. It is also the home of the monthly meetings of the Women's Institute and the Mothers' Union, and the Old Age Pensioners' Association has bingo sessions, plant sales and auctions.

A more serious use is made by Social Services for the preparation of meals to deliver to senior citizens. It opens its doors twice a year to the Cubbington Players for their dramatic productions, which they rehearse there, and at Christmas they present their Pantomime.

In 1997, by virtue of grants of £20,000 each from the District and Parish Councils and generous private donations, an extension was added to the original hall to provide a second function room with access for the disabled and wheelchair users. Toilet facilities have been improved to accommodate these latter.

During 1999 it is intended to refurbish the existing building, replacing the roof and windows, and modernising the heating system. This work is hoped to be completed before 2000.

THE BRITISH RED CROSS

The Warwickshire Branch of the British Red Cross made its headquarters in Coventry Road in April 1996, sharing a building with Mayfair Securities. The Red Cross houses its vehicle fleet here, and provides loans of medical care equipment such as wheelchairs. Apart from administration of the Branch, refugee support and 'message & tracing' services are also provided at the premises.

SNIPPETS

The men in the photograph on page 130 have been mostly identified. From the left: Mr Anderton, standing; Messrs Gibbs and Richardson with the motor-cycle combination; Mr Eales, sitting; in the line behind, Messrs Stevens, Draper, Norman Bass, two unknown, another Draper, and a Chamberlain; Mr Lambert, the Landlord, is on the far right.

Part of Joseph Russell's farm, Ham Barn on the Offchurch Road, (see picture on page 44, and reference page 181) was converted into a dwelling house between 1976 and 78.

The funeral of Miss Mary Bastock took place on the 26th of January, 1971. She had lived to see her hundred-and-first birthday.

The Spirit of Cubbington
The Revd. John Clarke, Minister of the Methodist Church, watches Mrs Amelia Giles perform the opening ceremony of the Church's Renewal Project on the 7th of September, 1996

The Annual Sunday School Concert, about the year 1946.
The Reverend P T Broadway is seated on the right

ILLUSTRATIONS

INDEX